AMERICAN
CHANGE
AGENT

AMERICAN CHANGE AGENT

A Life & Legacy of Seeking Diversity, Equality, and Inclusion

by DR. JOHN F. LEEKE, PH.D.
with ANANDA KIAMSHA MADELYN LEEKE

To request permission, contact ananda@anandaleeke.com

Author photos by Leigh Mosley, Leigh Mosley Photography
Book design by Gigi Mascareñas

ISBN 979-8-218-62798-0
First Edition

Published by Ananda Leeke Consulting
anandaleeke.com/drjohn

Follow and build community with @drjleeke on Instagram and facebook.com/john.leeke1; @anandaleeke on LinkedIn, YouTube, and Spill; and @anandaleeke.bsky.social on Bluesky.

DEDICATION

My African ancestors from the Akan people in Ghana and the Yoruba people in Nigeria

My indigenous ancestors from the Cherokee, Chickasaw, Mosopelea, Shawnee, and Yuchi tribes of Kentucky

My European ancestors

My immediate family, Theresa, Michael, Madelyn (Ananda), Mark, and Matthew

My extensive extended family that includes my daughters-in-law, Lu and Pamela; my cousins and their extended families; my nieces and nephews; and my godchildren and their families

My many friends, colleagues, and individuals who have contributed to my life's journey

TABLE OF CONTENTS

Letter to the Reader xi

Timeline of Dr. John F. Leeke's Life and Career xvii

A List of Acronyms Used in Book xxv

PART ONE:
BUILDING THE FOUNDATION
(1939–1968)

Chapter 1   The People I Come From 5

Chapter 2   From Indianapolis to Terre Haute to
              Washington, DC. 50

Chapter 3   From St. Augustine's Catholic School to
              Archbishop Carroll High School in DC . . . 65

Chapter 4   Following in My Parents' Footsteps at
              Indiana State Teachers College 98

Chapter 5   Dealing with Adversity 135

Chapter 6   New Beginnings: A Parent, a Teacher,
              and a Social Justice Activist 144

PART TWO:
THE NEA EXPERIENCE: CLIMBING THE LADDER OF EQUALITY AND INCLUSION (1968–1985)

Chapter 7   Our New Life in Maryland. 167

Chapter 8   The First Year at the NEA:
Task Force on Urban Education 178

Chapter 9   NEA Special Project on Urban Education:
The Urban Institutes. 187

Chapter 10   NEA Special Project:
The Project Urban Upswing 204

Chapter 11   Trying to Create Change in a Racially
Tense School District 213

Chapter 12   The National Training Laboratory of
Applied Behavioral Science (NTL):
A Major Influence on My NEA and
Consulting Career. 219

Chapter 13   Life in the Center for Human Relations . . 225

Chapter 14   The Rise of a Strategic Change Architect:
My Move to NEA's Instruction and
Professional Development Unit 233

Chapter 15   The Pursuit of the Doctorate 255

PART THREE:
STANDING IN MY OWN SHOES UNAPOLOGETICALLY AS I MOVE FULL FORCE TOWARDS GREATER SERVICE, GREATER PROGRESS (1985–2015)

Chapter 16   Establishing John F. Leeke Associates, Inc. 275

Chapter 17   DEI Innovator Elsie Y. Cross and
the EYCA Story 298

Chapter 18   The Story of the NEA Affirmative Action
UniServ Intern Program for Women and
Ethnic Minorities 325

PART FOUR:
THE FINAL ACT: LEAVING A LEGACY

Chapter 19   Life in Retirement. 357

Chapter 20   My Family 391

Chapter 21   Our Father's Journey:
How My Children See Me 426

Chapter 22   A Legacy Gift for You: Lessons Learned. . 433

Resources. 447

Acknowledgments 459

Author Bios 461

LETTER TO THE READER

Dear Reader,

Dr. William Edward Burghardt (W.E.B.) Du Bois, one of my greatest teachers, once wrote, "The return from your work must be the satisfaction which that work brings you and the world's need of that work. With this, life is heaven, or as near heaven as you can get." Dr. Du Bois's wisdom expresses the fulfillment I have received in my work as a change agent seeking diversity, equality, and inclusion. The book you are about to read takes you on a journey of selected stories from my life and career that I believe will help you understand the people, places, experiences, and thresholds of change that have shaped and impacted my work. Just in case you are unfamiliar with the phrase "a threshold of change," I want to make sure you understand that it is a moment in your life when you experienced a major shift in your beliefs, behavior, education, personal and professional growth, relationships, and/or environment that transformed who you are.

Before you dive deep into my life stories, it is important for me to open the door to my own vulnerability and confess that it has taken me several years to write this book. I started, stopped, and re-started several times. Why? Because I was afraid I didn't have the ability and confidence to write a book that had any value. As I struggled with my fear and lack of confidence as a writer, I reached the conclusion that writing this book was something I needed to do for myself. Reaching this conclusion helped me release the fear and move forward. I also felt I needed to give my children the gift of my book.

One of the greatest lessons I have learned while writing this book is the power of storytelling and its ability to change lives, cultivate leadership, build relationships, and create a sense of community. My storytelling perspective aligns with the position of the authors Heather Box and Julian Mocine-McQueen in their book, *How Your Story Sets You Free*: "If you are a human, you love stories. Why? We're hardwired to love stories because they help us understand our world and are essential to our evolution. We use stories to organize and communicate our surroundings and our past, present, and future. All humans have stories. They represent our unique experiences, lessons learned, and wisdom gained."

As you read this book, I hope you will come to know and appreciate the man I have become over the last eight decades. I have never viewed my life as one that has been planned. It has evolved into what I call "an emerging life." I hope you will see what I value, meet some of the people who were significant, and witness the many opportunities I had as I pursued a life commitment of change. Further, I hope some of the young people who are beginning their journey will gain inspiration and direction on how to navigate their life and career.

As you turn the pages, you may wonder whether you are in fact a change agent. I'm here to tell you that you are a change agent. Everyone is born with this ability. You just must choose to use it. Let's look at what it means to be a change agent. According to the organizational theory espoused by Richard Beckhart, author of *Agent of Change: My Life, My Practice*; Warren Bennis, author of *On Becoming A Leader*; Kurt Lewin, an author of *A Dynamic Theory of Personality*; and Edgar H. Schein, author of *Organizational Culture and Leadership*, a change agent, or agent of change, is someone who promotes and enables change to happen within any group or organization. My life as a change agent has been focused on planned change.

As you read, you will notice I indicate the race and gender of most of the individuals that become part of my life. This is deliberate as their identities have determined how they influenced my development and the outcomes of the different experiences. Race is not only significant in my life, but also in our society. It has always been and is currently impacting us today. I hope my stories will help you to see the patterns, trends, and alternatives to addressing the ongoing dilemmas facing our society.

Each chapter is introduced by a quote. Many come from African American change agents and civil rights and social justice activists. Some chapters include references to African American history. My daughter Madelyn (Ananda) and I think you might experience those references as a mini course in African American history. My hope is that you are inspired to learn more about history, especially given the current attack on dismantling African American history.

In Part 1: Building the Foundation, you will witness what I owe my ancestors. I owe them my thirst for knowledge and ability to stay focused with the legacy of emotional, spiritual, and economic stability. Many of them, including my mother, father, and maternal grandmother, were extremely organized. Their commitment to live in these ways became the internal architecture for who I am today.

When you reach Part 2: The NEA Experience, I will share the work I did with the National Education Association (NEA). All my NEA work is rooted in the commitment to develop strategies that improve educational opportunities for Black, Indigenous, and people of color (BIPOC), women, and the Lesbian, Gay, Bisexual, Transgender, Queer, Intersex, and Asexual (LGBTQIA) community.

Part 3: The Entrepreneurial Years explores how I was able to leverage my NEA experience into a consulting firm and collaborative partnerships that allowed me to expand my impact on people and systems in:

- The corporate world.
- Federal and state governments.
- Educational associations and school systems.
- National and local organizations.

Part 3 also explains what is required to work with people of differences on addressing systemic racism, sexism, oppression, inequality, and white supremacy. In my 60 years of doing this work, these issues have challenged American society at all levels. We have taken steps forward, but we have also taken steps backwards, especially under the presidencies of Richard M. Nixon, Gerald R. Ford, George H.W. Bush, William J. Clinton, George W. Bush, and Donald J. Trump. Under former President Barack H. Obama's administration, many embraced his mantra of "Yes We Can" and "Si Se Puede." Although some steps were taken to move the ball forward, Obama's administration encountered numerous barriers. What we have learned is change is incremental. It is a process. It is not for the faint at heart. It takes commitment, patience, organization, community, long-term strategies, and lots of flexibility. Let's bring them with us as we reach the final days of President Joe Biden's administration and prepare to elect Vice President Kamala Harris as the first African American, Asian American, and woman to lead the United States as President. Let's also move forward with her wisdom: "Change is never easy, but it is always necessary. Let's embrace it and make a brighter future for all."

Part 4: The Final Act: Leaving a Legacy takes you on a scenic tour of my life in retirement, shares my reflections on the relationships I have with my wife and four children, and offers you a glimpse into how my children have experienced me. It ends with key lessons I have learned that I think you can incorporate into your life, relationships, and career.

At the end of each chapter, I have included reflection questions that give you an opportunity to explore your life journey and aspects of what it means to be a change agent. For those of you who are interested in going a bit further, I have included a resource section with a list of books, journals, and magazines you can use to deepen your experience.

May you enjoy reading my book as I have enjoyed my life's journey.

Sincerely,
Dr. John
October 27, 2024

TIMELINE OF DR. JOHN F. LEEKE'S LIFE AND CAREER

1939   Born May 19, 1939 in Indianapolis, IN

1953   Completed eighth grade at St. Augustine Catholic Elementary School, Washington, DC

1957   Graduated from Archbishop Carroll High School, Washington, DC and enrolled in Indiana State Teachers College in Terre Haute, IN

1958   Joined Indiana Alpha Delta Chapter of Pi Lambda Phi Fraternity at Indiana State Teachers College

1960–61   Elected President of Indiana Alpha Delta Chapter of Pi Lambda Phi Fraternity

1961   Graduated from Indiana State Teachers College with a BA in Education and named in Who's Who in American Colleges and Universities

Married Theresa Bernadette Gartin at
St. Rita's Catholic Church in Indianapolis, IN

1962   Completed Certification Requirements in
Elementary Teaching from Indiana State
Teachers College

Hired as a teacher at Browne Junior High
School in Washington, DC

1962–68   Taught fifth and sixth grade at Brownell
Elementary School and served as a
Counselor at Scott Elementary School in
Flint, MI

1963   Michael David born August 28 in
Washington, DC

1964   Madelyn Cheryl born December 18 in
Flint, MI

1965   Mark Andrew born December 27 in
Flint, MI

1966   Graduated from University of Michigan with
a MA in Counseling

1967   Matthew Jay born September 17 in Flint, MI

1968	Family moved to Landover, MD
1968–69	Hired to work as a staff member on the Task Force on Urban Education at the National Education Association in Washington, DC
1969	Family joined St. Joseph Catholic Church, Landover (now located in Largo), MD
	Joined the National Training Laboratory of Applied Behavioral Science (NTL)
1969–70	Became Assistant Director of the Project Urban at the National Education Association
1970	Worked with the school district in Aliquippa, PA that was racially intense
	Developed and delivered the first Urban Institute in Battle Creek, MI
	Began doctoral studies at The Union Institute and University, Yellow Springs (now Cincinnati), OH
1970–71	Developed and delivered the Project Urban Upswing in Indianapolis, IN

1970–76	Worked as a staff member in the Center for Human Relations at the National Education Association
1971	Developed and delivered the second Urban Institute in Des Moines, IA
1976–85	Worked as a staff member in the Instruction and Professional Development Unit at the National Education Association
1977	Earned Ph.D. in Organizational Development at The Union Institute and University
1980–2016	Family moved to and lived in Lake Arbor in Bowie, MD
1982	Began serving as a class representative for Archbishop Carroll High School, Class of 1957
1985	Resigned from the National Education Association
	Established John F. Leeke Associates, Inc.
	Joined Elsie Y. Cross Associates, Inc. as a Senior Associate

1986	Renewed wedding vows and hosted a celebration at St. Joseph Catholic Church
1987	Began consulting relationship with the National Education Association and developing and implementing the NEA Affirmative Action UniServ Program for Women and Ethnic Minorities
1993–2016	Family purchased and vacationed in a beach house in the Oyster Harbor community that was originally incorporated and inhabited by African Americans in Annapolis, MD
1996	Family began hosting an annual Kwanzaa celebration
2009–present	Joined Facebook and began using other social media and blogging tools as a digital senior citizen www.facebook.com/john.leeke1
2011	Received an award for 25 years of dedication and commitment to the NEA Intern Program from the graduates of the NEA Affirmative Action UniServ Intern Program for Women and Ethnic Minorities (1987–2011)

2012–present	Served as a Maryland Democratic Party volunteer for President Barack H. Obama's campaign in Prince George's County, MD
	Launched *Dr. John: Change Agent	Change Advocate	Change Influencer* blog on Tumblr to share thoughts, opinions, and information, and raising questions about issues of race, diversity, and differences
	https://drjohnleeke.tumblr.com
2013	Closed consulting relationship with National Education Association
2013–16	Served as President of the Lake Arbor Homeowner Association
2014	Launched *Dr. John Leeke* YouTube Channel
	www.youtube.com/@drjohnleeke
2015	Ended relationship with Elsie Y. Cross Associates
	Attended the White House Conference on Aging and met President Barack H. Obama

2017	Closed John F. Leeke Associates, Inc. and began retirement
	Featured in *The Washington Post* article, "Swimming with the tide" (about life in retirement)
2017–present	Served as an Election Judge for the Anne Arundel County Board of Elections, member of the Black History Committee at St. Joseph Catholic Church, and Treasurer of the St. Joseph Community of Africans and Friends
2019	Received the National Black Staff Network's JEGNA Award
	Launched *Messages from Dr. John* podcast that featured reflections on civil rights, democracy, diversity and inclusion, politics, and voting on Soundcloud
	https://soundcloud.com/john-leeke
2019–2022	Served as President of the Parish Council at St. Joseph Catholic Church
2021	Celebrated 60th wedding anniversary with family at home

2022   Helped to establish St. Joseph Catholic
        Church's Men's Ministry

        Hosted *Dr. John Live!* Facebook
        conversations about the importance of voting
        during the 2022 elections

        www.facebook.com/john.leeke1/videos

2023   Became a widower when wife Theresa died
        on July 9

A LIST OF ACRONYMS USED IN BOOK

NOTE TO READER: This book includes many organizations with acronyms that are mentioned in the book. As you read, we invite you to use this list.

1. BIPOC – Black, Indigenous, and People of Color

2. CEA – Connecticut Education Association

3. CHR – Civil and Human Rights Division of the National Education Association

4. CIRCES – Combatting Institutional Racism, Culturalism, Ethnicism and Sexism (refers to the doctoral group)

5. CYO – Catholic Youth Organization

6. EYCA – Elsie Y. Cross Associates, Inc.

7. FEA – Flint Education Association (now known as the Michigan Education Association, Flint Office)

8. HBCUs – Historical Black Colleges and Universities

9. IPD – Instruction and Professional Development Division of the National Education Association

10. LGBTQ – Lesbian, Gay, Bisexual, Transgender, and Queer

11. MBTI® – Myers-Briggs Type Indicator®

12. MEA – Michigan Education Association

13. NBSN – National Black Staff Network

14. NCATE – National Council for Accreditation of Teacher Education

15. NEA – National Education Association

16. NEARO – National Education Association Retired Organization

17. NEASO – National Education Association Staff Organization

18. NSBA – National School Boards Association

19. NTL – National Training Laboratory

20. PDE – Project Demonstrating Excellence (name of doctoral dissertation)

21. PSEA – Pennsylvania State Education Association

22. RFC – Resources for Change

23. SJCAF – St. Joseph Community of Africans and Friends

AMERICAN
CHANGE
AGENT

PART ONE

BUILDING THE FOUNDATION

(1939–1968)

CHAPTER 1

The People I Come From

"I believe in pride of race and lineage and self; in pride of self so deep as to scorn injustice to other selves."

—DR. W.E.B. DU BOIS, a change agent, a sociologist, a historian, a civil rights activist, a Pan-Africanist, and an author

---

Dr. Du Bois's wisdom reminds me that having a strong understanding of who you are can make you angry at injustices and inequalities. It can also serve as armor and motivation for attacking these issues. While working at the National Education Association in 1968, I began to realize how race and class greatly influenced my life. Through this lens, my awareness of the injustices and inequalities, especially in education, expanded way beyond the Black middle-class background I was born into.

In writing this book, I have been able to trace my lineage back six generations in my mother and father's families. My daughter Madelyn (Ananda) and I accomplished this mighty task with the support of genealogical research conducted by my niece, Ellen T. Cook. In addition, we have used family stories and photos that I have acquired from my parents and cousin Barbara Jones Blueitt as well as maternal and paternal data from the African Ancestry DNA testing kits. African Ancestry reported that my matriclan test results were a 98.9 percent match to the Yoruba people's DNA. This means at some point in the 500-to-2,000-year history of my maternal lineage that there was a Yoruba woman. My patriclan test results were a 99.4 percent match to the Akan people's DNA. Receiving this information was exciting because it gave me a sense of confirmation that my roots go back to Africa.

The Yoruba people are a West African ethnic group that inhabit Nigeria, Benin, and Togo. They represent approximately 30 million people in the continent of Africa. During the eighth century, Ile-Ife, a powerful Yoruba kingdom, organized itself around well-structured city-states well before the arrival of the British colonizers. At the onset of the *Maafa*, the African Holocaust (i.e. the Atlantic slave trade), the Yoruba people from Nigeria and Benin were forcibly transported to and enslaved in America. Slavery expanded their religion across many borders—to Trinidad, Cuba, Saint Lucia, Benin, Togo, Brazil, Guyana, Haiti, Jamaica, to name a few.

Some prominent members of the Yoruba community include Moshood Kashimawo Olawale Abiola, a businessman, publisher, and politician who served as the Aare Ona Kankafo of Yorubaland; Oloori Kofoworola "Kofo" Aina Ademola, an educator who was president of the National Council of Women Societies; Adewale Akinnuoye-Agbaje, an actor, director, and fashion model known for his roles as Simon Adebisi in the television show, *Oz*, Lock-Nah in the movie, *Mummy*

Returns, Nykwana Wombosi in the movie, *Bourne Identity* and Kurse in the movie, *Thor*; Elizabeth Abimbola Awoli-yi, the first woman to practice as a physician in Nigeria and the first West African to earn a license of Royal Surgeon in Dublin; Oyeronke Oyewumi, a gender scholar and professor of Sociology at Stony Brook University; and Henry Olusegun Adeola Samuel, known professionally as Seal, a singer and songwriter who has sold over 20 million records worldwide.

The Akan people are also a West African ethnic group that inhabit Ghana and the Ivory Coast. The Akan culture made its way to the Americas during the African slave trade. Approximately 10 percent of all ships carrying enslaved West Africans included the Akan people. Many of the Akan people that were sold into slavery were Coromantee soldiers who played a major role in slave revolts and plantation resistance tactics in the Americas and the Caribbean.

Some prominent members of the Akan community include David Adjaye, an architect who designed the National Museum of African American History and Culture; Kofi Annan, the first Black man to serve as the United Nations Secretary and a Nobel Peace Prize honoree; Kwame Nkrumah, the first president of Ghana and the founder of the Pan-African movement that liberated African states from European colonialism; Esther Afua Ocloo, the Chairwoman of the Women's World Banking Board of Directors who helped millions of women start and run businesses; and Efua Theodora Sutherland, a playwright, a radio broadcaster, a creative director, and a teacher.

Possessing this information has helped me see my ancestors as a magnificent tapestry of blended blood. In addition to African ancestry, Native American and European ancestors are part of my tapestry. Arkansas, California, Kentucky, and Maryland are the current names of the occupied land of my Native American ancestors. The Quapaw lived in Arkansas. The Chumash, Alliklik, Kitanemuk, Serrano, Gabrielino Luiseno Cahuilla, and the Kumeyaay (Southern California); Modoc, Achumawi, and Atsugewi (Northeastern); Tolowa, Shasta, Karok, Yurok Hupa Whilikut, Chilula, Chimarike and Wiyot (Northwestern); and Bear River, Mattale, Lassick, Nogatl, Wintun, Yana, Yahi, Maidu, Wintun, Sinkyone, Wailaki, Kato, Yuki, Pomo, Lake Miwok, Wappo, Coast Miwok, Interior Miwok, Wappo, Coast Miwok, Interior Miwok, Monache, Yokuts, Costanoan, Esselen, Salinan and Tubatulabal (Central California) lived in California. The Cherokee, Chickasaw, Mosopelea, Shawnee and Yuchi tribes lived in Kentucky. The Accohannock, Assateaque, Choptank, Delaware, Matapeake, Nanticoke, Piscataway, Pocomoke, and Shawnee lived in Maryland. Denmark, England, France, Germany, Netherlands, and Scotland are the home of my European ancestors.

On my father's side, my family story begins with my great-great-grandfather Peter Leek who was born in 1799 in Maryland, and my great-great-grandmother Catherine Leek who was born in 1811 in Maryland. They had 14 children including my great-grandfather Leonard Leek who was born in Hagerstown, Maryland in 1825. The entire family of sixteen people was enslaved in Hagerstown until they escaped by way of the Underground Railroad. My daughter and I discovered their escape while researching family history on Ancestry.com. We found my great-grandfather Leonard's obituary that was published in the *Lansing State Journal* in 1927. When we read the title of the obituary, "Former Slave, 102, Dies at Home," we were amazed because we didn't know this part of our family history.

My great-grandfather Leonard's obituary provided the missing details of our family's journey from slavery to freedom. It also inspired my daughter to use Ancestry.com and Google search engine to dig deeper into our family history. Based on the year Leonard was born (1825), she determined our family escaped in 1839. His obituary told us they traveled by covered wagons, on steam ships, and at times walked for several days. They reached Cleveland, Ohio and were put on board the Keystone State steamer, one of several steamers sailing between Cleveland and Amherstburg, Canada. Amherstburg was a chief entry point for the Underground Railroad freedom seekers into Canada. Their journey to freedom was approximately 410 miles.

When my daughter visited the Doleman Black Heritage Museum in Hagerstown, she learned some historical facts that helped me understand how a family of sixteen might have planned their escape. There is a strong likelihood our family sought assistance from the Ebenezer African Methodist Episcopal Church that was incorporated by Reverend Thomas W. Henry in 1839. She used *The Underground Railroad in Hagerstown* brochure published by Visit Hagerstown to gather information about the route freedom seekers took to access the Underground Railroad. Most freedom seekers traveled on Jonathan Street to Chambersburg, Pennsylvania, the first major destination for people escaping from Washington County.

After researching our family history on Ancestry.com's Canadian census records, my daughter identified Peter and Catherine Leek and several of their children, including my great-grandfather Leonard and his brother Isaac. Isaac's family history is featured in the Amherstburg Freedom Museum. Her research taught us Leonard married my great-grandmother, Sarah E. Reider (born in 1846). They had a son, James Ebard Leek, my grandfather, in Colchester in Essex County in Ontario, Canada in 1871. We learned from Leonard's obituary that he remarried Anna S. Leek, died in 1927, and was buried in Mount Hope Cemetery in Lansing, Michigan. Learning my ancestors had the courage to escape slavery gave me deeper pride and gratitude for their sacrifices. It also showed me how I inherited their DNA as change agents.

My grandfather James (preferred to be called Ebard) married my grandmother Florida Jones who was born in Louisville, Kentucky in 1885. They had my father, John Leonard Leek (later changed to Leak and Leeke), who was born in Minneapolis, Minnesota in 1914. My grandmother Florida's family can be traced back through her father, John Henry Jones, my great-grandfather who was born in 1830 in California, and her mother, Sarah Ann Montgomery Jones (Hoke Hughes), my great-grandmother who was born in 1865 in Arkansas and died in Indianapolis in 1933. She was buried in Crown Cemetery near Butler University in Indianapolis. Sarah's parents were William Montgomery and Mary Jane Collins Montgomery (Washington), my great-great-grandparents. Mary Jane was born in 1832 in Alabama and died in 1912 in Indianapolis, Indiana. Mary Jane's parents were Carter Collins (born in Alabama) and Lilly Webb (born in North Carolina), my great-great-great-grandparents.

On my mother's side, my family story begins with Osborne Weir, Sr., my great-great-grandfather who was born in Greenville, Kentucky, and Caroline Smith Martin, my great-great-grandmother born in 1828 in Greenville, Kentucky. Osborne and Caroline married and had a daughter, Cratter Weir, my great-grandmother who was born in 1852 in Kentucky. Cratter married Henry Fred Roberts who was born in 1855. They had my grandfather Henry Osborne Roberts in 1875 in Morton's Gap, Kentucky. My grandfather Henry married my grandmother Eunice Ann Thomas in 1898. They had my mother, Frederica Stanley Roberts, in 1915 in Terre Haute, Indiana.

My grandmother Eunice was born to David Thomas and Francis "Fannie" Daniel Thomas in 1879 in Calhoun, Kentucky. My great-grandfather David was born to my great-great-grandparents Latt Mort and Martha Thomas in 1857 in Kentucky. My great-grandmother Fannie was born to John "Hence" Daniel, a Native American, and Ann Newton Daniel, an enslaved African woman, in 1863 in Kentucky.

Most of my early ancestors, which would include my maternal grandparents and paternal grandmother and great aunts and uncles, expressed their pride of race, lineage, and self through their education, community service, and entrepreneurial efforts at a time when American society did not support the freedom, equality, and upward mobility of African Americans. Their commitment to overcoming these struggles exemplified the seven principles of Kwanzaa my family has practiced for more than two decades. They include:

1. Umoja is unity in the family, community, race, and nation.
2. Kujichagulia is self-determination to define, create, and speak for ourselves.
3. Ujima is collective work and responsibility to build and keep our community together.
4. Ujaama is cooperative economics to build and manage our own stores, shops, and businesses.
5. Nia is purpose to make our collective vocation the building and developing of our community's greatness.
6. Kuumba is creativity in leaving our community more beautiful and beneficial than we inherited it.
7. Imani is faith in believing with all our heart in our parents, teachers, leaders, and the righteousness and victory of our struggle.

My ancestors' choices and commitment helped give birth to the man I am today.

Three days after I was born, my father, John Leonard Leeke ("John Leeke"), sent a letter typed on his office stationery to my aunt Mabel Roberts ("Aunt Mae"), my mother's eldest sister, expressing the joy and excitement he and my mother,

Frederica ("Freddie") Stanley Roberts Leeke, had when I was born on May 19, 1939. In the letter, he wrote:

Well to start off, he is the cutest baby I ever saw (not just because he is mine either), but everyone says that his features, skin & etc. are perfect. Eunice Ann and H.O. were over yesterday and they were tickled pink. He weighed seven and a quarter with fingernails, toe-nails and everything (I say the last because from my understanding, it is not common for them to come here without those little accessories).

Mrs. Roberts said he was a long baby and that he would be tall. Now to tell you about his hair, kid, it is really hot stuff. You know real-fine and not much of it. Everyone says that it will really be nice hair, and of course you know Freddie and I are really pleased with that. Next, he is about Freddie's complexion, the eyes, we are not quite sure about, you see we can't tell whether they are brown or black, but they are very nice eyes, you know, big and pretty. Well, that's enough on John Frederic. I am sure you know by this time that he is the latest in baby pulchritude, except he came here raising a racket.

His letter reminds me how my family stayed connected through love and stories. I became the beneficiary of this love that very day as my mother gave birth to me in my parents' apartment in Lockefield Gardens, the first Federal Government housing project in Indianapolis, Indiana.

Dr. Clarence A. Toles, my granduncle who was married to my father's mother's sister, Lavinia, delivered me with the assistance of my aunt Paulyne Roberts ("Aunt Paul"), my mother's older sister. Dr. Toles, a native of Kansas City, Missouri, was a graduate of the Emmerich Manual Training School and Indiana University School of Medicine. In addition to his medical practice, he was elected to serve as the Deputy Coroner of Indianapolis and the President of the Aesculapian Medical Society, the Indianapolis Chapter of the National Medical Association (NMA). The NMA is the oldest and largest organization representing African American physicians and health professionals in the United States since 1895. His memberships included the Alpha Phi Alpha Fraternity, Inc., the first intercollegiate Greek-letter fraternity established for African American men at Cornell University in 1906; and the Allen Chapel African Methodist Church.

At the time of my birth, Aunt Paul worked as a nurse at Homer G. Phillips Hospital, the only medical institution built to serve the needs of more than 70,000 African Americans in St. Louis, Missouri. John Leeke was employed as a resident manager in Lockefield Gardens. He was hired by Lionel Artis, an African American man who served as the Director of Lockefield Gardens. Lionel was also a Leeke family friend and my godfather.

My name, John Frederic, celebrates the first names of my parents. My father and I were named after my great-grandfather, John Henry Jones. Although I don't know much about him, I do know he and my great-grandmother Sarah Montgomery Jones raised 12 children, including William, Thaddeus, George, Suzanne, Lillian (Brown), Jessie (Gentry), Lavinia (Toles), Edna (died at 19), Sanoma, Betty, and my grandmother, Florida (Leeke). I was not able to find information about two of their children. Florida, a native of Louisville, Kentucky, and several of her siblings attended and graduated from college. Florida and her sister Lavinia became social workers. Lavinia graduated from Butler University and Indiana University. Lillian became a drama teacher. Thaddeus moved to Los Angeles to work as an actor and producer. He is best known for his work in the movie, *The Buccaneer.* William served in the military and worked for the U.S. Postal Service and the City Hospital in Indianapolis. Suzanne was a writer in New York City during the Harlem Renaissance and later returned to Indianapolis to work as a nurse before she died in her late thirties.

My grandmother was affectionately known as "Florida J." She was an exuberant woman with a lot of friends. She was very forthcoming and had a take-charge personality. After she married my grandfather James Ebard Leek, they lived in Milwaukee, Wisconsin. James and Florida J started their family in Minneapolis, Minnesota where Lillian Jane ("Jane") was born in 1913 and John Leonard in 1914. The family later moved to Gary, Indiana.

Both of my grandparents worked while raising their children. She earned a living as a dressmaker and a social worker. He owned a barber shop and ran it as an after-hours gambling house until his death in 1934. Several years after moving to Gary, they divorced. After the divorce, she changed the last name from Leek to Leak. A few years later, she changed it to Leeke which has made it more difficult to trace my family history.

During my father's teenage years, Florida J became a member of Sigma Gamma Rho Sorority, Inc., an African American sorority founded on the campus of Butler University in Indianapolis, Indiana. She served as a national officer in the role of Grand Anti-Grammateus from 1927 to 1929. She also became a charter member of the Epsilon Chapter (later became Alpha Sigma Sigma) in Gary.

Sigma Gamma Rho Sorority selected her sister, Lillian, a teacher, a wife of a local doctor, and a mother of one daughter, as an honorary member. She served as the President of the Indianapolis City Federation of Colored Women's Clubs, President of the Woman's Council, and member of the Women's Improvement Club of Indianapolis. Florida, Lillian, and their sister Lavinia were change agents and social activists committed to the upliftment of the African American community. Like Lillian, Lavinia was a member of the National Association of Negro Women's Clubs and served as the first vice president of the Indianapolis Chapter of the National Council of Negro Women (NCNW). Their friendship with Dr. Mary McLeod Bethune, the NCNW founder, strengthened their commitment.

In her career, Florida J held administrative positions at several colleges and taught school when she moved to Los Angeles and remarried. In the 1930s, she made sure her two children attended college. Jane studied French at Fisk University in Nashville, Tennessee. While at Fisk, she became a member of Alpha Kappa Alpha Sorority, Inc., an African American sorority founded at Howard University. When she graduated, she married her college sweetheart, Harry Schell, an attorney, and began teaching French at Theodore Roosevelt High School, more commonly known as Gary Roosevelt. Gary Roosevelt was one of only three high schools in Indiana constructed exclusively for African Americans. They had one child, Harry Jr.

My father attended the University of Illinois at Urbana-Champagne. Chemistry was my father's major. While there, he joined Kappa Alpha Psi Fraternity, Inc., an African American fraternity founded at Indiana University in Bloomington, Indiana in 1911. When my father transferred to Indiana State Teachers College (later became Indiana State University) in Terre Haute, Indiana, he met my mother, Freddie, the love of his life.

Although my father didn't have any brothers, he had a close relationship with his cousin William (Bill) Brown Jones, the son of my uncle, William Jones, one of Florida J's brothers. Bill was 10 years older than my dad. He was born and raised in Indianapolis, Indiana. He also attended Butler University and worked in the U.S. Postal Service. He married his wife, Anna, in 1929 and moved to Chicago to be with her. During World War II, he joined the U.S. Army and was stationed in the artillery division in northern Italy and Germany. He later entered officer training school and retired as a Major. When he left the military, he returned to working in the U.S. Postal Service.

My mother, Frederica "Freddie," a native of Terre Haute and a graduate of the Training High School of the Indiana State Teachers College, was a year younger than my father. When she was a junior in high school in 1930, she became a change agent when she and Ernestine Horvel (the aunt of my childhood friend Wally Webb) founded the A.Q. Club, an organization for their Black female classmates. They raised money through plays, operas, teas, seasonal balls, dances, fashion shows, garden parties, concerts, and other events to support needy families with food, the Phyllis Wheatley home, and the colored day nursery. They continued the organization while they were in college. During my parents' courtship, they attended garden parties at the home of her parents, Henry Osborne and Eunice Ann Thomas Roberts. They married there in 1937. The *Indianapolis Recorder*, a Black newspaper founded in 1898, covered their nuptials. The article was entitled "College Romance Culminates Marriage of Leeke-Roberts." Below is a copy of the text from the article.

The lovely home of Mr. and Mrs. H.O. Roberts of Terre Haute, Indiana, was the scene of the wedding of their youngest daughter, Frederica, and John Leeke, only son of Mrs. Florida J. Leeke, a prominent socialite of this city. The single ring ceremony was performed by the Rev. B.C. Winchester, pastor of the Second Missionary Baptist church in Terre Haute, and the bride and groom stood before an altar of ferns and palms.

Throughout the entire ceremony, melodious bridal airs were played by the accomplished Miss Dora Alice Smith, a school friend of both the bride and groom. The house was beautifully decorated with assorted fall flowers. There were no attendants. The bride was charmingly attired in white duchess satin, designed on princess style.

Attending it relatives from out of town were: Mrs. W.E. Brown, Dr. and Mrs. C.A. Toles, and Mrs. Leeke, of Indianapolis; Miss Pauline Roberts, head nurse in Hospital No. 2, in St. Louis, Missouri, and Miss Mabel Roberts, teacher in the Elkhart, Indiana schools, sisters of the bride. Mrs. Leeke is a graduate of the Indiana State Teacher's Training school, and both she and her husband attended the Indiana State Teachers College. The marriage is a culmination of a college romance, and the young couple will be at home to their friends in the Lockefield Garden Apartments of this city.

Growing up, I spent a lot of time with my grandparents on my mother's side. Her father, Henry Osborne Roberts, affectionately called "Ozzie" by Eunice, his wife of 64 years. I called him "Granny Man" and her "Grandmother." Granny Man's father, Henry, was a white man. His mother, Cratter, was a mixed-race woman. He had one sister named Lydia. His parents named him after his father and selected his maternal grandfather Osborne's first name as his middle name. He self-identified as a colored man. When he met Grandmother, she was working as a teacher. She was also a graduate of Franklin College. After falling in love, they married in 1898.

Grandmother's parents, David and Francis ("Fannie"), raised seven children: Ada, Bessie, Eunice, Clyde, Lucien, and Leslie Russell (Uncle Buck). My great-grandfather David was a farmer and a preacher. My great-grandmother Fannie was a seamstress, a hat maker, and a midwife. Fannie selected Ann as the middle name of my grandmother Eunice. Grandmother was a proud, outgoing, and statuesque woman who regularly held court on her front porch and dispensed advice to Terre Haute's African American community. She was an active member of her Second Missionary Baptist Church and the Bethlehem Chapter of the Order of the Eastern Star, Prince Hall Affiliation. She served as treasurer for 40 years. When she went out, she was dressed to the nines. Folks called her "Mrs. H.O." or "Miss Eunice Ann."

Utilizing her entrepreneurial skills as a seamstress, she developed a clientele that included the mayor's wife and many illustrious residents. She was known as one of the most skillful dressmakers in Indiana. In addition, she was instrumental in helping to organize research for the book *The Negro in the History of Indiana* by Dr. John W. Lyda, my grandmother's good friend. Dr. Lyda, a Terre Haute native, was a graduate of DePauw University, Indiana State Teachers College, and Indiana University. He taught at Paine College, Morgan State College, and the University of Texas at Houston before serving as the Director of the Graduate School of Education of Atlanta University.

Grandmother's fierce housekeeping schedule included

menus for each day of the week. Her Sunday dinner plates were filled with homemade rolls, Kentucky wonder green beans straight from her garden, and baked chicken that once lived in her backyard and were killed by Granny Man when he wrung their necks. Mondays were wash days. The wash tub sat in the middle of the kitchen while navy bean soup cooked on the stove and cornbread in the oven for dinner. On Fridays, she fried fish. She was a woman with a plan who wanted each of her children to have the opportunity to attend college and better themselves.

Like Grandmother, Granny Man was actively involved in his church, the Spruce Street African Methodist Episcopal (A.M.E.) Church and served as its treasurer for many years. He was also a Mason. Both my grandparents were members of the Board of Control of the Hyte Community, a social services organization established in 1941 to meet the needs of Black youth in Terre Haute. Grandmother was the secretary of the Board. Their community service demonstrated their role as change agents.

As an entrepreneur, Granny Man, like Grandmother, had a strong work ethic. He was famous for riding his bike to and from his various jobs as a furnace tender and a landscaper. In the wee hours of the morning, he would travel to his clients' homes to ensure they had enough coal to heat their furnaces. Maintaining his business required a high level of responsibility, discipline, and client trust and respect. Most of his clients were white people who owned large homes.

In spring and summer evenings, he would often sit on

the front porch observing the neighborhood happenings. My cousin Chester Paul's friend Bob Russell, one of Terre Haute's Black morticians whose funeral home was two blocks away from my grandparents' home, often stopped by to say hello. During his visits, Granny Man's dry humor showed up on the scene. He would tell Bob, "Don't worry, we'll call you when the time comes. You don't have to keep checking on whether I am still alive." As he got older, he would sit in the dining room nodding off to sleep.

Together, they had five children: Mabel, Paulyne, Chester, Maurice who died two months after birth, and my mother, Frederica Stanley. Mabel studied education and graduated from Indiana State Normal College, joined Zeta Phi Beta Sorority, an African American sorority established at Howard University, and became the first Black teacher in Elkhart, Indiana. Paulyne studied nursing and graduated from Homer G. Phillips Hospital in St. Louis, Missouri. Chester attended Indiana State Teachers College where he studied printing and met and married Alma Burnham, a library science major. Finally, Frederica attended Indiana State and studied home economics.

Granny Man and Grandmother's commitment to their family and educating their children, home ownership, church, community, and businesses created a template for me to use in my life when I came of age to marry and have a family. As you can see, my ancestors laid a very strong foundation for the life I was born to lead. Turn the page and learn what happens when I get to walk the path they carved out for me in my early years.

Francis "Fannie" Daniel Thomas, daughter of Ann and Hence Daniel, wife of David Thomas, and mother of Eunice Ann Thomas Roberts

Francis "Fannie" Daniel Thomas, wife of David Thomas, with her son Clyde

Bessie and Clyde Thomas, children of Francis "Fannie" Daniel Thomas and David Thomas

*Leslie "Uncle Buck" Thomas,
son of Francis "Fannie"
Daniel Thomas and
David Thomas*

*Leslie "Uncle Buck" Thomas
as an older man*

*Eunice Ann Thomas Roberts,
daughter of Francis "Fannie"
Daniel Thomas and David
Thomas, as a young girl*

*Eunice Ann Thomas Roberts
as a young woman*

Eunice Ann Thomas
Roberts and her sister
Ada Thomas, daughters
of Francis "Fannie"
Daniel Thomas and
David Thomas,
as young women

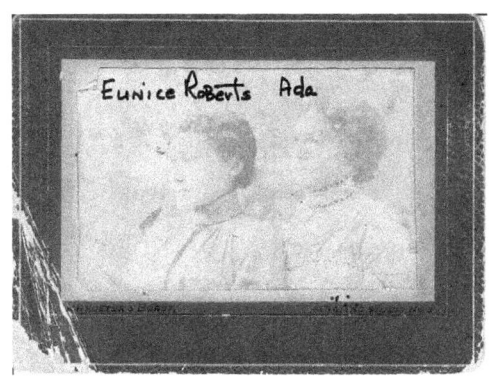

Eunice Ann Thomas Roberts as an
older woman dressed to the nines in
her Spruce Street neighborhood in
Terre Haute, Indiana

Eunice Ann Thomas Roberts as an
older woman walking in downtown
Terre Haute, Indiana in the 1940s

25

Henry Osborne Roberts, husband of Eunice Ann Thomas Roberts, as a younger man

Lydia Roberts, sister of Henry Osborne Roberts, and Eunice Ann Thomas Roberts

Lydia Roberts and her nephew, David Henry Roberts, son of Chester Henry Roberts and Alma Burnham Roberts

Dad.

Henry Osborne Roberts, husband of Eunice Ann Thomas Roberts, standing in the front yard of their home located at 1657 Spruce Street in Terre Haure, Indiana

Eunice Ann Thomas Roberts and Henry O. Roberts

Home of Eunice Ann Thomas Roberts and Henry Osborne Roberts located at 1657 Spruce Street in Terre Haute, Indiana (photo taken in 1968)

1657 - Spruce St
T.H. Ind

*Eunice Ann Thomas Roberts is seated in the fourth seat
(from the left) on the end of the third row (near children) at the
Oak Street Second Baptist Church in Terre Haute, Indiana*

*Henry Osborne Roberts standing in the front row
(second from the left) with his Mason brothers at the
Spruce Street AME Church in Terre Haute, Indiana*

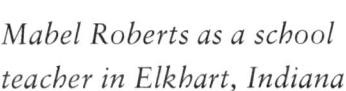

Mabel Roberts, first daughter of Eunice Ann Thomas Roberts and Henry Osborne Roberts

Mabel Roberts as a school teacher in Elkhart, Indiana

Paulyne Roberts, second daughter of Eunice Ann Thomas Roberts and Henry Osborne Roberts, as a young nurse who completed her education at Homer G. Phillips Hospital and School of Nursing in St. Louis, Missouri

29

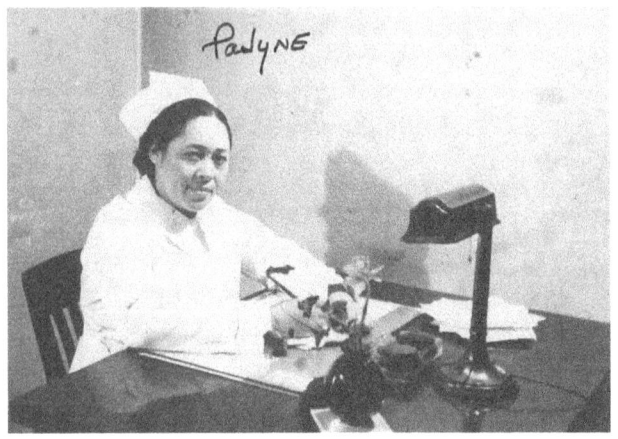

*Paulyne Roberts, second daughter of Eunice Ann Thomas
Roberts and Henry Osborne Roberts, working as
a public health nurse in Washington, DC*

*Paulyne Roberts in the 1950s
in Washington, DC*

*Paulyne Roberts and her sister
Frederica "Freddie" Stanley
Roberts Leeke in 1918
in Terre Haute, Indiana*

Chester Henry Roberts, son of Eunice Ann Thomas Roberts and Henry Osborne Roberts, and his youngest sister, Frederica "Freddie" Stanley Roberts Leeke

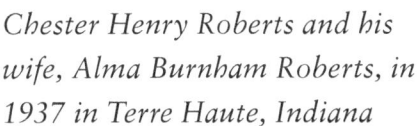

Chester Henry Roberts and his wife, Alma Burnham Roberts, with his sister Frederica Stanley Roberts Leeke in 1926 in Terre Haute, Indiana

Chester Henry Roberts and his wife, Alma Burnham Roberts, in 1937 in Terre Haute, Indiana

31

Chester Henry Roberts and his wife, Alma Burnham Roberts, in Wilmington, Delaware

The children of Chester Henry Roberts and Alma Burnham Roberts: David Henry, Chester Paul, Thomas Eugene, and Leslie Russell Roberts in 1937

Chester Henry Roberts and his daughter Paulyne Anne Roberts

Frederica Stanley Roberts Leeke, third daughter of Eunice Ann Thomas Roberts Leeke and Henry Osborne Roberts, as a toddler in Terre Haute, Indiana in 1916

Frederica Stanley Roberts Leeke, third daughter of Eunice Ann Thomas Roberts and Henry Osborne Roberts, standing in front of the Spruce Street Baptist Church in 1931

Frederica Stanley Roberts Leeke, third daughter of Eunice Ann Thomas Roberts and Henry Osborne Roberts, standing with a tennis racket in her hand in Terre Haute, Indiana in the 1930s

*Frederica Stanley Roberts Leeke and her fellow graduates of the
Training School of Indiana State Teachers College in 1932*

*Frederica Stanley Roberts Leeke as a young college student
majoring in Home Economics at Indiana State
Teachers College in the 1930s*

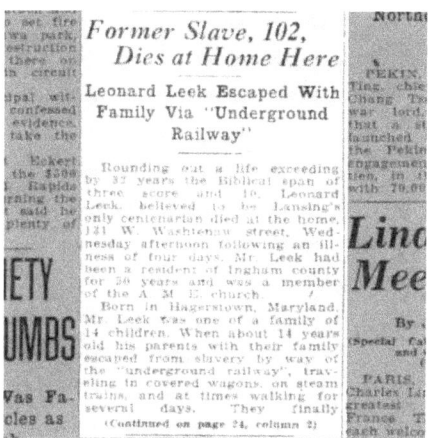

Page one of the obituary of Leonard Leek (Leak), the father of James Ebard Leak and grandfather of John Leonard Leeke, who escaped from slavery with his parents, Peter and Catherine Leak, and his 13 siblings, in Hagerstown, Maryland to Amherstburg, Canada in 1839

Page two of the obituary of Leonard Leek (Leak), the father of James Ebard Leak and grandfather of John Leonard Leeke and Lillian Jane Leeke Schell

Death Certificate of Leonard Leek (Leak),
the father of James Ebard Leak and grandfather of
John Leonard Leeke and Lillian Jane Leeke Schell

Sarah Ann Montgomery Jones (Hoke Hughes), wife of John Henry Jones, mother of Florida Jones Leeke (Leak and Leek), and grandmother of John Leonard Leeke and Lillian Jane Leeke Schell

Florida Jones Leeke (Leak and Leek), daughter of Sarah Ann Montgomery Jones (Hoke Hughes) and John Henry Jones, wife of James Ebard Leak, and mother of John Leonard Leeke and Lillian Jane Leeke Schell, as a young woman

Florida Jones Leeke (Leak and Leek), wife of James Ebard Leak and mother of John Leonard Leeke and Lillian Jane Leeke Schell, as an older woman

Lillian Jones Brown, daughter of Sarah Ann Montgomery Jones (Hoke Hughes) and John Henry Jones, as a young woman

Lillian Jones Brown, daughter of Sarah Ann Montgomery Jones (Hoke Hughes) and John Henry Jones, as an older woman

John Leonard Leeke and Lillian Jane Leeke Schell

*John Leonard Leeke and
Lillian Jane Leeke Schell
sitting on porch with cousin*

*John Leonard Leeke
and his sister Lillian
Jane Leeke Schell in
Michigan in 1922*

*John Leonard Leeke,
his sister Lillian Jane
Leeke Schell, and
their Leak cousins in
Michigan in 1922*

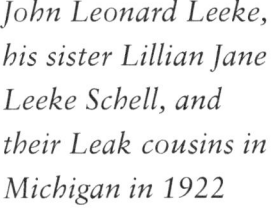

*Jessie Jones Gentry, daughter of Sarah Ann Montgomery Jones
(Hoke Hughes) and John Henry Jones, and wife of
George Gentry, as a young woman*

*Jessie Jones Gentry, daughter of Sarah Ann Montgomery
Jones (Hoke Hughes) and John Henry Jones,
and her husband, George Gentry*

Lavinia Jones Toles, daughter of Sarah Ann Montgomery Jones (Hoke Hughes) and John Henry Jones, wife of Dr. Clarence A. Toles, and mother of Barbara Toles Bluiett

Lavinia Jones Toles and her niece Lillian Jane Leeke Schell walking in Los Angeles, California in the 1940s

Lavinia Jones Toles, daughter of Sarah Ann Montgomery Jones (Hoke Hughes) and John Henry Jones, wife of Dr. Clarence A. Toles, and daughter of Barbara Toles Bluiett, as an older woman

In Memoriam

LAVINIA J. TOLES

*Suzanne Jones, daughter of
Sarah Ann Montgomery Jones
(Hoke Hughes) and John Henry Jones*

*Betty Jones, daughter of Sarah Ann
Montgomery Jones (Hoke Hughes)
and John Henry Jones*

*William Jones, son of Sarah Ann
Montgomery Jones (Hoke Hughes)
and John Henry Jones, with his
wife, Susan Jones*

Thaddeus Jones, son of Sarah Ann Montgomery Jones (Hoke Hughes) and John Henry Jones, as a younger man

Thaddeus Jones, son of Sarah Ann Montgomery Jones (Hoke Hughes) and John Henry Jones, as an older man

George Jones, son of Sarah Ann Montgomery Jones (Hoke Hughes) and John Henry Jones, with his wife and two sons

Martha Gentry and her husband Eddie, Florida Jones Leeke, Gene Gentry, Jessie Jones Gentry and her husband George Gentry, and others in 1956

Jessie Jones Gentry and her daughter Martha Gentry at Disneyland in 1970s

Jessie Jones Gentry in 1969

John L. Leeke with his cousin
William "Bill" Jones in
Chicago, Illinois in the 1960s

William "Bill" Jones, son of
William and Susan Jones, and
his wife, Ann Jones, in 1967

William "Bill" Jones, son of
William and Susan Jones,
in John and Frederica Leeke's
house in 1967

John Leonard Leeke at
Frederica Stanley Roberts
Leeke's garden party in
Terre Haute, Indiana in 1933

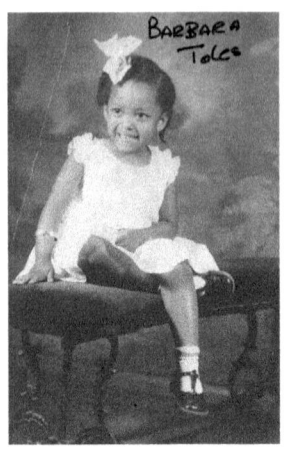

*Barbara Toles Blueitt,
daughter of Lavinia Jones
Toles and Dr. Clarence
A. Toles, as a child*

*Lillian Jane Leeke Schell with
her cousin Barbara Toles Blueitt
at the beach in Los Angeles,
California in the 1940s*

*Barbara Toles Blueitt, her husband, Marshall Blueitt,
and their children, Sonny, Yvonne, Michael, Stanton, Deborah,
and Adriana, on Easter in Indianapolis, Indiana in 1960*

Frederica Stanley Roberts Leeke, John Leonard Leeke, and their friends at her garden party in Terre Haute, Indiana in 1933

Frederica Stanley Roberts Leeke and John Leonard Leeke as college students at the Spruce Street Baptist Church in Terre Haute, Indiana in the 1930s

Lillian Jane Leeke Schell in the 1930s

Frederica Stanley Roberts Leeke, John Leonard Leeke, and Lillian Jane Leeke Schell at the beach in Gary, Indiana in 1938

CHAPTER 1 REFLECTION QUESTIONS

---

1. Individual: Think about the role of your ancestors in shaping your life. Identify one family member or adult for each stage of your early development: 1) childhood (1–12 years old); 2) teenage years (13–18 years old); and 3) young adulthood (19–22 years old). What did you learn from these people?

2. Individual: Were any of your ancestors change agents?

   NOTE: A change agent is a person who creates or supports the process of making a group, community, or organization grow and adapt in ways that improve the lives of others.

   Here are several change agent examples from my family:

   - *My great-great-grandfather Peter Leek and great-great-grandmother Catherine Leek and their fourteen children who escaped from slavery.*
   - *My grandmother Eunice Ann Thomas Roberts and grandfather Henry Oswald Roberts's participation as members of the Board of Control of the Hyte Community, a social services organization established in 1941 to meet the needs of Black youth in Terre Haute.*

3. Individual: Now that you have explored the impact your ancestors have had on your life, you're ready to take a deep dive into your life story. What's your life story (one or more experiences or events) that you want to tell and how will it help you and your family, friends, community, and colleagues? Do you have any thresholds of change in your life story?

   NOTE: A threshold of change is a moment in your life when you experienced a major shift in your beliefs, behavior, education, personal and professional growth, relationships, and/or environment that transformed who you are.

   Here's an example of a threshold of change that occurred in my family:

   - *When my grandmother Eunice Ann Thomas Roberts attended Franklin College and became a teacher, she was the first person that I know of who attended college in my mother's family. Her pursuit of education fueled her commitment to ensure her children received a college education which was passed down to my mother, myself, and my children.*

4. Group Discussion: Each person would have 3–5 minutes to share their responses with the group. As a group, list some of the similarities and differences highlighted in the sharing session. Also, discuss one or two lessons each person has learned.

CHAPTER 2

From Indianapolis to Terre Haute to Washington, DC

"The ache for home lives in all of us. The safe place where we can go as we are and not be questioned."

—DR. MAYA ANGELOU, a change agent, a poet, an author, a civil rights activist, and a professor

———————

Throughout my life, I have always felt I had several places I could go and feel welcomed and taken care of. That feeling is what helps me know I am in a safe place I can call home. It has guided me in how I have created a home with my family and a community with my friends, colleagues, church members, and neighbors.

Two years before I was born, my parents married and moved into Lockefield Gardens on Indiana Avenue in Indianapolis, Indiana in 1937. At the time, Indiana Avenue ("The Avenue") was known as the center of Black culture, commerce, and entrepreneurship in Indianapolis. It functioned as a "Black Main Street." It featured some of the Jazz Age's finest talent including Edward "Duke" Ellington, Cab Calloway, Ella Fitzgerald, and Wes Montgomery. The Avenue was also home to numerous Black newspapers, nightclubs, bars, businesses, and churches. America's first self-made woman millionaire, Madam C.J. Walker, built the Walker Building that housed her manufacturing company, a beauty school and salon, a ballroom, an auditorium/movie theater, a drugstore, a coffee shop, and professional offices there. All of this was located across the street from Lockefield Gardens.

When my parents moved into Lockefield Gardens, they were among the earliest residents of the first Federal housing project in Indianapolis. Living there was a big deal because the newly built community included more than just housing: it included a school, abundant green spaces for residents, and modern amenities with indoor plumbing in all 748 apartment units. It was also a big deal because my father worked there as a resident manager. He was hired by Lionel Artis, the Director of Lockefield Gardens. Artis was the first Black person to be appointed to a policy-making municipal agency in Indianapolis. He was also a family friend and a member of my father's Kappa Alpha Psi Fraternity. He knew my grandmother, Florida J, grandaunts Lillian and Lavinia, and Lavinia's husband, Dr. Toles. Like many other Black men during that era, my father worked a second job as a waiter in several restaurants.

While we lived in Indianapolis, I attended kindergarten at School 27, a segregated public school. My teacher was Hattie Mae Dulin Redford, one of the seven founders of Sigma Gamma Rho Sorority. Redford was the sorority sister of my grandmother, Florida J, and grandaunt, Lillian. I played with the children of my parents' friends, the Bowels, Hines, Ransom, and Robinson families. While we were playing one day in the apartment building's hallways, I jumped from one landing to the next, fell flat on my face, and ended up getting stitches in my chin at a local hospital. From that day forward, I was teased for pretending to be Superman. My Superman souvenir is a tiny scar that only I can see now. It is hidden by a lifetime of gray and white hair on my beard.

Throughout my family's life in Indianapolis, we spent time with my grandaunts Lavinia and Lillian. They were famous for having a Sunday family dinner like the ones in the movie, *Soul Food*. We also spent time with my parents' friends, the Haizlips. They managed and later owned the Willis Mortuary, one of the leading Black funeral homes located around the corner from Madame C.J. Walker's building. Because they didn't have any children and grew very fond of me, I was treated like their son throughout my entire life. In college, they opened their home, which was above the funeral home, to me for my weekend visits and during my student teaching. They even talked to me about seriously taking over their business when they retired. I told them I wasn't comfortable with the business and didn't want to study mortuary science. Like any good parents, they understood I had a different dream.

My grandparents' home on Spruce Street in Terre Haute became my home away from home. In *The Negro in the History of Indiana*, Dr. Lyda writes, "The words Terre Haute mean high ground. This city stands on the highest ground along the Wabash River for many miles in both directions." Spruce Street was referred to as the "Gold Coast" because middle-class Black homeowners created a flourishing neighborhood that spanned five blocks. Some of the homeowners included my grandparents; Dr. Winton Jones, the pharmacist; Huerta Tribble, the only Black police detective; James Ross, the chief maintenance engineer for the Elks Club; Helen Webb, an entertainer who played the piano at local clubs and events; Bob Russell, the owner of the Russell Funeral Home; and other professionals and entrepreneurs.

While I stayed with them on weekends and during the summer, I forged a bond with my four older cousins, David, Chester Paul, Thomas, and Leslie. They lived with their parents and our grandparents. I was always surrounded by extended family. Being the youngest of five male cousins, I did my best to keep up with them. They looked out for me and made me feel like their little brother. That was a special gift for an only child.

By the time my parents were ready to move to DC, I was six years old. My cousins were living in Wilmington, Delaware. Uncle Chester had gotten a job in the DuPont plant. Aunt Alma, affectionately known as Auntie, was a stay-at-home mother who was busy taking care of my five cousins, which now included their sister, Paulyne Anne. Thanks to her birth, I was no longer the youngest!

While my parents looked for permanent housing in DC in 1945, I lived with my uncle, aunt, and cousins for six months in Wilmington. Within this period, I was able to start first grade and develop a stronger bond with my cousins. It has lasted throughout my lifetime. Having these relationships helped me appreciate and cherish a close-knit family.

My family became a part of the second Great Migration, the mass movement of Blacks to cities in the North and West that began in 1940, when we moved from Indianapolis to DC in 1946. At that time, the city was segregated. That meant there were entire neighborhoods that were segregated, as well as specific establishments including schools, hospitals, churches, stores, restaurants, night clubs, movie theaters, beauty salons, and barber shops. It also meant Black people had numerous opportunities to create their own institutions and businesses that were strongly supported by their community. Being in DC was like living in Indianapolis. Both had thriving Black communities.

My parents purchased a three-story brick row house with a basement on 8th Street, NW. We lived there until my sophomore year in high school. Our house was located where the current Walter E. Washington Convention Center is now located. I had a large room on the second floor that looked out onto the street. My room was large enough for me to put up a Lionel train set and a small city of little plastic houses and other accessories. Aunt Paulyne, a nurse at Freedmen's Hospital, lived with us. She had a room across the hall from me. It was big enough for her bed, vanity set, chester drawers, and a reading chair. It reminded me of a master suite without a bathroom. We shared the second-floor bathroom. Several young men in their twenties and thirties who were just getting started in life rented rooms on the third floor and in the basement. Their rent money contributed to my family's income.

They were like big brothers to me. Living with them and my Aunt Paulyne created the same type of extended family experience I had in Indianapolis.

Our neighborhood had everything I needed as a child including Gregg's Barber Shop, where my father and I would get our hair cut on 7th Street, and several movie theaters, the GEM, Booker T., Dunbar, Howard, and Lincoln. Throughout my childhood, my parents and I spent time uptown and in the U Street neighborhood where the best of Black life happened. Having this experience made me feel safe. I thought I had everything I needed to enjoy a good life.

Today, U Street is known as the Greater U Street Historic District because it was home to the city's most important businesses, entertainment facilities, and fraternal and religious institutions owned and operated by African Americans. The city's leading African American citizens lived in the surrounding neighborhood. My parents loved to dine at Zanzibar, an upscale restaurant and bar located on 14th Street between U and W Streets. I ate breakfast regularly at the Waffle Shop, two doors down from Zanzibar's. The landscape of today's U Street is much different from when I was a boy. My daughter currently walks the same streets that I did, but because of time and gentrification, she eats breakfast at Café U or Busboys and Poets instead of the Waffle Shop. Many of the same landmarks are still there like the Industrial Bank, Lee's Flower Shop, and Mason's Building. Historical markers are placed on each street to educate newcomers about U Street's rich history.

Our family lived a middle-class lifestyle with my mother staying at home until I reached the sixth grade, and she began working as a secretary in the Federal Government. My father was the sole breadwinner who worked as a mail sorter for the U.S. Postal Service at the main location on North Capitol Street next to Union Station. He also leveraged his love of cards, numbers, and horses in gambling activities. On the weekends, he and my mother would host poker games in the basement. My mother would cook food. His fellow postal workers would come to eat and play cards on a regular basis. Each day he played the numbers with 327 as his favorite. He also spent a lot of time going to racetracks in Maryland, Delaware, and New Jersey. His life as a gambler had many ups and downs. When he experienced low cash moments, he would take his suits to the pawn shop. When times were better, he would go back and reclaim them. No matter what happened, we lived well.

John and Frederica Leeke in Indianapolis, Indiana in the 1930s

John and Frederica Leeke holding their newborn son,
John Frederic Leeke, in 1939

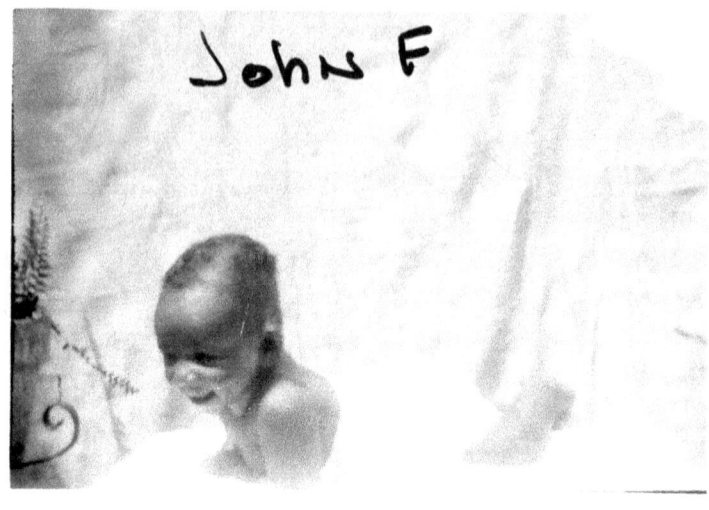

John Frederic Leeke as a baby in 1939

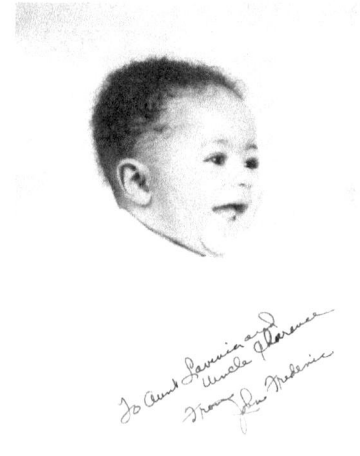

John Frederic Leeke as a toddler in 1939

Photograph of John Frederic Leeke given to his Aunt Lavinia Jones Toles and Uncle Clarence Toles in 1939

*John Frederic Leeke and his
Aunt Jane Leeke Schell at
Lockefield Garden Apartments
in Indianapolis, Indiana in 1939*

*John Frederic Leeke
as a toddler in his
grandparents' backyard
in Terre Haute, Indiana
in 1940*

John Frederic Leeke with his cousins David Henry, Chester Paul, Thomas Eugene, and Leslie Russell Roberts in Terre Haute, Indiana in 1941

John Frederic Leeke with his cousins David Henry, Chester Paul, Thomas Eugene, and Leslie Russell Roberts in their grandparents' backyard in Terre Haute, Indiana in 1941

John Frederic Leeke with his childhood friends Huerta Tribble and Winston Jones in Terre Haute, Indiana

John Frederic Leeke as a toddler at Lockefield Gardens Apartment in Indianapolis, Indiana in the 1940s

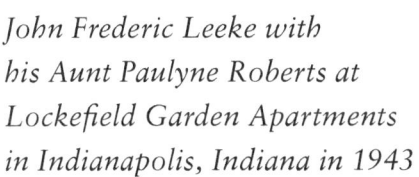

John Frederic Leeke riding his tricycle at Lockefield Gardens Apartments in Indianapolis, Indiana in the 1940s

John Frederic Leeke with his Aunt Paulyne Roberts at Lockefield Garden Apartments in Indianapolis, Indiana in 1943

John and Frederica Leeke in Washington, DC in the 1940s

John Frederic Leeke with his grandfather Henry Osborne Roberts and Aunt Paulyne Roberts standing near his parents' house on 8th Street, NW in Washington, DC in the 1950s

Henry Osborne Roberts and his daughters Paulyne Roberts and Frederica Roberts Leeke standing across the street from Frederica's house on 8th Street, NW in Washington, DC in the 1950s

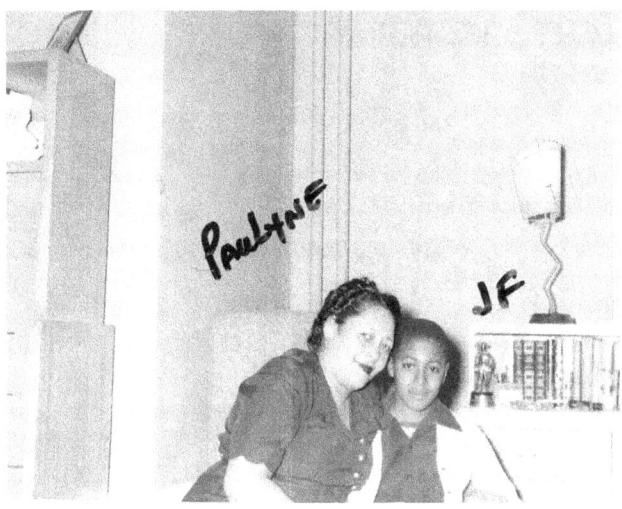

John Frederic Leeke with his Aunt Paulyne Roberts in his parents' home on 8th Street, NW in Washington, DC in the 1950s

John Frederic Leeke standing in front of his parents' home on 8th Street, NW in Washington, DC in the 1950s

CHAPTER 2 REFLECTION QUESTIONS

---

1. Individual: Think about where you and your family lived, attended church, went to school, worked, and participated in community and entertainment activities during your childhood. Who were the people, places, and events that impacted you?

2. Group Discussion: Each person would have 3–5 minutes to share their responses with the group. As a group, list some of the similarities and differences highlighted in the sharing session. Also, discuss one or two lessons each person has learned.

CHAPTER 3

From St. Augustine's Catholic School to Archbishop Carroll High School in DC

"None of us got where we are solely by pulling ourselves up by our bootstraps. We got there because somebody —a parent, a teacher, an Ivy League crony or a few nuns— bent and helped us pick up our boots."

—THURGOOD MARSHALL, SR., the first African American U.S. Supreme Court Justice, a change agent, a lawyer, and a civil rights activist

———————————

U.S. Supreme Court Justice Thurgood Marshall, Sr. is correct in acknowledging that none of us makes it alone. My life echoes Justice Marshall's words. I had plenty of support from my parents, family members, friends, nuns, teachers, coaches, and employers. I am who I am because of the people who have nurtured me.

Four of my life's greatest gifts came from the values my parents raised me with: structure, organization, responsibility, and socializing and having a good time despite any societal limitations resulting from segregation and other inequalities. I first want to talk about their passion for socializing and having a good time. It was something they learned early in their lives and were able to experience together when they met, dated, and married. My daughter Madelyn (Ananda) calls their way of being "joie de vivre," a French phrase that means the joy of living. Today, we both think they would be ambassadors of the Black Joy movement.

While writing this book, my daughter introduced me to the Black Joy movement when she asked me to visit the National Museum of African American History and Culture's website and read "Black Joy: Resistance, Resilience and Reclamation," an article written by Elaine Nichols. Our Black Joy conversation helped me name a family value I had practiced for decades. After reading the article, I reflected on the words of Kleaver Cruz, the founder of The Black Joy Project, a digital and real-world movement:

> *Black Joy is not ... dismissing or creating an 'alternate' black narrative that ignores the realities of our collective pain; rather, it is about holding the pain and injustice...in tension with the joy we experience. It's about using that joy as an entry into understanding the oppressive forces we navigate through as a means to imagine and create a world free of them.*

My daughter and I think the Black Joy my parents unconsciously possessed and instilled in me was preventive medicine because it can stand alongside the gifts of structure, organization, and responsibility in times when we experienced the pain and injustice of being Black. It was also an affirmation of who we were as a family. Our unconscious practice of Black Joy resonates with what Upset Homegirls co-founder Brandy Factory said, "Black Joy affirms that I am not a victim. I am an agent of change. It rejects the idea that violence, … injustice, discrimination, prejudice, and dominance over others are normal and acceptable actions." Factory's words offer another way of looking at how my parents and I have been change agents.

They lived out these values and made sure I learned how to use them in our family and home, and my education, extracurricular activities, and work ethic. Our house was run on a schedule. We ate dinner each night at around six o'clock. Sunday dinners were special because my mother always made her famous hot rolls. I also did chores and was responsible for keeping my room clean, washing dishes, vacuuming the carpets, and dusting throughout the house. My Catholic faith and education reinforced these values I have used in my life, marriage, role as a parent, and career. They helped me develop a sense of independence and confidence to do most anything. They also opened doors to many life experiences.

My parents' decision to enroll me in St. Augustine Catholic School, an all-Black elementary school, was a game changer for my family. I became the first family member to attend a private school. When I started school, my family was non-Catholic. While there, I began taking religious education classes every day. My mother also began studying to become a Catholic. I don't know why my mother decided to become Catholic. My hunch is that she may have been influenced by her sister Paulyne who had converted to Catholicism years before. She may have also been motivated by her friends, the Hines, who were Catholic. She and I joined St. Augustine Catholic Church, DC's oldest Black Catholic Church, together. The church was originally founded by former enslaved Black people in 1858 and dedicated in 1876. During its early years, a small population of white people attended Mass. That changed during the Jim Crow era. My father didn't convert but attended Mass on special occasions like Christmas and Easter.

By the time I reached the sixth grade, my mother began working at the Naval Air Systems Command, a part of the U.S. Department of Navy, in Arlington, Virginia. Most mornings, my dad would drive my mother to work and then give me money and drop me off for breakfast at the Waffle Shop at 14th and U Streets. My morning routine was not typical for most of my classmates who ate breakfast at home. All the waitresses knew me. Some days I would eat waffles. Other days I'd eat fried or scrambled eggs. Being able to order, eat, and pay for my breakfast made me feel very grown up. After breakfast, I'd walk three blocks to school. After school, I walked home, changed my clothes, and started my homework. After dinner, I completed my homework and had some time to play. Having the freedom to do these things enhanced my independence.

The Oblate Sisters of Providence, the oldest Black order of nuns in the United States, were in charge of the school. Their order was founded by Mother Elizabeth Lange, a Cuban woman of Haitian descent. The nuns knew how important it was for us to be well prepared. They stressed reading, math, and penmanship. Penmanship has stayed with me even today. I still receive compliments about how clear my printing and cursive writing are.

Mother Consolata, the principal, and the other nuns, taught me about service, leadership, responsibility, and team-work. I served as an altar boy and a school patrol. I joined because I was always following in the footsteps of the older students who were leaders and involved in both activities. I looked up to them as role models. As an altar boy, I had to learn Latin, clean and set up the altar, and assist the priest during weekday and Sunday Masses. One of the benefits was serving at funerals. All the altar boys liked to attend funerals because it meant we missed class, got to ride in the funeral car, and sometimes had lunch out with the priests.

In the fifth and sixth grades, I was a patrol boy standing on the corners and making sure my classmates safely crossed the street. I became a lieutenant patrol in seventh grade and cap-tain of the patrols in the eighth grade. In both capacities, I su-pervised other patrols which helped strengthen my leadership skills. These experiences were my first opportunity to manage a team. Every May, all patrols participated in a citywide pa-rade down Pennsylvania Avenue. I always looked forward to it because the students at St. John's Military School would vol-unteer to train us how to march with precision and style.

During my last two years, Mother Mary Consolata select-ed me to represent the school for different events hosted by the District of Columbia and the Archdiocese of Washington, DC. On one occasion, I was invited to take a photograph with

Archbishop Patrick O'Boyle (who later became a Cardinal) and two white Catholic students including an All Catholic athlete from Archbishop Carroll High School's first graduating class. It was published in the *Catholic Standard*, a weekly newspaper. My parents, Aunt Paulyne, and the rest of my family were thrilled. They shared the news with anyone who would listen.

In those years, I could go for weeks and only interact with Black folks except for the white pastor at St. Augustine's, Monsignor Gingras, and his assistant, Father George Joyce. They supported Archbishop O'Boyle's efforts to end segregation in the Archdiocese of Washington. For example, Monsignor Gingras led the discussions around the merger of St. Augustine Church with the all-white congregation of St. Paul Church. His efforts laid the groundwork for the merger in the early 1960s. Father Joyce, along with several Black male parishioners including Willis Thomas and George Dines, Sr., were instrumental in ending the segregated Catholic Youth Organization (CYO) League.

St. Augustine's athletic program gave me an opportunity to pursue my passion for baseball and basketball. By the time I started playing in the CYO League, they were integrated in terms of participation. Here's what this type of integrated participation looked like: Black teams were able to play white teams. My involvement in sports also taught me the value of teamwork, sportsmanship, and competition. I began playing baseball in the fifth grade. As the youngest player, I pitched and played in the infield. I joined the basketball team in the sixth grade. Mr. Chapman coached both teams. Our basketball practices were held at the historic Twelfth Street YMCA.

My love of sports included following my hometown team, the Washington Senators. I'd go see them play at Griffith Stadium, a 10-block walk from my home. Some of my favorite players included Bob Porterfield, a pitcher; Eddie Yost, a third baseman; Mickey Vernon, a first baseman; and Jim Busby, a centerfielder. There were no Black players on the team. I also attended several games played by the Homestead Grays, one of the Negro Leagues' preeminent clubs, that was based in DC and Pittsburgh. They won nine straight league titles from 1937 to 1948, and three Negro World Series championships in that timeframe. One of the highlights was seeing legendary slugger Josh Gibson, who is often compared to Babe Ruth.

When Jackie Robinson became the first Black baseball player in the Major Leagues in 1947, I fell in love with the Brooklyn Dodgers. Roy Campanella, a catcher; Don Newcombe, a pitcher; Pee Wee Reese, a shortstop; Gil Hodges, a first basemen; Duke Snider, a centerfielder; and Preacher Roe, a pitcher, were some of my favorites who helped beat the New York Yankees and win the World Series in 1955. I'd listen to the broadcast of their games on the radio. I fondly remember laying in my bed at night listening to Nat Allbright, an American sports announcer who used a ticker tape and embellishment to give a play-by-play radio broadcast of games he had never seen. He would describe each pitch and play, combined with sound effects to make the depiction more vivid to listeners. One that I remember was, "Snider steps in. The pitch comes. It's a long fly ball to deep center field and it's out of here onto Bedford Avenue."

Before the school year ended, I had a ritual of writing to my grandparents and asking them if I could spend the summer in Terre Haute. This ritual taught me how to be responsible for making arrangements for the things I wanted to do. It also taught me not to assume I could just show up at my grandparents' home and expect them to take care of me for the summer. I learned staying with them was a privilege. Naturally, they would write back and say they would love to have me. I traveled there by train while I was in the fifth to the ninth grades. This experience made my love of model trains come alive. Growing up, I owned a Lionel Train set. I would use the money I received from doing chores for the young men who rented rooms on the third floor of our family home to purchase train cars, parts, and plastic houses and buildings. On the days I had extra money, I'd walk downtown to a train shop and buy them.

My parents became acquainted with one of the Black Pullman Porters who would look out for me during my summer trips. I traveled with him regularly for several summers. He would also let me accompany him at each of the stops as he helped direct the Black and white passengers on and off the train. As the train departed, I stood with him at the rear of the car where people boarded. The lower half of the door was closed. We would watch the train move away from the station for three to five minutes. That was a big deal for me because everyone didn't get a chance to do that. It made me feel special and more grown up like one of the Pullman Porters.

The Pullman Porters were known as the ambassadors of hospitality. They came into existence a few years after the Civil War when George M. Pullman, a Chicago businessman, began hiring thousands of Black men—including many former slaves—to serve white passengers traveling across the country on his company's luxury railroad sleeping cars. They were underpaid, overworked, and endured constant racism on the job.

Despite the difficulties, working as a Pullman Porter became a coveted career that later helped many Black men escape the backbreaking field labor and move themselves and their families into economic stability. In addition, these men were able to travel throughout the country at a time when most Black people did not have access or money to make these kinds of trips. In 1925, under the leadership of A. Philip Randolph, the Pullman Porters organized and founded the Brotherhood of Sleeping Car Porters, the very first Black labor union to sign a collective bargaining agreement with a major U.S. corporation.

Because seating was not segregated on the train traveling from DC to Terre Haute in the Midwest, I was able to move around freely. Had I been in the south, I would not have had this opportunity because trains were segregated there until 1964. I'd go to the dining car to eat my meals. As the train stopped and the white conductor called out, "Next stop," and named each city, I would commit these names to memory. I slowly learned the geography of the Midwest. During these trips, I began thinking about working as a train engineer.

Those trips also taught me how to travel, a skill I used later in my work as a staffer at the National Education Association and as an organizational development consultant.

When I arrived in Terre Haute, I spent time with my grandparents, Aunt Mabel who came home for the summer from her teaching position in Elkhart, Indiana, and cousin Chester Paul who was a student at Indiana State Teachers College. My Aunt Mabel was emphatic about cleaning the house. She wanted everything in its rightful place. My cousin Chester Paul and I would often complain that we didn't want to go in the house after one of her cleaning storms because she nit-picked us on everything we did, but she loved us. When I wasn't running from my Aunt Mabel, I spent my days hanging out with my friends Warren Ross, Wally Webb, and Huerta Tribble. They would later become my college classmates, fraternity brothers, and lifelong friends.

Throughout the summers, I would have conversations with my grandmother who always told me "colored people" had to work twice as hard as white people no matter what it was. Her truth-telling reinforced the importance of me getting a good education and working hard in my life. She was a staunch Democratic as a result of President Franklin Roosevelt's New Deal and her work in the WPA. The New Deal was a series of programs, public work projects, financial reforms, and regulations established between 1933 and 1939. The WPA was one of the public work projects. On one occasion, she told me she would always vote for a Democrat even if they were a dog catcher. Like her, I have maintained the same stance given the current Republican Party.

Anytime she would send my grandfather to the grocery store with a detailed list, he would always call to ask questions about what she wanted. When the phone rang, she would say, "That's that old fool calling." The way she teased him was hilarious and playful all at the same time. It's a shame they didn't have their own television show called "Ozzie and Eunice."

By the time I reached the eighth grade in 1953, I had become an A or B+ student. My dream was to attend St. John Military Academy which at the time was located several blocks from St. Augustine. I always liked the uniforms they wore. St. John was a predominately white high school that had an unspoken quota on how many Black students would be admitted each year. The quota was no more than five. When it came time to decide where I would attend high school, the decision was essentially made by Mother Mary Consolata. She strongly recommended to my parents I take the entrance exam to attend Archbishop Carroll High School, a new all-boys Catholic high school that had opened in 1951.

Cardinal O'Boyle made a very clear statement this school would be integrated—open to all young men regardless of race. It became the first DC school to defy segregation before the landmark U.S. Supreme Court decision in Brown vs. Board of Education in 1954. In this case, the Supreme Court ruled that separating children in public schools because of race was unconstitutional. It ended legalized racial segregation in U.S. schools and overruled the "separate but equal" principle set forth in the 1896 Plessy vs. Ferguson case.

Cardinal O'Boyle selected the Augustinian Order to operate Carroll as a college preparatory institution. Being accepted at Carroll was a threshold of change moment in my life because it allowed me to explore leadership and develop long-term relationships which exist to this day in an interracial academic setting. Even though I was not aware of how unique an opportunity it was at the time, I interacted and developed friendships with my white classmates that only existed at school. We did not hang out or visit each other's homes because we lived and interacted in segregated neighborhoods. The entire experience prepared me for even more changes when I started my freshmen year at Indiana State Teachers College and joined an interracial fraternity.

Since 1992, Carroll has been a co-ed institution with a diverse student body and staff. Most students are from communities of color. More than 95% of the graduates have been accepted in colleges and universities across the nation over the past few years. I have continued my relationship with the school by being an active alumnus. I am very proud of how the school has maintained and strengthened its commitment to providing quality educational experiences to the youth of the Washington community regardless of race, gender, religion, or class.

In my first year at Carroll in 1953, there were just three grades, freshmen, sophomores, and juniors, because the first class entered in 1951. It was still a predominantly white school. On my first day, I became a member of the Carroll brotherhood with the required tie, shirt, sport jacket, and trousers. We all started the day in the same way. Depending on whether we had after school events or athletic team practices, many of us ended the day with a loosened tie and the same shirt, sport jacket, and trousers. Why? We were expected to keep up the image of a Carroll student even when we were headed home.

My class schedule was highly structured. The school day began at 9 a.m. and ended at 3 p.m. Throughout the day, I changed classes and was taught by different teachers. History was one of my favorite classes because my favorite teacher, Mr. John Carroll (outside of school we called him J.C.), made history come alive. J.C. was an eccentric, impeccably dressed man with slicked back hair who wore three-piece suits and cowboy boots. He carried an old cloth briefcase. When he came in the room, he would throw the briefcase on the desk like a college professor. He lectured as he told a lot of stories which baptized me into taking copious notes for the first time in my life. Everyone was mesmerized by his stories. He emphasized concepts not facts. His essay exams were new for me. I later mimicked his style in my teaching career at Brownell Elementary School in Flint, Michigan.

One of J.C.'s stories about how the U.S. government entered World War II is something I can still remember hearing. Listening to him was like watching a movie; his language was so vivid I could visualize the conflict that occurred when the Imperial Japanese Navy Air Service attacked the U.S. naval base at Pearl Harbor in Honolulu, Hawaii in 1941. I learned there were some U.S. officials who knew the attack was coming. However, they were unable to deliver the message to the White House in time to avoid the attack. At the time, the

Japanese Navy had promised to call the strike off if the U.S. discovered it in advance. J.C.'s story taught me to explore the story behind the major story for a complete understanding of what happens in history.

Unlike J.C., Father James Deery, my freshmen teacher for Religion, was scary. Unfortunately for me, Father Deery also taught Biology in my sophomore year and French in my junior year. He was small in stature and seemed to be extremely strong. I heard stories about his military service and how he became shell shocked. His condition, when triggered, caused him to act out against students. One story involved him picking up a student who was a running back on the football team and weighed almost 200 pounds. He threw him and the chair out of the classroom. That's why we called him crazy.

No matter what subject he taught, Father Deery believed in pop quizzes at the beginning of each class. His teaching style was unique. When he entered the classroom, he would pull out from underneath his Augustinian robe half sheets of paper that had four questions we were required to answer. He kept us on our toes. Whenever we have class reunions, we always share stories about him.

The lunch hour at Carroll gave each student an opportunity to choose who we spent time with. By choice, our cafeteria resembled the 11 a.m. church hour on Sundays in America. It was one of the most segregated times of my day. In my class of 209 students, there were 19 of us who were Black. All of us attended some years of college. Four earned doctorate degrees. Three reached the rank of Colonel in the military.

One became a priest. Others made contributions in education, industry, law enforcement, and fire prevention. We have lived productive lives as citizens in our communities. After graduation, we began to have reunions with each other about every five years. Most of us have remained in touch. I believe our closeness is a result of the time we spent together at school. For example, we made a conscious choice to sit together during our lunch hour because it was necessary. It was one of the only times we were able to check in with each other, laugh, share stories, and plan our weekends.

In my junior year, a priest attempted to break up our lunch gathering by demanding we stop sitting together because it didn't look good. He wanted us to sit with other students. Although he was not explicit, we knew he was referring to the white students. Because we were accustomed to respecting and following the priests, we didn't resist him. For the next couple of days, it felt forced and awkward. Eventually, we returned to our usual table. Our decision invited him to issue another demand. This time we were prepared and argued the table next to us was filled with mainly white athletes. When we questioned why he hadn't asked them to sit at different tables, he got the message and left us alone. Our experience represents a pattern of over-policing Black students' behavior that still occurs in our schools today.

Although I was one of the few Black students at Carroll, I didn't experience many of the racial difficulties faced by my peers in the segregated South. There didn't appear to be any overt prejudice or bias exhibited by the priests. They were equal opportunity employers when it came to discipline! On the whole, the Black guys were less likely to get in trouble because we knew we would let our elementary teachers down as well as our parents. This was a time when home and school were generally on the same page.

The Black and white guys who participated in athletics got along very well. I had played against many of the white guys in the CYO League in elementary school. All the teams were integrated. The coaches did not seem to show any favoritism. During the fall of my junior year, I was one of the last to be cut from the junior varsity basketball team. It was my first major disappointment. After getting over it, I asked Coach Bob Dwyer if I could be one of the team managers. He agreed to my request. My decision helped me become one of the three varsity team managers in my senior year. Five of my fellow Black classmates, James Howell, William Wells, Ronald Jenkins, Arnold Hart, and Reginald Johnson, were playing on the varsity team. That made our year of winning 23 games special. It was something we could also enjoy. What's more, I, like them, earned an athletic letter. I received it at the annual Athletic Banquet. My father, a mail sorter for the U.S. Postal Service, was front and center to see me in all of my glory. Once I had my letter, I had it sown to my school sweater and wore it proudly. My daughter also borrowed and wore it proudly when she attended Carroll basketball games while she was a junior and senior at Elizabeth Seton High School in the 1980s. Now the sweater proudly lives in my closet.

One of my high school memories I will never forget was

the lynching of Emmett Till, a 14-year-old Black boy from Chicago who was visiting his extended family in Mississippi when he was murdered after whistling at a white woman. I recall seeing the photos of his bloated face in *JET Magazine*, a weekly publication founded by entrepreneur John H. Johnson. His mother insisted that these photos be shared with the public so that they would know how vicious the mob was. Years later, I revisited these memories when I visited the Smithsonian's National Museum of African American History and Culture and saw Emmett Till's casket on display. The lesson I learned from his death was to never do anything with a white girl or woman because that meant death in a most horrible way. It took me a long time to be friendly with white women in a professional setting. That did not happen until I was a teacher at Brownell Elementary in 1963 at the age of 24.

Because I socialized in the Black world, my high school experiences, especially in my junior and senior years, filled my calendar with weekly activities that were fun and exciting. I dated and had several long-term relationships with girls who attended all-girl Catholic schools as well as DC public schools. Attending debutante balls and junior and senior proms were the norm for me. During my senior year, my classmates and I would huddle together before we left school to share details about weekend parties and dances. This information helped me map out and select the best places to have a good time. Most weekends, I ended up going to house parties and public dances in Northeast and Northwest DC.

At house parties, I'd wear my Carroll athletic sweater with

a shirt, a pair of slacks, loafers, or suede bucks. The host parents would supervise who came in and out of their home. We had to abide by their rules which meant we couldn't come in and out like a revolving door. On some occasions, my classmates and I would go to parties that we were not invited to. Sometimes, the parents would question us before allowing us to enter their home. We'd tell them we attended Carroll, expecting them to give us the keys to the kingdom because of our school's reputation. This strategy didn't always work. Once we got into the party, we joined others in the basement. A colored light in a dark room with music playing on a record player greeted us. We'd pair off with girls, dance, talk, laugh, get numbers, and drink punch and soda before leaving for home. If the party wasn't poppin', we'd leave and find another party.

On some occasions, I went to public dances that were held in a big hall located at 15th and Q Streets, NW. They cost money to attend. Anybody and everybody who lived in and near DC was there. It was mostly high school students. We spent most of our time dancing to fast songs. Because the room was crowded, you could smell their sweat and funk. There wasn't a lot of time for chatting with girls, so all we did was dance. Because fights often broke out, we had to be more cautious. That's one of the reasons we didn't make them a weekend priority.

Most Sunday evenings, you could find me at St. Martin's Catholic Church's Marteen Club. Being a member and serving as an officer allowed me to attend meetings and informal dances with other teenagers who went to Catholic and public schools. Father Cremona, a white jovial priest at St. Martin's, was our advisor who organized the meetings in the basement hall. We really loved him because he respected us as young men and women. He expected us to follow his rules, but he didn't police us. Each week, he purchased the latest 45 (7-inch) records and helped to manage our meetings and dances himself. The meetings and dancing began at 6 p.m. and ended like clockwork at 9 p.m. Unlike house parties, all the lights were on when we danced. During slow dances, Father Cremona would put his hand between boys and girls to make sure we didn't get too close. At special dances, he would allow us to invite one or two guests. I would often bring one of my classmates. On those occasions, parents would chaperon. Afterwards, I walked or took the bus home.

In the fall, I went to football games on Saturdays. During the basketball season, I worked as a team manager at games that were held during the week and throughout the weekend. My classmate Jim Howell was an outstanding high school basketball and football star. He was also an all-star basketball player at American University and later became the first Black referee to officiate an NCAA final game of the National College Championship. Speaking of Carroll athletic stars, John Thompson, Jr., a member of the Class of 1958, played on the basketball team that won the record 55 games over a two-year period. Thompson later became the first Black basketball coach of Georgetown University and the first Black coach to win the NCAA College Basketball Championship in 1984. Edward A. "Monk" Malloy, a white student, was a member of the basketball team during my senior year and the only sophomore to make the varsity team. Malloy was also a member of the historic team that won 55 games. He later played for the University of Notre Dame, became a priest, and returned to Notre Dame to serve as a professor and president from 1987 to 2005.

Throughout my high school years, I continued to be a good student, graduating in the top third of my class of 209. My grandparents traveled from Terre Haute to attend my graduation. We have a family photo that commemorates the event. They are standing proudly with me, my parents, and my Aunt Paulyne. Everybody in that photo had strong ties to the city I would eventually return to for college. My college choice was based on two requirements. First, I needed to go to a school that would help me pursue my dream of becoming a coach. That meant I needed a degree in education. Second, I wanted to go away to school. Indiana State Teachers College quicky became the best option. Going there made financial sense because I was able to live with my grandparents who were thrilled to welcome me.

After graduation, I got my first real paying job at a shoe store owned by a Jewish family on 7th Street between N and O Streets, NW. It was one of the stores where many young Black men, especially those from Baltimore, would come to get their shoes. They couldn't try on shoes in Baltimore. My job responsibilities included stocking the shoes in the backroom and cleaning the store. The owner also had me go and get his lunch and dinner from the nearby deli. After a couple of weeks, I began to wait on customers. I was working about 60 hours a week and paid $35. At first, I was excited about having the job because I was saving some money that I could use when I went to college. After several weeks, I became concerned that I had no time to do anything else. I was working late on Friday, all day on Saturday from 9:00 a.m. to 10:00 p.m., and every other Sunday. From Monday through Thursday, I worked from 9:00 a.m. to 4:00 p.m. On those days, an older Black man worked part-time. He also worked on the weekend.

I spoke to the owner about changing my schedule. He wasn't too happy with my request, but reduced the number of hours and increased my pay to $40 a week. After several more weeks, the older Black man announced he would be taking some vacation time. I thought this might give me an opportunity to increase my pay by working a few more hours. When the owner approached me about working more hours, it did not include a pay increase. When I questioned him about a pay increase, he got upset and said, "No, this is what we do to cover employees." His response made me angry. When I took my dinner break, I called my father and discussed the situation and my thoughts about quitting. He suggested I have some more discussion with the owner. When I returned and was back in the stockroom, the owner came back and made a comment that reinforced his previous statement, "I guess you really don't have to work." I responded, "No. I don't really have to work. I am working now to save money for my college expenses." I ended the conversation with, "I think you will need to find someone else." We parted ways at the end of the week. One silver lining from this job was the shoe sales experience I gained and would later use as a husband and father when I applied for a part-time job at Sears in Flint, Michigan.

One of the last things I did before leaving for college was a road trip with my father to a racetrack in Atlantic City. He was a gambler who religiously played the numbers and horses. His hustle was real. In fact, it was so real, I adopted it in other parts of my life. I packed up John Leeke's hustle and took it to college when I held a variety of jobs as a waiter and cashier. On the day he wanted to take the trip, I didn't want to go because I only had a few more days left at home. I wanted to spend time with my girlfriend Doris. My mother convinced me to go. One of the wildest driving experiences I ever had happened during this trip. We were going down the highway when my father asked me to drive. I asked him if we should pull over. He casually said, "Just slide underneath me." That's exactly how we switched seats as the car was still running! I was nervous and scared. He was confident and cool as a cucumber. When the day races were over and he hadn't done that well, he told me he wanted to go to another racetrack in Delaware for the evening horse races. After he won and broke even for the day, we headed home and arrived in the wee hours of the night.

John Frederic Leeke wearing Junior Commando shirt in his house on 8th Street, NW in DC in the 1940s

John Frederic Leeke posing for his First Communion at St. Augustine Catholic Church in the 1940s in DC

John Frederic Leeke in his altar server uniform in his home on 8th Street, NW in DC in the 1950s

*John Frederic Leeke and his father, John Leonard Leeke,
standing in front of his Aunt Paulyne Roberts's apartment
off Benning Road, NE in DC during the 1950s*

*John Frederic Leeke and his father, John Leonard Leeke,
standing in front of the family Mercury Monterey
car on the Ohio Turnpike*

*John Frederic Leeke, Uncle Chester Henry Roberts,
and cousin Leslie Russell Roberts at his home
on 8th Street, NW in DC*

*John Frederic Leeke's Roberts cousins, Thomas Eugene,
Leslie Russell, Chester Paul, and Paulyne Anne, in the 1950s*

*John Frederic Leeke's sixth-grade birthday party with his
St. Augustine Catholic School classmates at his home
on 8th Street, NW in DC*

*John Frederic Leeke and his male St. Augustine Catholic School
classmates at his sixth-grade birthday party that was held at
his home on 8th Street, NW in DC*

From St. Augustine's Catholic School
to Archbishop Carroll High School in DC

The ✝ Catholic Standard

Washington, D. C., Friday, September 26, 1952

Vol. II, No. 39 — Entered as Second Class Matter at the Post Office, Washington, D. C. — PRICE, 10¢ $3 per Yr.

In This Issue

- *The 500th Birthday Of Johann Gutenberg's Bible, The First Printed Book. Pictures On Page 12.*

- *Should The Garb Of Nuns Be Modernized? Read The Holy Father's Comments. Page 14.*

- *Film Critic W. H. Mooring Describes A Hollywood Movie Censor At Work. Page 11.*

Archbishop Urge Back N To Aid

The support of loy. the "good sign" needed greater devotion to Ch.

Archbishop O'Boyle ington archdiocese this respond with new and scription drive, which b

Again the paper will have the services of the 32,000 pupils of the Catholic grade and high schools of the archdiocese as subscription agents, and this year they will be aiming at a new and bigger list of prizes.

This year the circulation effort will be conducted in two parts: the intensive three-week "Drive" beginning Monday, and an extended six-month "Campaign" beginning Monday, Oct. 20, and ending on April 19, 1953.

Drive Grand awards are two one-year tuition scholarships, one to a boy and one to a girl, to any Catholic university or college in the archdiocese, or two two-year tuition scholarships, one to a boy and one to a girl, to any archdiocesan high school participating in the drive.

These grand awards will be
(Continued on Page 24)

READY TO COMPETE FOR SUBSCRIPTION PRIZES in the *Standard's* subscription drive are these four representatives of the 32,000 boys and girls in the grade and high schools of the Archdiocese. The drive begins on Monday. Archbishop O'Boyle is reading the impressive prize list to Bernadette Lapp, of the eighth grade of Calvert School; Joan Meehan, a senior at Immaculata Conception Academy; Charles May, a second-year student at Archbishop Carroll High School, and John Leeke, of the eighth grade at St. Augustine's School.

Catholic Standard article featuring John Frederic Leeke posing with Archbishop O'Boyle and other students who participated in the Catholic Standard's *subscription drive*

John Frederic Leeke wearing his St. Augustine Catholic Church's Catholic Youth Organization's (CYO) baseball team uniform on the steps of his house on 8ᵗʰ Street, NW in DC in the 1950s

John Frederic Leeke's eighth-grade graduation class at St. Augustine Catholic Elementary School in DC in 1953

*John Frederic Leeke served as a manager for Archbishop Carroll
High School's Basketball team during the 1956–57 school year*

*John Frederic Leeke and John Leonard Leeke attend father and
son banquet at Archbishop Carroll High School in DC in 1957*

John Frederic Leeke with his parents, Frederica and John L. Leeke, on the day of his graduation from Archbishop Carroll High School at his home on 7ᵗʰ Street, NE in DC in 1957

John Frederic Leeke and his grandmother Eunice Ann Thomas Roberts at his home on 7ᵗʰ Street, NE in DC in 1957

Indiana State Teachers College
Terre Haute, Indiana

OFFICE OF THE REGISTRAR

April 18, 1957

Mr. John F. Leeke
2921 -7th St., N.E.
Washington, D.C.

Dear Mr. Leeke:

Your application for admission to
Indiana State Teachers College has been
received. We appreciate your interest
and hope your college career will prove
to be beneficial and satisfactory to you.

The enclosed form is to be filled in
by your principal after you have graduated.
When this record is returned to us it will
complete your transcript of credits and
admit you to this college unconditionally.

Very truly yours,

James H. Ringer

James H. Ringer
Registrar and Director
of Admissions

JHR/bal

Acceptance Letter to Indiana State Teachers College

John Frederic Leeke with his Archbishop Carroll High School
classmates Richard Gaither and Samuel Malachi
leaving a relative's home in Dayton, Ohio,
on the way to Indiana State Teacher's College in 1957

CHAPTER 3 REFLECTION QUESTIONS

---

1. Individual: What values did you receive from your family, church, school, or community?

2. Individual: Did those values include Black Joy or something similar like joie de vivre (joy of living)?

3. Individual: How do your values show up in your life today?

4. Individual: Think about where you went to elementary, middle school, and high school. What people and experiences influenced your development? Did you experience any thresholds of change?

5. Group Discussion: Now that you have explored your values and primary and secondary educational experiences, you're ready to take a deep dive into how they will help inform you and your family, friends, community, and colleagues in a group discussion.

   Each person would have 3–5 minutes to share their responses with the group. As a group, list some of the similarities and differences highlighted in the sharing session. Also, discuss one or two lessons each person has learned.

CHAPTER 4

Following in My Parents' Footsteps at Indiana State Teachers College

"Education is the passport to the future,
for tomorrow belongs to those who prepare for it today."

—MALCOLM X, a change agent, a Muslim minister,
and a human rights activist

———————————

Malcom X has not been the only person who has stressed the role education plays in reaching one's dreams. Education was what my ancestors encouraged me to pursue. My teachers and mentors urged me to pursue my education continuously. I took everything they taught me about education and packed it in my bags when I traveled by train to attend my freshmen year at Indiana State Teachers College, an integrated institution like Archbishop Carroll High School, in Terre Haute in August 1957. At the same time, the 85th U.S. Congress passed the Civil Rights Act of 1957, the first federal civil rights legislation since the Civil Rights Act of 1875. President Dwight D. Eisenhower signed the bill on September 9, 1957. President Eisenhower's proposed bill provided federal protection for African American voting rights because most African Americans living in the South could not vote due to various state and local law restrictions. Opponents were able to remove several of the Act's provisions which later limited its immediate impact on African American voting rights. However, the U.S. Commission on Civil Rights and the U.S. Department of Justice's Civil Rights Division were successfully established by the act. It laid the groundwork for the Civil Rights Act of 1960, the Civil Rights Act of 1964, and the Voting Rights Act of 1965.

College was a significant growth experience. Even though I was living with my grandparents and shared the second floor of their home with my best friend and Carroll classmate, Sam Malachi, I was solely responsible for creating my own schedule and routine. I used my class schedule to carve out time to eat lunch and hang out with friends on campus. Since the campus was approximately 14 blocks from their home, Sam and I would walk together most days. We'd start on Spruce Street where my grandparents and other Black middle-class families owned homes. Their street was located next to other streets where mostly white people lived. Our walk would take us down these streets. We rarely encountered white people because we left very early in the morning. Other days, we would get a ride from Warren Ross, one of my childhood buddies who lived two houses from my grandparents. Four of my other friends and neighbors, Wallace Webb, Huerta Tribble, Joyce Cheatem, and Virginia Holloway (Grundy), also attended Indiana State Teachers College, a predominately white institution. We were part of the largest number of African American students to enter the institution at the same time.

By the time I arrived on campus, it had undergone significant changes from the time it was established by the Indiana General Assembly as the Indiana State Normal School in 1865. As the State Normal School, it educated elementary and high school teachers including my Aunt Mabel. In 1929, the Indiana State Normal School was renamed as the Indiana State Teachers College. When I graduated in 1961, it was renamed Indiana State College due to an expanded mission. The Indiana General Assembly renamed it to Indiana State University in 1965 due to the expansion of its student population and the degrees offered.

Indiana State was on a quarter system and later transitioned to the semester system in my sophomore year. All freshmen were required to take Sociology, Government, and Economics. These three courses were very easy for me because of the classes I took in my senior year at Carroll. The Carroll curriculum was similar to these classes. Also, I had earned a B or better in my Carroll classes. Most of my professors lectured to a room of 75 students. There was no interaction among students. We listened and took notes. Thanks to my Carroll experience, I was well prepared.

I have always been an early morning person. When I wake up, my mind is fresh and ready to take in information and experiences. I learned early on that scheduling my classes in the morning and very early afternoon was the best way for me to learn. Creating this schedule helped me sustain the structure I had grown accustomed to at Carroll and St. Augustine's.

Declaring a major wasn't difficult for me. On my way

to Terre Haute, I had stopped in Indianapolis to see family friends. During my stay with the Hazlips and socializing with the Hines, I took time to think about my future. Before I left DC, I thought about majoring in History because I loved studying it in high school. However, I decided to major in Physical Education (P.E.) and to minor in Business because that was the route to coaching. I reasoned that Business would be my backup plan if I didn't pursue a career in education.

Just like high school, I continued to maintain an active social life in college. The Student Union became my home away from home. Throughout my four years, I played bid whist—a partnership card game that is popular in African American culture—daily for two to four hours. We played in an area of the Student Union Cafeteria the Black students claimed and called "The Grill." As we entered "The Grill," we congregated in a section to the right with tables and booths. The food counter and line were across from us on the left side.

Starting in my first year, I began to play and quickly became one of the best players. Card playing came naturally to me and may have been a skill I picked up from my father. I used to play with him. During our tonk card games, he would talk to me about keeping track of what cards had been played and projecting the cards held by other players as the game progressed. The games I played with my classmates included a lot of trash-talking. I took great pride in what I was able to dish out, especially since I was winning most of the time. By the time I completed my freshman year, I felt I had earned my *B.S.* degree in *whistology* and my doctorate in my junior year. I had quite a reputation within the Black student community. It increased when I teamed up with Billy Worrell, a good friend from New York who helped me get a job as a banquet waiter at the Deming Hotel, one of the two major hotels in the downtown area. The Deming Hotel was named after Demas Deming, financier and philanthropist. It occupied the site of the old Congregational Church which was one long block from the Terre Haute House, the second major hotel. In 1963, Indiana State University purchased the Deming Hotel and made it a men's dormitory and later a conference center.

Beginning in my sophomore year, Billy and I maintained a regular seat at the card table in "The Grill" and took on all comers. We did our best to arrange our class schedules so that we could start playing during lunch and stay for most of the afternoon. That didn't always happen given some of the classes did not fit into card-playing plan. When were able to play, we were so glued to our seats that we had to have our friends get our lunch. We felt like we had a responsibility to help weed out some of the incoming students who mistakenly believed they could defeat us. Unfortunately, their efforts caused them to lose and to miss some of their afternoon classes. Our card games found their way into our weekends at classmates' homes and during our breaks at the Deming Hotel.

My weekends often included a visit to Big Shoe's Barbecue (a.k.a. Shoe's), a well-known spot on the South Side of town, with my friends. My grandmother often told my cousin Chester Paul and me that she didn't want us to go to that part of town. She referred to it as "Baghdad" which meant it was dangerous and should be avoided. I chose to ignore her because my experience was different because I never had any dangerous encounters. Shoe's was a place where there was sawdust on the floor and newspapers were used as tablecloths. It was a low-budget establishment that catered primarily to African Americans. They had the best barbecue ribs I had ever tasted. My friends and I would stay there two or three hours eating the slabs of ribs and coleslaw. We washed it down with beer and soda.

Unlike DC, Terre Haute did not have many social gatherings on the weekends. Consequently, I would travel the hour and a half to Indianapolis (Indy) whenever I got a chance. In my first and second years, my friend Wally would get his family's car and drive us back and forth. We stayed with his aunt and uncle. His mom and aunt were my mother's childhood friends. Once I set foot in Indy, I would contact the Hines family and talk to their daughters, Ann and Rita Jo, to find out where the parties were. They hosted some of them and always pointed me in the direction of fun. My weekend adventures gave me a chance to reconnect with the children of my parents' closest friends like the Robinson and Bowles families. These experiences taught me two things. One, Indy and DC folks partied the same way. Two, whether I stayed in Terre Haute or traveled to Indy, I was always surrounded by extended family.

My social life changed in my junior year. Why? Well, when I came home at the end of my sophomore year, my parents gave me an older Pontiac. The gas indicator didn't function, which meant I had to keep a manual record of how much gas I purchased and the number of miles driven. On several occasions, I ran out of gas. It's funny now looking back, but one time the car stopped at a railroad crossing. It was one of the major crossings where there were at least six or seven train tracks. I was alone at night and had to push the car across the tracks to a safe position before walking on foot several blocks to get gas.

I had some memorable experiences with that Pontiac, including the time I volunteered to drive my Carroll classmate Lloyd Hall (Class of 1955) from DC to Ohio State University in Columbus. My plan was to head back to Terre Haute after the Christmas break. Lloyd asked me if I would be willing to pick up several women who lived in DC and were attending Wilberforce College. When we arrived at their home, they weren't ready. Instead of leaving at 4 p.m., we didn't take off until two hours later. I was the only person allowed to drive my temperamental car. I didn't trust anyone else to get behind the wheel because they wouldn't know how to operate it if something went wrong. When we arrived in Ohio, I dropped off Lloyd first. One hour later, I dropped the women off. It was 3 a.m. in the morning when I got back on the road. Shortly after leaving them, I began to get sleepy. Instead of stopping, I fought sleep and made it to Richmond, Indiana. While there, I got coffee and walked around which helped me stay awake until I arrived in Indy. After driving through Indy, I stopped again for more coffee before driving 72 miles to Terre Haute. Now here's when it gets crazy. Once I got to Brazil, Indiana which is 20 miles from Terre Haute, I started to doze off at the wheel. Luckily for me, my guardian angels were watching out. I made it safely to the Pi Lambda Phi Fraternity house at 6 a.m. After unloading my car, I tried to sleep, but found myself wide awake. So I went to class and vowed to never volunteer to drive folks I didn't know back to school.

During the second half of my freshmen year, I joined a racially diverse group of men who were exploring the idea of forming a fraternity. My friends and I were attracted to the group's diversity of members and campus involvement. Several were older men who had been in the military and were taking advantage of the GI Bill to finance their education. I, along with a couple of my Terre Haute buddies, Warren, Wallace, and Huerta, attended some of the initial organizing meetings. At the time, there were no Black fraternities and sororities on campus. There were four national fraternities and seven national sororities, and none had any men or women of color. Greek life was very significant on campus. Most of the social life and control of student activities were determined by the Greek organizations.

The men who began meeting and discussing the formation of a new fraternity on campus shared two critical principles: (1) they wanted the fraternity to be open to all regardless of race, creed, nationality, or religion; and (2) they did not want to have the demeaning type of hazing that historically took place during the pledge period which was the norm in most Greek organizations. Eventually, we formed a local fraternity chapter called Alpha Delta which was recognized on campus and became a part of campus life.

During my sophomore year, the Alpha Delta Chapter members started researching how we could become a part of a national fraternity. Our research led us to Pi Lambda Phi Fraternity, Inc. ("Pi Lam") which was founded by Frederick Manfred Werner, Louis Samter Levy, and Henry Mark Fisher. They decided to establish the first non-sectarian fraternity in the United States that was "a fraternity in which all men were brothers, no matter what their religion; a fraternity in which ability, open-mindedness, farsightedness, and a progressive, forward-looking attitude would be recognized as the basic attributes." When we read their creed, it mirrored our values as a fraternity.

The Creed of Pi Lambda Phi Fraternity

That all men are created free and equal.
That no society of men can flourish unless members of that society are endowed with the opportunities and privileges of freedom.
That freedom implies the elimination of prejudice.
That the elimination of prejudice means a better understanding 'twixt men.
That it is incumbent upon me to fight for such freedom, even with my life.
That because my country is dedicated to the highest standard of freedom and justice for all men of all creeds, I hereby pledge allegiance to my country, and to its national symbol.

In its early years, Pi Lambda Phi was a fraternity located mostly in the East. The members were predominately Jewish. Its motto was "Not Four Years, But a Lifetime." Its colors were purple and gold. We were chartered as Indiana Alpha Delta Chapter of Pi Lambda Phi Fraternity, Inc. in 1958. Looking back, I had no idea that this would mark another threshold of change in my life.

Our chapter was very well-rounded. We participated in all campus-wide activities. Campus Review and Songfest were two major competitions that all Greek organizations and an independent campus group participated in. Campus Review was a theatrical production which involved acting, singing, set design, and script writing. Songfest was a singing contest. All the brothers were involved. The brothers who had knowledge, skills, and experience took the lead. I participated every year.

I fondly remember the year we performed the production of *Goodheart for President* and finished in third place. I played one of the three main characters. It was my first time participating in a play. As a newbie, I was intrigued by the storyline which focused on a presidential election. We had lots of late-night rehearsals. I was able to memorize my lines and get through the performance without blowing it. Although this experience was fun, it taught me to stay in my lane as P.E. major.

In my senior year, we won first place in the Songfest competition. I participated in every practice, but prior to the performance, our director told me, "I just want you to mouth the words." My feelings weren't hurt because it was a well-known fact: I couldn't hold a tune to save my life. This fact remains true today even though I was married to the founder and director of the St. Joseph Catholic Church's Gospel Choir.

The fraternity did well academically. We maintained first or second place in academic ranking among the fraternities. We also had some of the leading athletes on the basketball, track, and wrestling teams. One of the proudest moments was during the year I served as the Rex (President) of the chapter. The mother of John Dow, an African American basketball star from East Chicago, Indiana, gave our chapter a significant contribution. We used it to make some needed fraternity house improvements. Mrs. Dow's gift was significant because very few people would have expected an African American family member to have the financial capacity to be so generous.

My fraternity experience gave me the opportunity to be a part of the beginning and building of an organization committed to equality. With the support of my chapter and the Greek community, I was elected treasurer of the sophomore class. In addition, I served as a pledge leader, vice president, and representative to several campus organizations. At the end of my junior year, I was elected president of the chapter. That summer, I traveled to the fraternity's 65th annual convention that was held at The Americana in Miami Beach, Florida. I served as my chapter's representative. At the beginning of my senior year, I ran our fraternity house with the assistance of a house mother and a faculty advisor. There were 20 brothers living in the house. Also, I was a member of the 1961 Homecoming committee, Interfraternity Council, and the Indiana State College President's Council.

My college career began at the same time the Little Rock Nine, a group of African American students, were enrolling in the all-white Central High School in Little Rock, Arkansas in 1957. Their attendance at the school was a test of the 1954 U.S. Supreme Court ruling in *Brown v. Board of Education* that declared segregation in public schools unconstitutional. Arkansas Governor Orval Faubus ordered the Arkansas National Guard to block the students' entry into the school. President Dwight D. Eisenhower sent in federal troops to escort the Little Rock Nine.

Unlike them, my days at Indiana State were not racially charged. Throughout my four years, there were no civil rights sit-ins and demonstrations on campus. However, campus life was not devoid of acts of racial prejudice, bias, and discrimination. For example, my interactions with fraternities and sororities were not always pleasant, especially at some of the social activities. Each of the fraternities owned houses. Sororities were allowed to have a section of one of the women's dormitories to hold their meetings and social events. Each of the fraternities would partner with a sorority. Because our chapter was interracial with a number of African Americans and two native Hawaiians, several sororities chose not to partner with us. During the pledge season, several fraternities questioned prospective members, "How would you feel having your girlfriends dance with Black guys?" They also asked, "How would you like having a Negro tell you what you can or can't do?" Blatant comments that used the word "nigger" were also said. We were able to overcome these racial slights, and I believe it made us all stronger and prepared to live and work in an integrated world.

The first time I was directly called a "nigger" happened during a road trip with my fraternity brothers to see our college play against the great Oscar Robinson and his University of Cincinnati teammates. Two of my fraternity brothers, Warren and Wallace, were on our college team. On our way home, we stopped to get gas at a truck stop. In those days, an attendant would pump your gas. We waited for someone to come out, but they never came. After several minutes, I went inside to ask about getting someone to come out. The white gas attendant replied, "Will someone help this nigger?" He repeated it several more times. I could see the white men inside were all looking at me. I was stunned and quickly returned to the car and drove off. I didn't tell my brothers what happened until we were further down the road because I didn't want them to get upset and do something that would get us hurt. That turned out to be a wise decision because some of the brothers would have wanted to confront the men.

During the Christmas break of my senior year in 1960, I was asked by my fraternity brother Fred Dobens, a national fraternity field representative, to serve as a pall bearer for Jack Buchheit, our fraternity brother and Executive Director, in Williamsburg, Virginia. Jack died in an airplane crash. Fred and Jack were white men. I met Jack when he visited my college's chapter. Fred was one of the first people I met when I joined my chapter. When he served as president during the 1959–1960 school year, I was vice president. I got to know both well when I drove them to visit the chapter at the University of Illinois at Urbana-Champagne. On the way back, the roads were slick. As I was driving, I lost control of the car as it slid into a ditch. When the car stopped, we got out and were unharmed. That was a scary experience. As it was happening, I envisioned the headlines of the newspaper reading, "Undergraduate Fraternity Brother Drives Car in Ditch and Kills Executive Director and Field Representative." Fortunately, that didn't happen. We were all safe. That experience gave us a lot of time to talk. It also created a lifelong bond.

My trip to Williamsburg marked my first visit to a southern state. When I arrived by bus, I observed several Black people step off the sidewalk and into the street as they passed a white person. After Jack's funeral, we had dinner at the home of a white woman who had been like a mother to Jack when he was attending William and Mary College. The table was set formally with what I am sure was her finest China and silverware. Throughout the meal, I noticed her staring constantly at me and thought, "She is probably having a fit with me sitting at her table and using her finest." Later, Fred and I discussed my experience. He didn't think she was thinking what I had mentioned, but after sharing what I had been taught by my family, he seemed to understand.

In addition to my fraternity activities, I was a member of three organizations: the Newman Club, a Catholic student organization; the Spartan Club, an organization whose membership included men who were in the Health, Physical Education (P.E.), and Recreation Department; and Circle K, a men's service organization for the campus and community. I also worked part-time as a waiter. Near the end of my first year, my friend Billy Worrell helped me get hired as a banquet waiter at the Deming Hotel. I worked mainly on the weekends and learned to perfect my skill of waiting in my first year. My friend Warren's father helped me get a second job as a cafeteria cashier at the Elks Club. Many of the Indiana State professors ate lunch there. I also got free lunches.

My friends and I helped each other throughout our high school and college lives. Just like Warren and Billy helped me get jobs, I was able to help two of my Carroll classmates attend Indiana State. During the Christmas break of my freshmen year, I spoke to John Sullivan, a former football star, and William (Royce) Wells, a basketball star. They had earned the status of All Catholic during our high school years. When I learned the news of them not attending college, I wanted to help them have the same experience I was having. I didn't want them to miss out. When I asked them if they wanted to attend Indiana State, they gave me permission to speak to the coaches. I used my contacts as a P.E. major to approach the football and basketball coaches about their athletic success. They were interested and offered them athletic scholarships. Wells played for a couple of years and graduated in 1963. Sullivan played on the football team, but left school at the end of the 1958 season. He returned to DC, got married, and had a child.

At the start of my senior year, I met Theresa B. Gartin, a very attractive student majoring in Elementary Education from Indianapolis. Within the first week of meeting her, I asked her out. On our first date, I picked her up from Shear House, one of the women's residential houses on campus. We went to play cards at Warren and Janet Ross's home. Naturally, we played bid whist. Theresa and Janet were partners against Warren and me. They beat us and talked a lot of trash given my reputation as being one of the best players. We dated most weekends, going to fraternity activities and Shoe's Barbecue, and just spending time getting to know each other. At the time, I wasn't aware that our paths had crossed previously. In our conversations, I learned she knew some of my family friends I would visit and party with on the weekends in Indianapolis. It wasn't until much later that I realized she was already aware of who I was.

Our relationship grew and during the Christmas break, I went home and broke off the longtime relationship I had with high school sweetheart Doris. I even left early to return to school and stopped to see Theresa on my way back to campus. Our relationship was now very strong. When she informed me that she would not be returning for the second semester, I was very upset and unhappy. I knew I had to make a bigger effort to see her. When I found out I was doing my student teaching at Eastwood Middle School in Indianapolis, I knew we would be able to see each other regularly.

Eastwood Middle School was located on the Eastside of Indianapolis and was one of the school districts in Marion County. I taught physical and health education. Eastwood was a predominantly white school. Having a car made it possible to get to and from where I was staying with my cousin

Chester Paul and his family for several weeks. I lived with the Hazlips, family friends, for the remainder of my time. While I was there, Mr. Hazlip tried to convince me to go into their mortuary business because they didn't have children and wanted to leave it to me. I had other plans and stayed on track with my goal to become a coach.

In May, I graduated on a beautiful Spring sunny day. Dressed in my black cap and gown, I marched across the stage when they called my name. When I received my diploma, I became my grandparents' first grandchild to graduate from what had become the family alma mater. Many members of my family and extended family were in attendance including my parents, grandparents, Aunt Mabel and Aunt Paulyne, girl-friend Theresa, and the Hazlips. I remember my grandmother being dressed up and so very proud to see me graduate. After the ceremony, my grandparents hosted a small, intimate celebration at their house. Some of my fraternity brothers and fellow graduates, Warren, Wally, and Huerta, dropped by to celebrate with me. Little did I know it would be one of my last life moments my grandmother would get to witness.

The next chapter of my life had already begun. Prior to graduating, I started my job search for a teaching position. Looking back, I believe I was naive. I thought that having received my undergraduate degree, earned a teaching certificate, served as a leader, and named in Who's Who in America, the school systems were just waiting to hire me. Afterall, I was a P.E. major and still had the dream of coaching. I applied in Indiana, Ohio, and Missouri. I quickly learned there were only a few coaching jobs open for Blacks. Those positions were in the segregated Black high schools. They generally went to former outstanding players. In Indiana, there were only three Black high schools, Crispus Attucks in Indianapolis, Roosevelt in Gary, and Lincoln in Evansville. Likewise, there were very few P.E. positions at the junior high level. I got excited when a recruiting team from St. Louis came to campus and interviewed me for an elementary school P.E. position. It was a newly created position. I thought I had a real shot. It wasn't until late June when I made a trip to St. Louis and found out I should have applied for a Missouri teaching certificate. They informed me all the positions had been filled. As it turned out, I didn't receive any offers. This happened in 1961, a good bit before school systems began clamoring for Black male teachers. Disappointment became the emotion of the day. It left me feeling like I had made some bad choices. This experience represented another threshold moment of change. It was the first time in my adult life that my progress was significantly stalled.

I guess as they say, "When one door closes another one opens." Several things happened to shift my reality. My grandparents' health was failing. Although my grandmother had been able to see me graduate, her health had deteriorated to such a degree that she was pretty much bedridden. The family was facing some critical decisions. Aunt Mabel was still teaching in Elkhart and had a few years before retirement. For several years, she would come home in the summer and do many things to help her parents around the house. Aunt Paulyne was a public health nurse in DC and really didn't want to come home. My mother was working for the Navy Department. It would have been a difficult choice for her to leave my father and her job. We held a family meeting, and they proposed that since I didn't have a job and was considering going back to school to pursue an elementary teaching certificate, I would serve as my grandparents' caregiver. In exchange, the family paid for my tuition and purchased my new car, a Renault.

My elementary teaching certificate required me to take 18 hours of classes and complete a student teaching assignment at an elementary school. I completed my course work in one semester. The following semester, I did my student teaching at the all-Black Booker T. Washington Elementary School. It happened to be located two blocks from Shoe's Barbecue. By this time, I had proposed to Theresa. We planned our wedding for the Thanksgiving holiday weekend so family and friends could attend. We married on Saturday, November 25, 1961 at St. Rita's Catholic Church. This was Theresa's family parish. She had gone to elementary school there. Her family, especially her father, was very active in the church.

St. Rita's had recently completed the building of a new church. It was a very beautiful and modern facility. The pastor, Father Bernard Strange, was well known and had served this Black congregation for several years. Father Strange officiated our wedding. The wedding party included both sets of our parents; Theresa's niece, Janet, the flower girl; and Chester Paul, Jr. (C.P.), the ring bearer and my cousin Chester Paul's young son. Theresa's best girlfriend, Madelyn, served as her maid of honor; Veronica, her younger sister, was a bridesmaid. Fred Dobens, one my fraternity brothers, was my best man. Wallace Webb, a childhood friend and fraternity brother, served as a groomsman. Like my parents' wedding, our nuptials were covered by the *Indianapolis Recorder.*

My grandmother passed away of cancer on January 2, 1962. I remember that day because she had been in a lot of pain. Theresa and I were in the kitchen. Her bedroom was located next to the kitchen. She called out my name. When I entered the room, she was no longer alive. My grandfather made his transition six months later. During his last months, I was responsible for bathing him, cutting his hair, and shaving him. He had a stroke and went into a coma a few days before he died at home. They were married 65 years.

During our first months of marriage, Theresa worked as a clerk typist with Vigo County Redevelopment Agency while I completed my certificate program. I finished it in April. As a newly married couple, we went to Mass regularly at the neighborhood Catholic Church. We spent time with some of our college friends, including Charles and Jenny Grundy, Billy Worrell and his girlfriend Mary Helen Webb (my friend Wally's older sister), and Warren and Janet Ross, at our various homes and Shoe's Barbecue. We also attended my fraternity's social events and took trips to visit family and friends in Indianapolis.

After completing the certificate program in March, I knew I had to wait a few months before applying for teaching positions. In interim, I started working as a Correctional Counselor at the Indiana State Penal Farm in Greencastle. Greencastle was 30 miles from Terre Haute. I had no idea why the position was titled Counselor because I never did any counseling. The function of the job was mainly serving as someone who would process inmates when they arrived at the Penal Farm. The Penal Farm was a minimal security facility. Individuals assigned to the Farm were men who had been convicted of minor offenses with sentences lasting no more than a year. Many of the men were there because of child support, drunk and disorderly behavior, robbery without a weapon, minor assault, drug possession, and other minor types of offenses. The men came from all over the state, but mostly from the major cities in Indiana. Their ages ranged from 17 to over 70. There were some who had committed more serious offenses, but not murder, kidnapping, or offenses which, if convicted, would carry long-term sentences. According to the Pew Research Center, in 1960, the white male incarceration rate was 262 per 100,000 U.S. Residents, and the Black male rate was 1,313, meaning that Black men were five-times as likely as white men to be incarcerated. This held true even in 1962 when most Penal Farm inmates were Black.

I would normally process on average six to eight individuals per day. The form I used to interview required information about previous offenses, convictions, length of sentences, and the number of incarcerations. I would always ask what the inmates were in for, even though it would be on the sheet. Hearing their descriptions was often very interesting. Some would want to convince me they hadn't done anything wrong. During my six-month tenure, I had the opportunity to interview several individuals who left a significant impact on me. The first person was a white man who was in his fifties. He was a career criminal.

During the interview, he asked me if there was a list of offenses on the sheet. There was and he instructed me, "Check all except for murder and kidnapping." He revealed that he had served time in several states and proceeded to describe in some detail what life was like in the different institutions. According to him, the federal institutions were the best places to serve time. He advised, "If you were going to commit a crime, do something that would be a federal one." He also talked about "white collar" offenses and how the institutions that housed these inmates were like "country clubs." He rated California as having the best system because they really worked at rehabilitation, providing counseling and education programs, and boasting great facilities. He warned me about prisons in states like Texas and Mississippi. In fact, he said, "They still have chain gangs." Talking with him was a real education for me! He helped to convince me I didn't ever want to get involved in the prison system.

I will never forget this next individual and his story. I spent three hours talking with this Black man because I had never met anyone like him. In our conversations, he shared a significant portion of his life history. He was in his late thirties and sentenced to the Farm for a year. He had already been in the Marion County (Indianapolis) jail for 17 months awaiting his trial. He had been arrested on drug charges and admitted he had been a big-time drug dealer. He was also involved in other criminal activities. One of the interesting things he shared was his role as an entrepreneur with a legitimate construction business that had several large contracts. He was a master in the masonry trade and owned five homes, numerous cars, and moving vans. He used the vans to transport stolen goods across the state line and maintained an apartment in Chicago that he only visited once a month to pick up drugs. He had been arrested numerous times, but retained a well-connected lawyer and was never convicted. In fact, he said there were times when he would be in the courtroom before a judge and his lawyer would just say to him, "It's over, let's go." He never knew what had happened.

Finally, he was arrested without an escape hatch. That's when his world began to unravel. I learned he had been on drugs since he was 17 years old and had never experienced withdrawal until he was in the Marion County jail and went through a month-long withdrawal. He arrived a strong and healthy man. During his stay, he lost over 30 pounds. By the time I interviewed him, he had regained his physical stature. The most impactful memory I carry was what he shared about his drug use. He discussed how he had been using it for so long it was difficult to find veins to insert the needle. He shared how shooting into the veins of his neck eventually affected his voice. I cringed hearing some of the areas of his body where he inserted needles. I realized then I would never go near illegal drugs. In addition, I was convinced that if I was ever arrested, I would make every effort possible to avoid having to spend time inside a prison.

There was one time where I feared I might be harmed. The interview started as usual with me asking the basic questions to a white man in his early twenties convicted of a minor assault. As he talked, there were moments when he would start to ramble. He became quite animated and then normal again. I got a little concerned and remembered what the director had once said: "If at any time something doesn't feel right, end the session, and call to have the individual removed." Despite how I felt, I did not listen to my intuition and continued the interview. He started sharing a story about a time when he got upset with a Negro man and picked up a bat and began hitting him. He said, "I ain't afraid of anyone. I can take care of myself." At that moment, I thought he might do something to me. The office was rather small. It had a desk which I sat behind and a chair for the inmate. I would have to go past him to get out of the room. I did get him to switch to a different topic and began to close the session. In my report, I indicated he should be seen by a psychologist. Much later, I was informed he had been assigned to a psychologist and was in isolation until he could be transferred to another institution. When I think back to this experience, I realize it was a potentially dangerous situation. It also reminds me of the *Pressure Point*, a 1962 movie where Sidney Poitier, a Bahamian American, played a psychologist dealing with a white man, played by Bobby Darin, in a prison. In the movie, the psychologist discovers the prisoner is racist and anti-Semitic, and was arrested for sedition due to his Nazi sympathies.

While I was working at the Penal Farm, I continued my

search for a teaching position. I applied for jobs in the Midwest, especially in Indiana, Ohio, and Michigan. I received favorable responses from Pontiac and Flint, Michigan. Both school systems invited me to come for an interview. Billy, one of my college friends, also had interviews in these cities. We drove to the interviews in my new blue Renault. As we were coming around a curve which was more like a turn, the car's wheel axle snapped which caused it to flip over and roll down the middle of the two-lane highway. The car ended upside down. It happened in the middle of a bright, sunny day just outside of Defiance, Ohio. (As a side note, Defiance also holds a special place in my memory because *Scandal*, my favorite TV show written by the brilliant Shondra Rhimes and featuring Kerry Washington as Olivia Pope, the head of a crisis management firm, had a long-time story line based in the city.)

Back to the car accident. Once the car came to a halt, we asked each other, "Are you hurt?" We both answered we were alright. Miraculously, we got out of the car without any bruises or scars. We were so very fortunate that there was no traffic coming in either direction. A man came out of his home to check on us and made a call to the state police. The car was taken away and later totaled. We were driven to Defiance where we decided to take a bus back to Terre Haute. We both felt the accident was a sign telling us Michigan wasn't the place for us.

Recognizing we needed to make a move, Theresa and I decided DC would be the best place for me to try and get a teaching position. She could also get a job working for the Federal Government as we sorted out our new life and living arrangements in my parents' home. My friend Billy also moved to DC when he received an appointment letter to teach science at Paul Junior High. Just like Billy, I eventually received an appointment too.

John and Frederica Roberts Leeke on steps at the Student Union building on the campus of Indiana State Teachers College in 1933

John F. Leeke's fraternity brothers, Indiana Alpha Delta Chapter of Pi Lambda Phi Fraternity, 1959

John F. Leeke as President (Rex) of Alpha Delta Chapter of Pi Lambda Phi Fraternity at Indiana State Teachers College in Terre Haute, Indiana in 1960

John F. Leeke attended the Pi Lambda Phi Fraternity's 65th annual convention as his chapter representative at The Americana in Miami Beach, Florida in 1960

Pi Lambda Phi Fraternity house where John F. Leeke lived in 1960–61

Pi Lambda Phi Fraternity brothers participated in the Campus Review Competition's performance Goodheart for President *that featured John F. Leeke, Herbert Shigemoto, and Bart Richardson in 1960*

125

Photo from the Terre Haute Tribune-Star *of the Pi Lambda Phi Fraternity's Rex Ball that was held at the Deming Hotel in Terre Haute, Indiana in 1961*

Photo from Terre Haute Tribune-Star *featuring Alpha Delta Chapter of Pi Lamba Phi Fraternity winning the annual Songfest competition in 1961*

TERRE HAUTE STAR, FRIDAY, SEPTEMBER 30, 1960.

PLAN INDIANA STATE HOMECOMING — Plans for Indiana and Saturday, Oct. 7 and 8, are being completed by the big right: Miss Pat Drake of Walkerton, bands; Miss Mary Jane ington, announcements; Miss Ann Taylor of Terre Haute, general chairman; Miss Ellen McNabb of Evansville, business manaing: Miss Arlene Liechty of Brazil, program, Miss Irene Sopp queens; Bill Warrick of South Bend, queen's float; John verdale, parade marshall; John Guth of Brazil, parade mar-Hammond, pep rally.

State's forty-fourth annual Homecoming, to be held Friday student Homecoming committee. They are, seated, left to Deatrick of Worthington, bands; Miss Nancy Meade of Washeral co-chairman; Hal Sharpe of Terre Haute, general co-ager, and Miss June Knight of Terre Haute, publicity. Standof Hammond, dance; Miss Page Townsend of Covington, Leeke of Washington, D. C., awards; John Whitaker of Clo-shall; Bill DuChane of Terre Haute, dance, and Dan Peifer of

Indiana State Homecoming Social Events Planned for Oct. 7 and 8

Although highlights of Indiana State Teachers College's forty-fourth annual homecoming, Friday and Saturday, Oct. 7 and 8, will be the queen coronation, huge parade on Wabash Avenue, the Indiana State-Butler game, and the Blue and White Dance, many other social events are planned by sororities, fraternities, and other campus groups for students, faculty and alumni.

On Friday evening, Oct. 7, five dances are scheduled. The Independent Students Association dance will be in the Student Union Building, the Lambda Chi Alpha Fraternity is scheduled in the Mayflower Room of the Terre Haute House, Tau Kappa Epsilon Fraternity is sponsoring a dance at the Country Club of Terre Haute, the Theta Chi Fraternity dance will be at the Allendale Lodge, and the Sigma Phi Epsilon Fraternity dance is planned at the Wayne Newton Post, American Legion, Hall. All the dances will start at 9 o'clock.

+ + +

THE PRE-PARADE events planned for Saturday, Oct. 8, will be as follows and the chairmen are named: 7:15 o'clock in the morning, "I" Women's Breakfast, Student Union cafeteria, Miss Florida Lowry, chairman, Women's Physical Education Department, Indiana State; 7:30

and other events will be as follows: Eleven o'clock in the morning, Alpha Sorority Alums punch bowl, Terre Haute House Mezzanine, Mrs. Charles Evrard, co-chairman, R. 2. West Terre Haute, and Mrs. Joseph L. Bisch, co-chairman, 207 Woodridge Drive; Reeve Hall coffee hour, I. S. T. C. Reeve Hall, Betty Weber, chairman, I. S. T. C. Reeve Hall; 11:30 o'clock, Sigma Phi Epsilon Fraternity luncheon, Louise's Restaurant, W. Ernest Long, chairman, 3939 Riley Avenue; 12 o'clock noon, Alpha Alums luncheon, Terre Haute House Mezzanine, Mrs. Evrard and Mrs. Bisch, co-chairmen; Alpha Omicron Pi Sorority luncheon, Terre Haute House Mayflower Room, Karen Rickard, co-chairman, I. S. T. C. Burford Hall, and Miss Donna Schumpert, co-chairman, 7 Jackson Boulevard; Alumni of Foreign Tours luncheon, Deming Hotel Silver Room, Dr. Betty Foster, chairman, 526 Deming Street; Burford Hall luncheon, I. S. T. C. Burford Hall, Sandra Uland, chairman, I. S. T. C. Burford Hall; Chi Omega Sorority luncheon, Student Union Building east ballroom, Molly Alkire, chairman, I. S. T. C. Burford Hall; Delta Gamma Sorority luncheon, Shrine Temple, Mary Jo Swink, chairman, I. S. T. C. Burford Hall; Epsilon Pi Tau Fraternity luncheon, Eat-A-Teria. Ethan Svendsen,

and Gary Toothman, co-chairmen, 441 North Eighth Street; Order of Diana Mothers Club luncheon, Deming Hotel Pine Room, Mrs. Donald Sharpe, chairman, 1601 South Sixth Street; Phi Delta Kappa Fraternity luncheon, Y. W. C. A., Dr. Charles Hardaway, chairman, R. R. 7, Box 442. Terre Haute; Sigma Kappa Sorority luncheon, Terre Haute House, Pat Bartley, chairman, I. S. T. C. Burford Hall; Tau Kappa Epsilon Fraternity luncheon, Deming Hotel, Larry Fuqua, chairman, 401 South Seventh Street; Theta Chi Fraternity luncheon, Fraternity House, Nelson Miller, chairman, 451 North Eighth Street; Union Hospital School of Nursing alumni luncheon, Gourmet Room, Deming Hotel, Mary Arnett, chairman, Union Hospital School of Nursing, and Zeta Tau Alpha Sorority luncheon, Throckmartin's, Jackie Strahle, chairman, 4 Washington Street.

+ + +

AFTER - THE - GAME events include: 4 o'clock in the afternoon, Poets Club Tea, Language-Mathematics Building, Mary Jo Swink, chairman, I. S. T. C. Burford Hall, and Press Club open house, Student Union Building, Lola Sims, I. S. T. C. Reeve Hall, and Bob Bartlett, I. S. T. C. Parsons Hall, co-chairmen; 5 o'clock, Sigma Phi Epsilon Fraternity buffet, Fraternity House, Ray Martin, chairman, 801 South Fourth Street, and Inter-Varsity Christian Fellowship picnic, Deming Park, Linda Granlund, chairman, I. S. T. C. Burford Hall; 5:45 o'clock, Music Alumni dinner, Student Union Cafeteria, Dr.

Oct. 8, will culminate the weekend's activities.

The pep rally will be at 7 o'clock on Friday evening, Oct. 7,

John F. Leeke represented Pi Lamda Phi Fraternity
on the Homecoming Committee at
Indiana State Teachers College in 1960

*John F. Leeke and Theresa B. Gartin Leeke talking on campus
at Indiana State Teachers College in 1960*

*John F. Leeke and Theresa B. Gartin Leeke standing
in front of her parents' home on Cornell Street
in Indianapolis, Indiana in 1961*

*John F. Leeke and
Theresa B. Gartin Leeke
attending a Pi Lambda Phi
Fraternity event in 1960*

*John F. Leeke and Theresa
B. Gartin Leeke heading
to the Pi Lambda Phi
Fraternity's Rex Ball in 1961*

*Theresa B. Gartin Leeke on her
wedding day at St. Rita Catholic
Church in Indianapolis, Indiana
in 1961*

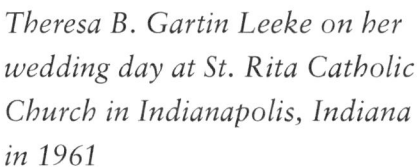

Architectural Beauty Of St. Rita's Scene Of Gartin-Leeke Marriage

The modern architectural beauty of St. Rita's Catholic Church, 1821 N. Arsenal, lent the perfect background for the brilliant morning ceremonies which on Saturday, Nov. 25, united in marriage, Miss Therese Bernadette Gartin, daughter of Mr. and Mrs. Robert W. Gartin Sr., 1447 Cornell, and John Frederick Leeke, son of Mr. and Mrs. John L. Leeke of 2729 Seventh, N. E., Washington, D. C.

The handsome couple recited their marriage vows, read by Rev. Bernard Strange, priest of St. Rita's, before an altar banked with vases of large white Fuji mums with gold accessories.

The former Miss Gartin attended Indiana University and Indiana State Teachers College. She is second anti-basileus of Alpha Sigma Chapter of Sigma Gamma Rho Sorority.

A June, 1961, graduate of Indiana State Teachers College, the groom was treasurer of his sophomore class at Indiana State and is past president of Alpha Delta Chapter of Pi Lambda Phi Fraternity. He was recently elected to "Who's Who In American Colleges and Universities."

The bride entered on the arm of her father, in a bouffant taffetta dress with a portrait neckline trimmed in lace and sequins. Her dress was designed with a

THE BRIDAL PARTY: Mr. and Mrs. John Leeke (center) take time out to cut their three-tiered wedding cake at a reception along with members of their bridal party who are (from left to right) Fred Dobens, best man of New York City; Miss Veronica Gartin, sister of the bride, maid-of-honor and Miss Madelyne Carol Grace, bridesmaid. (Recorder photo by Jim Burres)

draped buffled back which was caught with large roses and dropped to a chapel train. It was highlighted with a three-tiered illusion veil secured by a Swedish crystal crown and she carried a cascade bouquet of white Fuji mums and a white orchid.

Miss Veronica Ann Gartin, the bride's sister, was maid-of-honor and Miss Madelyne Carol Grace was bridesmaid. They were lovely in topaz peau de de satin gowns

which featured portrait necklines and bell shaped skirts—accented by delicate tiny bows at the princess waistline. Their accessories, ivory pearl earrings and beige gloves, were sparked by dyed-to-match satin bow hats highlighted with veils.

Little Miss Janet Cheryl Gartin, niece of the bride, was flowergirl. The ringbearer was Master Chester Paul Roberts Jr., cousin

Continued on Page 8

en Sponsors Have g With Director

onsors gathered in the home of their Christ- ?, in the home of their director, s hostess, where they enjoyed a

Architectural
Continued from Page 4

of the bridegroom.

The groomsmen were Fred Dobens of New York City, national executive of Pi Lambda Phi Fraternity, best man, and Wallace Webb of Terre Haute and Richard Parris of Brooklyn, N.Y., members of Pi Lambda Phi, ushers.

The mass was sung by Mrs. Maxine Ferguson with Charles Howcott of New York, a member of Pi Lambda Phi, presiding at the organ.

Following the double-ring ceremony was a reception in an adjoining church hall. Hostesses were members of Alpha Sigma Chapter.

They included Mrs. Hattie Redford, founder; Mrs. Effie Allen, Miss Nellye Russell, local basileus; Mrs. Vivian Benedict, Mrs. Rosemary Carpenter, first anti-basileus and Mrs. Mildred Hall.

Out-of-town guests were from Washington, D.C., Elkhart, Cincinnati, Terre Haute, New York

Article from the Indianapolis Recorder *that featured John and Therese Leeke's wedding in 1961*

Parents of John and Theresa Leeke on their wedding day in 1961:
John L. Leeke and Frederica Roberts Leeke and
Dorothy Mae Johnson Gartin and Robert W. Gartin, Sr.

Theresa and John Leeke's wedding party included her father
Robert W. Gartin, Sr., her sister Veronica Gartin,
her best friend Madelyn Grace, her niece Janet Gartin,
his Pi Lambda Phi Fraternity brothers Fred Dobens and
Wallace Webb, and his nephew Chester Paul Roberts, Jr.
Father Bernard Strange officiated the service.

John F. Leeke standing on the steps of the Student Union building on his graduation day at Indiana State Teachers College in 1961

John F. Leeke and his Pi Lambda Phi Fraternity brothers Wallace Webb and Warren Ross standing on the steps of the Student Union on their graduation day at Indiana State Teachers College in 1961

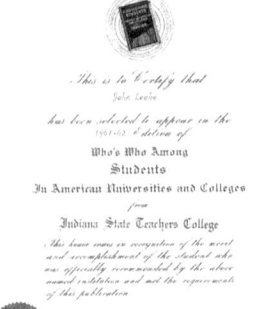

John F. Leeke was named in the Who's Who Among Students in American Universities and Colleges in 1961–62

John F. Leeke's 1961 graduation portrait

This Diploma makes known that

Indiana State Teachers College

on the Nomination of the Faculty has admitted

John Frederic Leeke

to the degree of

Bachelor of Science

and therefore is entitled to all the Honors, Rights and Privileges appertaining to that degree.

Given in the City of Terre Haute, Indiana, this *eleventh* day of June in the year of Our Lord Nineteen Hundred and Sixty-one.

In Witness Whereof, the Seal of the Institution and the Signatures of the President and the President of the State Teachers College Board are hereunto affixed.

Alexander M. Bracken
President State Teachers College Board

Raleigh W. Holmstedt
President

John F. Leeke's diploma from Indiana State Teachers College

CHAPTER 4 REFLECTION QUESTIONS

---

1. Individual: Think about your life from the ages of 18 to 22. What people and experiences influenced your development? Did you experience any thresholds of change? How did they impact you?

2. Group Discussion: Now that you have explored your young adult experiences, you're ready to take a deep dive into how they will help inform you and your family, friends, community, and colleagues in a group discussion.

   Each person would have 3–5 minutes to share their responses with the group. As a group, list some of the similarities and differences highlighted in the sharing session. Also, discuss one or two lessons each person has learned.

CHAPTER 5

Dealing with Adversity

"And I prayed to God to make me strong and able to fight, and that's what I've always prayed for ever since."

—**HARRIET TUBMAN**, a change agent, a conductor on the Underground Railroad, an abolitionist, and a social justice activist

---

All my life I was told, and trusted, God was present in my life. I believed God always protected me. Until I reached the age of 23, I never had an opportunity to call on God for help. Much like Harriet Tubman, I reached out through prayer which became a lifeline for strengthening my faith. I learned, like her, how to rely on God to make me strong and able to fight.

Clint Eastwood has always been one of my favorite actors. He starred in the 1967 movie, *The Good, the Bad and the Ugly*. My life has had good, bad, and ugly moments. The year following my college graduation was one of my bad and ugly years because it was frustrating and challenging. Theresa and I had spent the last seven months getting to know each other as wife and husband, taking care of my grandparents until their deaths, my getting a teaching certification, and taking a job, and her working. Shortly after arriving in DC, I interviewed with the principal at Browne Junior High School in Northeast. Browne was part of a larger school campus with Spingarn High School, Phelps Vocational High School, and Charles Young Elementary School. The Langston golf course was located across the street. It is a celebrated historic facility that has been instrumental in the growth of the game of golf for African Americans. It was named after John Mercer Langston, the first African American elected to serve as a Congressman from Virginia's 4th District, the founding dean of Howard University School of Law, and the first President of Virginia State University, a historically Black college.

My Browne interview was very interesting and memorable. As the principal reviewed my application and resume, he remarked, "I see you were a Physical Education major. You have an elementary teaching certificate and have most recently been working at a penal institution. I have just the job for you. Social adjustment teacher for boys." I had no idea what the job entailed. I just knew I needed a job as time was running out. I quickly accepted, completely unaware that I was walking into a very difficult threshold of change year. This would be the year where I would witness what is now called the school-to-prison pipeline. The school-to-prison pipeline refers to the process through which students are pushed out of schools and into prisons because they are profiled and treated harshly by disciplinary policies and practices. Most of these students are from Black and Brown communities and families with lower socioeconomic backgrounds.

On the first day of school, I was shown to my classroom which was a windowless converted locker room with a group shower area off from the gym. It wasn't the size of a regular classroom. My desk was placed in the front of the room surrounded by 15 student desks. There were no books or teaching materials. I was given a list of 10 male students who were to show up on the first day. Five of those students showed up. An hour later, 10 more arrived who were not on the list. I had no information about them, not even their names or the reasons they were assigned to my class. They were told to just go to Room 104. Many expressed their anger about being assigned to my room. I later learned my classroom was the dumping ground for boys who got into trouble. There was a similar room for the girls. All of this left me confused, upset, and wondering what I had gotten myself into.

Each day was different. Many days were chaotic, and I spent a significant amount of time breaking up fights and crap games played in the shower area, and calming students down. In between those moments, I looked for ways to engage students when issues popped up that they could easily relate to. For example, we had a lively discussion over the course of several days that focused on the choices some of them made after the citywide football championship game at RFK Stadium. After the game, a few of my students decided to join the crowd of boys who were randomly attacking people as they walked to their cars. All members of my class were excited to talk during the discussion. Those who were involved in the random attacks bragged about their behavior. As I listened,

I realized the discussion could be a teaching opportunity to help them rethink their perspective and choices. They were respectful and listened to me as they had respected and listened to each other. When we had these discussions, their anger disappeared. They demonstrated a natural brilliance. One I wish could have been cultivated throughout their academic life.

After a couple of weeks of trying to corral some textbooks and figure out how I could be useful with these young men, the principal pulled me aside and told me in no uncertain terms, "I didn't hire you to teach them. I hired you to keep them quiet and out of the way." That's when I really knew I was a glorified policeman without a gun or a club. I began to question the last five years of preparing for a teaching career. I got additional confirmation of my role when I received a copy of my draft deferment which indicated I was a teacher of incorrigible boys. I felt like I was in the same prison environment as my students: Caged with no place to go.

Amid this challenging experience, Theresa and I started going to pray Novenas, a prayer service, at St. Mary's Catholic Church in Chinatown on Monday evenings. We prayed I would get a new job and we would start a family with a new baby. Those evenings of prayer brought us great comfort. I developed a camaraderie with several teachers who were working with students like mine. They included the Social Adjustment teacher for girls, the seventh-grade teacher for basics students, and the younger Physical Education teacher. These students were referred to as "basics" which meant they were below grade level. Some had disciplinary problems. We shared our lunch period together which gave us an opportunity to swap stories and strategies and commiserate. The award-winning singer Roberta Flack was also one of my colleagues. At that time, Roberta taught music and sang in the evening and weekends at the famous Mr. Henry's on Capitol Hill. Her song "Killing Me Softly with His Song" later became one of my favorites.

One thing I learned was how to maintain discipline under difficult circumstances. It wasn't a skill or a class I took in college. This required on-the-job training. I witnessed how young men between the ages of 13 to 16 were placed on the track to failure. This school-to-prison pipeline was unfolding before my very eyes. With these thoughts in my head, I spent many depressing days and sleepless nights wondering how I could help them and find a better teaching position. After all, I had a wife to support and a dream of a coaching career to manifest. By December, my efforts to secure a transfer to another school had not materialized. I decided to finish out the school year as I continued my job search.

During this time, I considered giving up on teaching because I perceived that I wasn't cut out to be a teacher. I had become a policeman without a gun. My choices in how I handled the students when they fought were not always the best. Looking back, I realize I could have done better. On one occasion, I watched the shop teacher step back from a fight that broke out in front of his classroom. Curious about his approach, I asked him why he had let the students fight. He told me, "Sometimes I let them wear themselves out." When I became extremely frustrated, I put his advice into practice. I'd instruct the students to move their chairs and desks to create an open space where the two fighters could go at it for a while until they got tired, or one had gotten the best of the other. I knew this wasn't right, but the room would then be quiet as everyone, even those who were just watching, became exhausted. A couple of times, I thought I would be in trouble with the principal, especially when one student reported I had encouraged and allowed a fight. Much to my surprise, the principal suggested that in the future I take the students into the gym and let the Physical Education teacher supervise their fights.

I also spent time counseling a few of the young men with some success. One 16-year-old student demonstrated a strong desire to learn. His interest was encouraging. My first step was to ask his teachers for his textbooks. They were cooperative and happy to help. They never disclosed what I was doing to the principal. Once I had the books, we talked about his classwork and determined where we were to begin. Together, we mapped out his lessons and homework. This went on for several weeks. Once we had completed a portion of his work, I told the student I would submit a written recommendation to the principal indicating he be allowed to return to his regular classes. When I didn't get a response, I made a visit to the principal's office. That's when the principal told me my student would have to get three to four teachers' recommendations. Unfortunately, none of them had direct experience with him. There was no way he could meet the principal's requirements. In challenging the principal's decision, I learned he had already made up his mind about blocking any effort to help this student. He exclaimed, "His mother went to the superintendent's office and complained." His words wreaked of hopelessness for my student. I tried my best to delay delivering this bad news, but there was no way around it. When he asked about his recommendation, I told him we had to keep trying. He knew I was hiding the truth. A few days later, he told me, "Mr. Leeke, I know you have tried to help me, but you are not enough." That conversation was the last one we had. He dropped out of school the same day. I never found out what happened to him.

As the year progressed, I tried to help several other students with similar results. These experiences left me disheartened because everything that happened to my students was done by people who looked just like them. The Black educational leaders made decisions that had lifetime repercussions on children that could have been their own. That was hard for me to swallow, especially since it was 1963 and many students in the South were marching and protesting mistreatment by whites. At the same time, Dr. Martin Luther King, Jr., the Southern Christian Leadership Conference, and the Alabama Christian Movement for Human Rights organized a massive direct action campaign to attack the city of Birmingham's segregation system by putting pressure on its merchants during the Easter season, the second biggest shopping season of the year. Under Dr. King's leadership, the groups held a Good Friday march that landed him in the cell where he penned his famous "Letter from Birmingham Jail." Weeks later, 1,000 students ditched their classes to march two-by-two out of the 16th Street Baptist Church and found themselves arrested. One week later, Americans witnessed thousands more students being knocked off their feet by high-pressure water hoses and violently attacked and harassed by police dogs and angry white people. They watched these horrendous acts on their television screens in the comfort of their own homes. The students' courageous efforts brought victory to Birmingham's Black community. As a result, city officials were forced to reach a tentative agreement to end segregation.

Fortunately for Theresa and me, life did turn around. I decided to reconnect with the Flint, Michigan school system. I sent a letter following up on my interview that I was forced to cancel as a result of a car accident the previous year. Their response was favorable. I was invited to come for an interview at their expense over the spring break. After successfully completing the interview, I was offered a teaching position in one of the elementary schools during the 1963–64 school year. Their offer was a much-needed second chance at pursuing a teaching career. Naturally, Theresa and I were excited. We had one more reason to celebrate: Theresa was pregnant with our first child. We were going to be parents, moving to a new city at the same time, and facing a threshold of change together.

CHAPTER 5 REFLECTION QUESTIONS

———————————

1. Individual: Think about the adversities or challenges you faced in the early days of your career. What mindset and people helped you overcome these experiences? What lessons did you learn?

2. Group Discussion: Now that you have explored your experiences, you're ready to take a deep dive into how they will help inform you and your family, friends, community, and colleagues in a group discussion.

   Each person would have 3–5 minutes to share their responses with the group. As a group, list some of the similarities and differences highlighted in the sharing session. Also, discuss one or two lessons each person has learned.

CHAPTER 6

New Beginnings:
A Parent, a Teacher, and
a Social Justice Activist

"Life is a succession of lessons
which must be lived to be understood."

—HELEN KELLER, a change agent, an author,
a disability rights advocate, a political activist, and a lecturer

---

At 24, I hadn't acquired an arsenal of lessons to guide me into the new beginnings Theresa and I were about to face without family support. It was the first time in both of our lives where we lived the lessons. We used our faith and trust in God and each other to pave the way to understanding.

On the evening before the March on Washington, where Dr. King gave his memorable "I Have A Dream" speech in 1963, I drove from DC to Flint. I needed to be there for my new teacher orientation, but I delayed my departure hoping to be present for the arrival of Michael David, our first child. We agreed to name him after Theresa's cousin, David Michael, the son of her father's baby sister. She was very close to him. Michael came, of course, on his own timetable. When I arrived in Flint and called home, my mother told me my father had taken Theresa to the Columbia Hospital for Women. Michael arrived during the early morning hours of August 28th. I met him a few days later when I flew back home for the weekend. When I saw him for the first time, I was excited. The one thing I remember about his first weekend was I got very little sleep because he needed our attention every two hours. We were busy getting his bottles of milk and changing his diapers. That weekend, he baptized us into parenting.

When I returned to Flint, I threw myself into teaching. Theresa and Michael stayed with my parents for several months before traveling to stay with her parents in Indianapolis. Flint was essentially a neighborhood school system at the elementary level. I had been assigned to teach Social Studies and Language Arts to a fourth and fifth-grade combination class at Brownell Elementary School. Brownell was a brand new all-white school with a population of approximately 250 students. It was located on the expanding Northwest side of Flint. I didn't realize it at the time, but this was part of the white flight movement from the center of Flint to the underdeveloped Northwest side. There were only two Black teachers, me and a woman who taught at another grade level. She had more teaching experience than me and had come from another school in the city. The staff were primarily women and three men, including a male principal. I was the youngest teacher with the least amount of experience. I have always been curious as to why I was assigned to an all-white school.

Was I selected because of my earlier experiences as a student at an integrated high school, college, and fraternity? I am not sure if these considerations were raised by the hiring team, but it makes sense these experiences made me a good fit.

During my first several months in Flint, I lived at the local YMCA, which was located 15 minutes from Brownell. Living at the YMCA gave me an opportunity to develop friendships with several Black men my age who were attending the General Motors Institute (GMI). We played basketball three to four nights a week. Because Flint was a six-hour drive to Indianapolis, I would visit Theresa and Michael every other weekend. While I was away, I found comfort in knowing they had her family's love and support up close and personal.

On the weekends when I wasn't in Indianapolis, I used my time to look for permanent housing in Flint. The city didn't have much in the way of apartments or houses I could afford. I was able to find a three-bedroom rambler house for sale on the Southwest side of town. It was approximately 20 years old and in a predominately Black middle-class neighborhood. The house had a large backyard surrounded by six-foot hedges. Many of the residents worked in automobile factories. One weekend, Theresa came up to check it out. She liked it just as much as I did. Afterwards, we began the process of purchasing our first home. The lending institution required me to secure some additional income. I found a part-time job in Sears's shoe department. The job allowed me to use the experience I gained while working in a shoe store at the end of my senior year in high school. I kept this job throughout our time in Flint. Working at Sears gave our family a discount on clothing, shoes, and household goods.

We moved into 1835 Whittlesey Street in March 1964. We also began attending Christ the King Church, a Black Catholic Church led by Father Norman DuKette, a Black man who was originally from DC. Shortly after joining, Theresa introduced herself to Father DuKette and learned that he needed a choir director and an organist. As a result of her years of experience as a choir director at St. Rita's, she was a perfect fit. Being a part of the church community gave us an opportunity to meet other young families such as the Lathams and Mollays. Monica (Mollay) Latham and her husband, Joe, became very close friends. Our families have remained close since our time in Flint.

Weeks after moving into our new home, we found out we were expecting our second child. I was hoping and praying for a girl. On December 18, 1964, Madelyn Cheryl was born at St. Joseph's Hospital. She was named after Theresa's best friend and maid of honor, Madelyn Grace, and niece, Janet Cheryl. She shared the same godfather as Mike, Hallet Saunders. Her godmother Cheryl was the daughter of Hallet and Martha, Mike's godmother. By the time Mark Andrew showed up on the scene on December 27, 1965 at Hurley Medical Center, we were committed to giving all our children names that began with the letter M. The final member of the "four M's," Matthew Jay arrived at Hurley on September 17, 1967. He was named after J. Matthew Shaw, a close friend of my parents who rented a room in my childhood home on

8th Street, NW. Henry and Mona Dawson, our neighbors and fellow church members, were his godparents.

Being an only child motivated me to want to have more than one child. However, I am not sure it meant four! Having a large backyard allowed us to do things with the kids. We had a swing set and a sandbox they enjoyed playing in. Since Michael was one of the first to walk, he and I would cut the lawn together. He'd follow me with his little lawn mower while I cut the grass with the big lawn mower. We were quite a team. Establishing structure and family rituals were very important to Theresa and me. We started having dinner each night around 6 p.m. That ritual continued throughout their high school years. We also had a bedtime ritual of hugs and kisses that lasted until they were pre-teens.

Because I was skilled at cutting hair, my sons Michael and Mark became regular patrons in my kitchen barber shop. Every few weeks, they would get to sit on the kitchen stool for their haircuts. Apparently, Michael really enjoyed watching me cut hair. He had the brilliant idea of cutting some of Mark's hair and then putting it back as if he hadn't touched it. When Theresa and I discovered Mark's missing hair, we thought something was wrong. Turns out Michael was the culprit. When we asked Mark why he let his brother cut his hair, he looked around with his big eyes and tried to act like we weren't talking to him. Naturally, Michael was punished, and Mark was warned not to let anyone cut his hair except me.

On Sunday mornings, we would spend time getting the kids dressed for church. Once we arrived at Mass, Theresa would leave us to direct the choir and play the organ. My job was to make sure they sat still and behaved in the pew. Thanks to Theresa's child rearing, the four M's made my job easy. We loved taking rides around the city in our small Renault. Everyone was excited when we purchased a Ford station wagon with the seats facing in the back. It gave the kids room to stretch out and play. Whenever we were out, people would comment about how adorable they were. Their comments reminded me of how proud I was to be their father.

Flint was a great place to raise our family from 1963 to 1968. Unfortunately, present-day Flint is a shadow of what we knew it to be. While we lived there, there were four major automobile manufacturing plants located in the city: General Motors Corporation's Buick Motor Division, Chevrolet Truck Division, Fisher Body Division, and AC Spark Plugs Company. These plants helped the city grow into an automobile manufacturing powerhouse. They also created stable employment and helped the city achieve one of its lowest unemployment rates ever. Because employment was booming between the 1940s and 1960s, many Black people migrated from the South to Flint. They were a part of the Second Great Migration, the movement of more than five million Black people from the South to the Northeast, Midwest, and the West.

Flint was also the home of the Community School concept created by Dr. Frank Manley, the father of the Modern Community School Movement, and his philanthropic friend, Charles Stewart Mott of the Mott Foundation. They shared a belief that the "spirit of teamwork" could be used to solve community problems with available resources. They brought their belief to life in the 1960s through the application of six community education programs:

1. Community involvement
2. Facility use
3. Adult programming
4. Youth programming
5. Classroom enrichment through community resources
6. Coordination, cooperation, and delivery of community services

Every school in their system had a Community School Director who managed the programs. The schools were open from early morning until 10:00 or 11:00 p.m. During the day, classes were offered to children, youth, and adults. Afterschool programs, activities, and classes were held in the evenings. The school allowed entire families to participate. Theresa took advantage of some of the community school programs including a sewing class and several evening classes offered by the Michigan State University's Extension Center on the Flint Community College campus. Michael and Madelyn attended Tot Lot, a cooperative nursery school located in the Jewish Community Center near the Flint Community College campus. Since it was a cooperative nursery school, parents had to manage the school and provide food. Theresa served as a parent volunteer. Tot Lot was not a part of the Mott Foundation's Community Schools. The Mott Foundation funded the Community Schools. Its mission was to promote a just, equitable, and sustainable society. It also established the Mott Fellowship to build community education leaders in 1963.

Being able to finally teach students the way I had been prepared and dreamed about was a true blessing. During my first year at Brownell, I had two groups of students. I taught language arts (grammar, spelling, and reading) and social studies (history) to fifth graders in the morning and a combination of fourth and fifth graders in the afternoon. Although I really enjoyed teaching, it was a challenge because I had to learn Michigan history for my fourth-grade class. The fifth graders had American history. In my second and third years, I had one group of fifth graders and another group of fifth and sixth graders. I taught World History to the sixth graders. My history courses at St. Augustine and Carroll served as a template for my class preparation. I followed the syllabus and the district and state requirements which did not include Black history. It wasn't something I realized I needed to do until I became actively involved in the Flint Education Association and advocated for Black history to be included in the curriculum.

In English and Reading, I taught the basics and called on some of my previous experiences as a student and student teacher. I enjoyed introducing the students to diagramming sentences as a way to learn sentence construction. I had them write different types of reports, such as book reports, which had specific guidelines they were to follow. I implemented a weekly spelling contest on Fridays. The students enjoyed the friendly competition. It was a fun way to end the week. Looking back, it was a blessing I stayed at the YMCA and by myself because it gave me extra time to prepare during my first months at Brownell. Teaching got easier in the following years because I was able to build upon my lesson plans from the first year.

Most of these students seemed to enjoy school and were motivated. There were a few, mainly boys, who needed to work harder and required extra attention and more parent-teacher conferences. Most parents were very cooperative and saw our work as a team effort. It was a team effort. During those years, in addition to working at Sears, I sold World Book Encyclopedias which gave me an additional opportunity to visit the students' homes and to interact with their parents. I did get to know one of my students' fathers, Mr. Boze. He introduced me to the Flint Education Association (FEA). I'd also see parents while I was working at Sears. I am not sure how they viewed me, a Black man, teaching their children. I didn't sense anything amiss from the students. However, I may have been one of the few Black teachers they had in their school life. I, myself, didn't have a Black male teacher until I was working on my doctorate.

Earning my Master of Science Degree in Counseling at the University of Michigan (U of M) became a major focus in my second year at Brownell. I chose U of M because they had professors who would come to Flint and teach classes in the evenings at Flint Community College. Taking two classes every semester and driving to Ann Arbor to take classes in the summer became my regular routine for two years. While I was studying for my master's degree, Theresa was busy parenting our children. I would not have been able to complete this degree without her full-time support. My coursework helped me learn about the school system's plan to place an elementary counselor in five of its schools as a pilot program. When it came time for me to complete my counseling practicum, I asked my supervisor if I could work with elementary school students. Once my request was granted, I was in a better position to seize the opportunity before me. That's why I say timing is everything.

Upon completion of the practicum and my master's degree, I was assigned to Scott Elementary School on the Southwest side which was five minutes from home. Out of the five counselors selected, two were Black. I was the only man and the youngest in the group. Scott was an integrated school with Black and white students. Like the student body, the staff was predominantly white. There were three Black teachers, one male and two female. In total, there were four of us on staff. With the support of a wonderful principal and what I learned at the U of M, I created a system that allowed me to work with individual students and in small groups. I helped them explore different ways of studying. I worked with teachers on how to respond to the needs of a given child and assisted them with administering standardized exams. My group meetings with parents focused on topics such as how they could help their children with homework and ways to detect learning challenges. Because I had so much freedom and flexibility, I think the principal was grooming me at some point to be an administrator.

Being a part of a teacher's union and engaged in community activities was foreign territory for me. Here for the first time, every teacher was expected to become a member of the FEA. I joined but did not get actively involved due to family and work responsibilities and graduate studies. Mr. Boze, an active FEA member, convinced me to make a short-term commitment to work on the committee responsible for selecting the first Executive Director. This experience turned out to be a terrific one because I learned how to review resumes, select candidates, and then establish relationships with key FEA leaders. Once again, I stood out as the only Black member of the committee.

During my second year at Brownell, the FEA initiated its first round of formal contract negotiations with the school system. Teachers negotiating with a school board put Michigan on the map within the national teacher labor movement. Negotiations did not go well at first, and the membership voted to go on strike. This was a difficult time because I was the sole provider for my family and had never faced financial uncertainty. However, I not only voted for the strike, but volunteered to be our building contact. Most teachers joined the strike, including a white male teacher who taught fourth grade math in the classroom next to mine. We talked regularly about his support of the strike. On the first day of the strike, however, I was very surprised to see him cross the picket line in front of my eyes. The strike was successful and only lasted a few days. It impacted staff relationships. For example, it changed my relationship with the white male teacher. I no longer trusted him which meant we did not talk frequently.

When I began working at Scott in 1966, I became more involved in the FEA and was selected to be a delegate to the National Education Association (NEA) Convention in Minneapolis, Minnesota. This marked the first of many conventions I would attend in my career. It was an eye-opening experience to witness the democratic process where the delegates presented, discussed, and voted on resolutions and new business actions which determined the direction of the next year. Two significant actions were taken at this first convention: the merger approval of the NEA and American Teachers Association (ATA), the Black teachers organization; and the election of Elizabeth Duncan Koontz, a Black woman from North Carolina, as the president-elect. Koontz later became the first Black NEA President in 1968. These actions contributed to the NEA's decade of growth and change.

In 1967, the FEA selected me to be a part of a 10-member team which included teachers, administrators, parents, and community activists to attend a weekend conference at the Michigan Education Association's (MEA) Battle Creek Conference Center. The conference was sponsored by the NEA, the U.S. Justice Department, and the MEA. Samuel Ethridge, Director of the NEA Center for Human Relations, was the organizer. Samuel brought together teams from 17 of Michigan's urban areas. Trainers from the National Training Laboratory of Applied Behavioral Science (NTL) facilitated the conference sessions. During the sessions, I experienced for the first time Blacks and whites engaged in very heated discussions about what was happening to Black people in their schools. I will never forget listening to a very angry, passionate, and articulate Black man. He was about six feet and two inches tall with a full beard and a large Afro. He stood in front of a large fireplace, holding court. His passionate words about how whites were unwilling to accept Black members in different roles within the organization and changes to make education better for the Black community captivated everyone. It also scared some white people and left several in tears. Our discussions reflected the turbulent times we were living in, especially in urban centers. My dream for making change came to life while attending this conference.

That weekend conference produced several recommendations for change in the MEA and later became known as the conference that "never ended." I left Battle Creek charged up and committed to take action to change conditions in Flint. Shortly after returning home, I went to see Malcolm X, the national spokesman for the Nation of Islam (NOI), an organization of Black Muslims, speak at the IMA Auditorium. He was a very dynamic speaker who talked about Black people taking control of their own destiny. His inspiring words gave me much to think about. Little did I know we shared the same birthday. He was born fourteen years before me. Watching the discipline of the NOI men that Malcolm X led and the way they controlled the crowd impressed me. His remarks and the Battle Creek conference were certainly the beginning of my social activism.

Meeting and working with the 10 members of the Battle

Creek team opened the door for me to establish a long-term collaborative relationship with Gloria Fauth, a white woman who was a very active FEA member and leader in the Flint schools. Gloria had recently returned from attending the NEA Human and Civil Rights Annual Conference in Washington, DC. Through our efforts, we convinced the FEA, the Flint Community Schools, the MEA, and the NEA to sponsor a weekend conference similar to the one in Battle Creek in 1968. We used the Battle Creek model to recruit Flint conference participants. They were recruited from four teams built around the four high schools and their feeder junior and elementary schools. Each team had teachers, administrators, high school students, parents, and business and community leaders.

The Flint conference was very successful because it recommended increasing the number of Black administrators and counselors and expanding the curriculum to include Black perspectives. By the start of the school year, several Black people were appointed as principals and assistant principals. At the same time, I began organizing Black teachers and encouraging them to get more involved in the FEA. In following the wisdom of Malcolm X, I decided it was time to bring them together for a meeting to discuss our own destiny and how we could improve conditions for Black students. Unfortunately, FEA leadership and some of the Black teachers were not thrilled by my efforts. I don't think they were ready for such a progressive approach. Although the school superintendent was not pleased, he told me he would not get in my way. The FEA leaders contacted the NEA to have someone come help me understand the inappropriateness of my actions. Lucky for me, the NEA sent Larry Billups, a Black staff member, who helped me understand how to continue what I was doing without getting in trouble with the FEA leadership. He counseled me on how to strategically address the issues without threatening the white leadership. Larry's intervention helped me get into what the late Congressman John Lewis called "good trouble." Meeting Larry in Flint was also the beginning of a long and productive relationship.

While I was getting into "good trouble" in 1968 by continuing to advocate on behalf of Black teachers and students, the U.S. faced a year of turmoil with the Vietnam War and civil rights protests in the streets and on many college campuses. Howard University students took over the Mordecai Wyatt Johnson Administration Building to seek a greater voice in student discipline and the curriculum. The Kerner Commission released a report that examined the causes of race riots in American cities in previous years, which declared the nation is "moving toward two societies, one black, one white—separate and unequal." Dr. Martin Luther King, Jr. was killed at gunpoint in Memphis. After his death, riots erupted in major cities that destroyed many Black neighborhoods. There was a shootout between the Black Panthers and the police in Oakland, California that killed Bobby Hutton as he tried to surrender. President Lyndon B. Johnson signed the Fair Housing Act that banned discrimination in housing on the basis of race, color, religion, or national origin. The Poor People's Campaign held the Solidarity Day Rally for

Jobs, Peace, and Freedom in DC. Robert Kennedy was killed shortly after he had announced he was running for president in Los Angeles. Police and the Illinois National Guardsmen went on a rampage, clubbing and tear-gassing hundreds of antiwar demonstrators, news reporters, and bystanders at the Democratic National Convention. During the national anthem at the Olympic Games in Mexico City, Tommie Smith and John Carlos received the gold and bronze medals in the 200-meter dash and raised their fists in protest of violence toward Black people. As a result, the International Olympic Committee stripped them of their medals.

Like the nation, my life was undergoing great change. Samuel Ethridge invited me to be on a panel at the Human Relations Seminar prior to the NEA Representative Assembly meeting in Dallas. That's also the same time I interviewed with George Jones, Director of the Task Force on Urban Education at the NEA, for a staff position. George was appointed Director shortly after the Task Force and its members were named in March of 1968. The Task Force was voted on and approved during the NEA's annual convention in 1967. Prior to his appointment, he had worked for the NEA for a little over a year as a staff member in the Field Services Division. Before joining the NEA, he had served as the Executive Director of the American Teachers Association, Secretary of the Alabama Teachers Association, and Dean at both Miles College and Alabama State College. Both colleges were historically Black colleges and universities (HBCUs).

When I returned from Dallas and shared the news that

George had offered me the position, Theresa was not excited. This was the second job opportunity that had come my way in the past two years. The year before when I attended the NEA Convention in Minneapolis, a representative of the Follett Book Company interviewed me for a book salesman position. He later came to Flint and took Theresa and me out for dinner. During the dinner, he offered me a position in Queens, New York City. We turned down his offer because we didn't think it would be a great fit for our family.

Accepting the NEA position was risky because it was a one-year contract. George felt my contract would be extended after the Task Force assignment concluded because the NEA was in the process of hiring numerous Black staff. Theresa had reservations about where we would live. She really liked Flint because we had established a community of support in our church and neighborhood and leveraged the educational resources that were available to our family. By the time we were contemplating a move, our family of four had increased by two more sons, Mark Andrew and Matthew Jay. After much discussion about the benefits of living in the Washington, DC metro area, Theresa agreed to move. We were on our way to our next adventure.

The Leeke Family's first house,
1835 Whittlesey Street, Flint, Michigan

John Leeke and his son
Michael cutting the grass with
his toy lawn mower

Michael playing in
the sandbox

*John Leeke cutting his son
Michael's hair*

*John Leeke holding his
daughter Madelyn and
standing by his son Michael
in the living room*

*Michael and Madelyn playing
with their red wagon*

*Michael and Madelyn
sitting on their hassocks
in the living room*

(L–R) Mark, Matthew, Michael, and Madelyn Leeke

John Leeke sitting with his children, Michael, Madelyn, Mark, and Matthew, on Easter Sunday

Theresa Leeke sitting with her children, Michael, Madelyn, Mark, and Matthew, on Easter Sunday

CHAPTER 6 REFLECTION QUESTIONS

---

1. Individual: Think about the first time you began to navigate and integrate your career, relationships, and community or civic involvement. What were some of the key moments and lessons you learned during this period?

2. Group Discussion: Now that you have explored your experiences, you're ready to take a deep dive into how they will help inform you and your family, friends, community, and colleagues in a group discussion.

   Each person would have 3–5 minutes to share their responses with the group. As a group, list some of the similarities and differences highlighted in the sharing session. Also, discuss one or two lessons each person has learned.

PART TWO

THE NEA EXPERIENCE: CLIMBING THE LADDER OF EQUALITY AND INCLUSION

(1968–1985)

CHAPTER 7

Our New Life in Maryland

"Transition is psychological; it is a three-phase process that people go through as they internalize and come to terms with the details of the new situation that the change brings about. Because transition is a process by which people unplug from an old world and plug into a new world, we can say transition starts with an ending and finishes with a beginning."

—WILLIAM BRIDGES, a change agent and an author of
Managing Transitions: Making the Most of Change

Life offers a myriad of transitions that cause you to leave the old life behind as you move forward into a new life. The transition is what takes place in between leaving the old life and starting the new one. That in-between place is not always easy to navigate. It is filled with emotional, psychological, and physical concerns. Before I had a wife and children, I experienced transitions that only impacted me. Becoming a husband and a parent made transitions more complex and challenging because I was now faced with concerns, such as the uncertainty of what would happen, the fear of making the wrong decisions, and the pressure to ensure my family was taken care of.

Making the transition to the DC area was much more complicated than when we left Terre Haute as a couple in 1962. This time around we had a house to sell and the responsibility of finding housing for a family of six in a relatively short timeframe. With the support of one of my fellow teachers who worked with me at Sears and was licensed as a realtor, we put our house up for sale. Three days later we had a buyer. She was a single 40-something Black woman who was able to pay cash which made the sale happen quickly. After going to settlement, the NEA paid to bring Theresa and I to DC to search for housing. Prior to leaving, I asked my father to contact a local realtor since we only had a few days to find a new home. We narrowed our search to Prince George's County, Maryland. After he picked us up from the airport on Friday evening, we looked at houses on Saturday, Sunday, and Monday. Our final stop for the day was Kenmore, a predominately white neighborhood in Landover. There were 94 homes on four streets. The realtor took us to 3113 Manson Place, a two-story house with a large backyard. It had three bedrooms, two bathrooms, a kitchen, a dining room, a living room, and a basement. The owners were an older white couple. After inspecting the property, we learned about the elementary and junior high schools located nearby which meant our kids would be able to walk to and from school. In addition, my commute to the NEA would only take less than 30 minutes. Theresa and I had found our family's new home.

The next part of our transition was moving our family to Landover before my first week of work that started the day after Labor Day. We left Flint at the end of August 1968. The Mayflower Moving Company helped to pack our belongings. When we arrived in Maryland, we checked into the Holiday Inn in College Park. We stayed there for several days until we closed on the home and our furniture arrived. After we moved in, I flew back to Flint and drove our second car, the Renault, back to our new home. Looking back on this hectic move, I know God was looking out for us because everything fell into place.

As we settled into our new life, we learned we were the third Black family to move on our street of 19 homes. During this time, whites were moving away from our community. One year after we arrived, only three white families remained; they were all gone within the next year. White flight refers to the migration of white residents leaving neighborhoods when people of color begin to move in. White flight also gives people of color an opportunity to own homes and create communities. That's what happened in our case. Our family made long-lasting connections with other Black families in the neighborhood. Burgess and Catherine "Cat" Coleman lived across the street and became very close friends. They had two daughters, Valerie and Brenda, who were several years older than our children. They became our go-to babysitters. Stanford, the youngest Coleman, was Matthew's age. They became the best of friends. Stanford also became the unofficial fifth M. He was always at our house and ended up eating lots of dinners with us before he went home to eat dinner with his family.

Theresa used the Montessori method of education to prepare our children for kindergarten. Developed by Maria Montessori, an Italian physician, it emphasizes independence and views children as naturally eager for knowledge and capable of initiating learning in a supportive environment. Although Theresa and I attended Catholic schools, we wanted our children to be educated in the public schools. As an NEA staff member and former teacher, I felt a deep commitment to public education. Michael was the first of our children to attend kindergarten at Kenmore Elementary School. He paved the way for the rest of them. When he was in second grade, Madelyn in first grade, and Mark in kindergarten, Theresa enrolled Matthew in a nursery school at a Lutheran Church in Greenbelt. Not wanting to be left out, Stanford enrolled too.

When we first moved to the area, we visited St. Ambrose, a predominately white Catholic church, but didn't find it to be welcoming. We also regularly attended Mass at St. Anthony's in Brookland, my parents' neighborhood in DC. My mother was a member of the church. A year later, we learned about St. Joseph's Catholic Church in Landover, a predominately Black church located five minutes from our home. Everyone welcomed us. It felt like a family and reminded us of Christ the King Church in Flint. There were also several families with children the same ages as ours. After joining St. Joseph's, we enrolled the children in the Confraternity of Christian Doctrine (CCD) classes that met on Saturday mornings and taught them how to be Catholic. Theresa was asked to start a choir in 1970. Our sons became altar boys. All our children received their sacraments of First Communion and Confirmation.

Living in Maryland gave our children the opportunity to deepen relationships with my side of the family. My parents and Aunt Paulyne lived in DC and were able to visit regularly. My parents and Aunt Paulyne would host the children several times a year, which gave Theresa and me a break. We also celebrated birthdays and major holidays together. We took many short road trips to see my Aunt Alma "Auntie" and cousins Tom, Russ, and Anne Roberts who lived in Wilmington, Delaware. Tom, Russ, and Anne had children that were either a little older or the same age as our children. They grew up playing together in the summers and attending many family weddings, graduations, and celebrations together.

Our children's early years were deeply enriched by Theresa's decision to return to college to pursue a career as a teacher at Prince George's Community College and the University of Maryland at College Park. Because I was traveling a lot, she would take them with her to various classes and on field trips. For one summer, she took a Geology class that required collecting rocks. They had a good time learning about them and visiting Luray Caverns, the largest caverns in the eastern United States. She used what she was learning to guide our children through their formative years. For example, she emphasized their use of imagination and creativity. They were always drawing pictures, coloring, building things with Legos, and playing with their homemade Playdough that Theresa helped them make from scratch. Michael became the ringleader in designing a mud swimming pool in the backyard in the summers, an igloo in the front yard in the winters, and cardboard musical instruments that helped them pretend to be the Jackson Five.

While Theresa was a college student, she became a member of the Phi Sigma Chapter of Sigma Gamma Rho Sorority, which allowed her to serve as an undergraduate advisor to young women attending Bowie State University, a historically Black college located near our home. Our children regularly visited the campus and learned firsthand what it was like to attend homecomings and football games. After she earned her associate degree from Prince George's Community College, Theresa enrolled in the University of Maryland to complete her bachelor's degree and chartered Eta Beta Chapter. Working as the undergraduate advisor to the chapter meant that she was responsible for training and mentoring nine young women. They quickly became a part of our family and helped to expose our children to college life on a predominantly white campus. Throughout Theresa's time at the University of Maryland, our children were able to explore the campus, use the pool in the summers, spend time in the Student Union, and eat the famous homemade ice cream made from cows that were housed on campus. These experiences represented some of the many ways we exposed our children to living full lives.

Theresa Leeke sitting with her children,
Madelyn, Mark, Matthew (on lap), and Michael

Leeke children standing
outside of their home

Leeke children dressed up
on a cold day

*Leeke children playing
in the living room*

*Leeke children decorating
the family Christmas tree*

*Leeke children standing
with their father John,
grandmother Frederica,
and Aunt Paulyne Roberts
at their grandparents'
home in Northeast DC*

Leeke children standing outside of their grandparents' home in Northeast DC

Michael, Mark, and Matt and his childhood friend Stanford dressed up as pirates

Leeke children playing with neighborhood friends in their backyard

Neighborhood children playing with Leeke children in their backyard

Leeke Family's first dog,
Dandy

Leeke Family's second dog,
Clarence

John L. Leeke and grandson Mark after his 6ᵗʰ grade graduation
from Kenmore Elementary School

CHAPTER 7 REFLECTION QUESTIONS

---

1. Individual: What were some of the transitions you faced as you continued to build your life and career? What was their impact on your life and career?

2. Group Discussion: Now that you have explored your transitions and their impact, you're ready to take an even deeper dive into how they can help inform you and your family, friends, community, and colleagues in a group discussion.

   Each person would have 3–5 minutes to share their responses with the group. As a group, list some of the similarities and differences highlighted in the sharing session. Also, discuss one or two lessons each person has learned.

CHAPTER 8

The First Year at the NEA: Task Force on Urban Education

"A system of education is not one thing, nor does it have a single definite object, nor is it a mere matter of schools. Education is that whole system of human training within and without the school house walls, which molds and develops men."

—DR. W.E.B. DU BOIS, a change agent, a sociologist, a historian, a civil rights activist, a Pan-Africanist, and an author

─────────────

Dr. Du Bois's wisdom serves as a call to action for anyone committed to transforming an educational system so that it meets the current and future needs of its students in a holistic and equitable way. I believe everyone that participated in the NEA Task Force on Urban Education shared this commitment with me. Our diverse collective of educational institutions and individuals with unique expertise created a unity and synergy I had never seen or experienced before in my career. It was overwhelming and exciting all at the same time.

Nervous is the best word to describe how I felt on my first day at the NEA. My team had been working together for a few weeks. I was the last member to come on board. When

I arrived, George Jones and the Assistant Director Father Joseph "Joe" Devlin, a white Jesuit priest who was on release from his Provincial, greeted me. Father Joe had been working in the NEA Center for the Study of Instruction. They showed me around our suite of offices and introduced me to Linda Morris and Janet Tarkington, the other staff members who were both white women. Linda worked in the NEA Teacher Education and Professional Standards Department (TEPS). Janet had been working as a secretary in different NEA units for several years. Jane Power, another white woman who did not work in our office suite, was a technical writer in the Publications Division and assigned to work on the Task Force.

The Task Force was charged with a three-fold responsibility: (1) to identify and explore the most critical problems of urban education; (2) to design immediate and long-range plans through which the 1.1 million-member NEA, in cooperation with its departments, 50 state associations, and hundreds of large urban locals, can most effectively contribute to the solution of urban education problems; and (3) to recommend to other appropriate agencies, public and private, contributions they can make to help alleviate these problems. The Task Force was composed of 18 educators. They included classroom teachers, supervisory and guidance personnel, administrators, college and state department of education personnel, and representatives from the U.S. Office of Economic Opportunity. NEA Past President Irvamae Applegate, a white woman and the Dean of the School of Education at St. Cloud State College, chaired the Task Force. The vice-chairman was

Oliver Lancaster, a Black man in the Office of Inter-group Education in the Philadelphia, Pennsylvania school district. In addition, there were two consultants: Mario Fantini, a white man who was program officer for the Division of Education and Research for the Ford Foundation; and Robert Havighurst, a white man who was professor of Education at the University of Chicago.

Five departments of the NEA provided staff and financial resources to this effort. They included the American Association of School Administrators, the Association of Classroom Teachers, the Association for Supervision and Curriculum Development, the Department of Elementary Principals, and the National Association of Secondary School Principals. Staff assistance was also provided by the NEA Center for Human Relations, the Center for the Study of Instruction, the Division of Field Services, and the Research Division. These individuals and organizations represented the NEA's last diverse group of education entities working together on a single, focused issue. The individuals were some of the most experienced and knowledgeable educators in the United States at the time. In addition, this experience cemented my activist role and led to the achievement of some of my personal and professional goals, which I valued and utilized for a lifetime.

As staff, we planned and held regular meetings as well as four larger weekend-long gatherings at different sites across the country to hear from teachers, parents, and others about conditions existing in the urban schools and to gather suggestions on how to fix problems. We spent many days reviewing reports as well as talking with other education experts. I learned so much about the inner workings of educational institutions, especially how public schools function and their impact on children in urban environments.

My Task Force work represented the most intense and extensive research experience on a critical, comprehensive, complex, and sensitive issue I had in my early career. In addition to our research work on the report, we spoke at several meetings and conferences on some of the hot education topics at the time, such as school decentralization and community school control. Community school control was a big issue in New York and was spreading throughout the country. As a diverse team, we showed up looking like the characters in the television series *The Mod Squad*: George, a distinguished professor; Joe, a Catholic priest; Linda, a young hippie; and me, a young man with a large Afro. I met and formed connections and friendships with people that have lasted many years. While I developed many lasting relationships during this time, the ones I developed with my fellow staff members were the most significant. For example, George was my mentor, manager, colleague, and friend, and became like a father to me. Getting to know Father Joe marked the first time I had a significant personal and professional relationship with a Catholic priest. He wasn't your typical priest. Being a Jesuit, he was super intelligent and the principal writer of the Task Force Report. We had long conversations about the Catholic Church, including my questions about the sacrament of confession and the increase in priests and nuns leaving their orders.

One of the more memorable trips the staff took together was to Seattle, Washington. The NEA had a policy that any air travel over three hours qualified for first class. The Seattle trip was a four-hour flight from Dulles International Airport to the Seattle-Tacoma International Airport. As we discussed our upcoming presentation, the stewardesses began serving us shrimp cocktail appetizers followed by a salad and an entrée. I was given a choice of three entrées. I selected steak, a baked potato, and a vegetable. Red and white wine were served with the meal. Dessert and after-dinner drinks wrapped up our first-class feast. What a great NEA perk!

We completed our work in June 1969 and the report, *Schools of the Urban Crisis*, was presented to the NEA Representative Assembly at their annual meeting later that summer. I think the report's introduction could very easily be made today. It states:

> *This report deals with urban education, or, more specifically with public education in urban America. It focuses on the character and quality of education offered to millions of poor children—black, Spanish speaking, and white—who inhabit the inner cores of our metropolitan areas. These are the children who attend the schools of the urban crisis. This report deals with schools: schools which are now undergoing a state of unparalleled emergency, suffering from decay, neglect and continuing deterioration. Not every school in every large city is facing this crisis, but too many are.*

Forty-two recommendations were included in our report. Many addressed urban school reorganization, the educational experience, staffing, financing urban education, and the challenges to the NEA. The following 10 recommendations remain applicable today.

1. The school must work in a cooperative manner with young people and the police and courts to improve their relationships.

2. Local teacher organizations, urban and suburban, should develop an attack on socioeconomic biases, prejudice, and racism.

3. Instructional materials used in all areas of the curriculum must accurately reflect the different ethnic, economic, racial, and social backgrounds and attitudes of America's pluralistic composition.

4. Increased attention must be paid to the mobility of urban children across arbitrary school boundaries in our large urban school systems.

5. Special emphasis should be placed on assisting new and beginning urban teachers.

6. There should be widespread staff involvement in developing staff evaluation techniques. Evaluation should be used to improve rather than to criticize or condemn the teacher's performance.

7. School systems should initiate programs that will provide incentives and inducements for attracting capable and competent persons to enter urban school systems.

8. More representatives of ethnic and racial minority

groups must be employed in professional and executive staff positions in all phases of education.

9. All segments of the education profession must receive training and experience which will enable them to work effectively with parent, citizen, and community groups.

10. Funding of urban educational programs should be flexible, permitting the application of resources to the areas of greatest need as analyzed and determined at the local and community level.

The most notable recommendation was the proposed creation of an NEA Special Project on Urban Education. This project would be responsible for originating and coordinating urban education activities. After the report was accepted and adopted, the Special Project on Urban Education was funded for $82,000. The amount of funding provided was much less than the funding for the Task Force Report. George was selected to serve as the Director. He asked me to stay on as the lone professional staff person. In our conversation, George told me my role was to go to the field and work with our local and state associations on implementing the recommendations. His role would be to handle the many in-house interactions. With his blessing, I was on my way to making greater change.

Schools of the Urban Crisis:
Task Force on Urban Education Report

*George Jones at the podium
with Oliver Lancaster, Irvamae
Applegate, John Leeke, and
Father Joseph Delvin*

*John Leeke standing at the
podium to introduce the*
Schools of the Urban Crisis:
Task Force on Urban
Education Report

CHAPTER 8 REFLECTION QUESTIONS

---

1. Individual: Go back and read the Task Force's 10 recommendations. How do these recommendations relate to what is happening in schools and state legislatures today? How would you use the recommendations to address today's current issues?

2. Group Discussion: As a group, identify action steps that could be used to address today's current issues. If you want to take a deeper dive as a group, formulate an action and then determine how you will bring it to life within your own family, workplace, and/or community.

   Each person would have 3–5 minutes to share their responses with the group. As a group, list some of the similarities and differences highlighted in the sharing session. Also, discuss one or two lessons each person has learned.

CHAPTER 9

NEA Special Project on Urban Education: The Urban Institutes

"Whatever you do, strive to do it so well that no man living and no man dead and no man yet to be born could do it any better."

—DR. BENJAMIN E. MAYS, a change agent, a Baptist minister, a civil rights leader, Dean of the Howard University School of Religion, and President of Morehouse College

───────────────

Writing this book has given me a deeper appreciation for the people and experiences I encountered while working on the NEA's Special Project on Urban Education. At 85, I am just realizing how significant this part of my career was as a 20-something year old Black man who was given free reign by a 40-something year old Black man to design and implement a program that had never been done before. I brought everything I knew and experienced to the table, including my commitment to excellence that I inherited from my ancestors. My daughter Madelyn (Ananda) often reminds me it is known as "Black Excellence," the very thing Dr. Benjamin E. Mays talks about in his wisdom quote on striving to do so well that no one could do it any better than you.

One of the first activities of the NEA's Special Project on Urban Education was to assist local teacher associations in getting organized to address existing problems in their school communities. Drawing on my Flint experiences, I developed a work plan for the Urban Institute that identified seven urban communities where the NEA had strong local affiliates. The plan called for helping each local association build a team of 25 individuals from a high school cluster area in their city. It is also called for developing a training program to prepare the teams to address the most pressing and challenging issues in their school communities. This plan was included in a position paper I prepared to describe the type of work the Urban Institute would do. I used the paper to introduce the Urban Institute to association, school administration, and community leaders in the different cities; the training teams; and others who would be involved. See the position paper below.

URBAN INSTITUTE

The National Education Association, in addressing itself to the major issues in urban education today, proposes to co-sponsor a week-long Institute for the purpose of assisting several urban communities to begin making meaningful changes in their school system. The Institute will have training as its major focus to help educators, students, parents, and other citizens to work as partners in deciding what they want to happen in their schools.

Specific Objectives

1. To organize and train a "back home" team. This team would define the goals and objectives of the school system, and review the current programs offered in the schools to accomplish these goals.

2. To demonstrate new techniques for constructive dialogue among disparate groups within a community and develop models for different approaches to cooperative action among parents, school staffs, students, and other school-community environmental related personnel and agencies.

3. To design more meaningful ways to influence pre-service and in-service education, with concerns for human relations and the social environment of the child.

4. To develop possible action plans (model) for intervention and attempts to bring about needed changes and improvements of the schools.

It is proposed that selected cities from states within NEA Regions be invited to take part in this Institute.

Each selected city would send a team of 25 participants to the Institute. The team members are to be selected from a high school district (feeder schools included).

Each team would be made up to include the fol-

lowing: six classroom teachers (Elementary, Jr. High, and High School); three parents; six students (juniors and seniors); four administrators (Elementary principal, Junior High principal, Senior High principal or assistant, and someone from central office); three community groups or organization (one business representative, one city government official, and one college or university representative).

Selection of team members should be carried out by members and representatives from the teacher association, school, and community. Selection should be based on the following criteria:

1. *In selecting student participants, juniors should be taken over graduating seniors.*
2. *The make-up of the team should be as mixed as possible to reflect differences in race, ideology, gender, and age.*
3. *No one should be considered ineligible to participate because they are considered to be too militant or too reactionary.*
4. *Team participants should have in common the ability to be articulate, the desire to try and communicate towards the solving of problems, and if possible, some mixed group experience.*
5. *Parents should be from the high school cluster, having children enrolled at one of the levels K-12.*

6. *Participants representing community organizations should reflect those groups which play rather vital roles in the day-to-day life of this particular team community.*

7. *The representative from the business community could come from the broader community, but it would be highly desirable if he/she has a definite connection with the chosen area.*

8. *The college/university representative could come from the broader community but having some very visible contact with the chosen area. It is also desirable that it be someone knowledgeable concerning urban education.*

9. *The city government representative would represent the broader community. It would be desirable to have an individual who is in a position of knowledge and decision-making authority.*

10. *The desired team composition as set forth should be flexible enough to allow for adaptation to each local set of conditions. If, for the purposes of the Institute, the availability of some individual or organization not included in the contemplated team composition is considered more important than one which is included, then that person or organization should be the one invited to participate.*

Institute Design

Participants would meet in several different kinds of groupings during the week-long Institute. It is envisioned that at various times there would be:

    a. *Small heterogenous groups*

    b. *Homogeneous groupings (e.g., student groups, teacher groups, etc.)*

    c. *Temporary or "ad hoc" groups for exploration of a topic*

    d. *Back-home team group meetings to work out specific designs for action*

    e. *Plenary group*

Assistance in planning and conducting the Institute will be sought from people connected with or trained by the National Training Laboratory. The Institute staff, Director and facilitators will spend several days in special pre-conference training. Use will also be made of consultants who are knowledgeable in the areas of curriculum, organizational structure, staff preparation, development, and utilization.

Sponsoring or Cooperating Agencies

NEA through the Urban Project and Center for Human Relations will be the overall Institute coordinator. Other NEA units will contribute consultative services and resources to the Institute. Cooperation will be

*sought from State Education Affiliates, State Depart-
ments of Education, and private foundations. Local
participants and local education associations would
underwrite the cost of transportation. The local board
of education would cover the expenses of substitutes
for professional staff, and the local city or community
agencies cover the salaries of parents or others who
have to miss a week of work in order to attend.*

*Pre-conference activities will be coordinated by
the staff of the Urban Project/Center for Human Relations. This would include meeting with representatives in each selected city to discuss the Institute, help
with the selection of the teams and preparation of lit-
erature to be used in the Institute.*

Follow-up

*The Institute is considered as the initiation of a long
range (3–5 years) program with follow-up activities to
participating communities being coordinated by the
NEA staff. The staff will make on-site visits to the Institute for the purposes of assisting the team in carrying
out their plans. There will also be provision for at least
one formal one or two-day workshop for the team in
their individual communities following the Institute.*

MAKING THE PLAN A REALITY AND GETTING THE JOB DONE

Once George Jones, Director of the NEA Task Force on Urban Education, and I had prepared the plan, we faced the challenge of getting it implemented due to a very limited budget. That meant we had to be very creative and seek out support. The first task was securing a team to conduct the first Institute. George suggested we contact someone with National Training Laboratory (NTL) experience who would partner with me as lead trainer and co-director. George recommended Bill Moore, Director of the Model Cities program in Chicago. He met Bill at an NTL Lab. Bill and I began to build our relationship which lasted many years. He got familiar with the plan and began to think about how to staff the Institute. Together, we built a staff structure and began discussing where we could recruit trainers. We decided to tap our networks. Bill spoke to some of his colleagues. I sought out individuals from the NEA, State affiliates, and others. Once we had our prospective list, George began making formal contact, and getting managers' approval.

One of our critical concerns was including a diverse staff. At this time, there were not many minorities available. Those who were invited to participate were excited and enthused about what we were attempting to do. Some of the individuals selected have remained close colleagues including Larry Billups, Kate Kirkham, F.J. Johnson, and Dale Robinson. Larry and I met during my Flint days. Kate was a staff member in the NEA's Training Academy. F.J. Johnson was a staff member in the Association for Classroom Teachers. Dale was an Executive Director for one of the local affiliate chapters in Michigan. I also tapped two individuals from my past, Gloria Fauth, who was still working in Flint, and one of my fraternity brothers, Michael Ard, who was the Director of the Black Student Center at Indiana State College.

Our next major task was identifying local affiliates to participate in the Institute. George began contacting the State Executive Directors in Indiana, Michigan, and Ohio to get their support and suggestions as to which local associations to approach. I then contacted the presidents and staff to go over the plan and secure their commitment. Once secured, I began visiting each of the sites in Columbus and Dayton, Ohio; Fort Wayne and Indianapolis, Indiana; and Grand Rapids and Pontiac, Michigan to do the prep work. The prep work included me training them on how to select and build a 25-member team. Doing this work meant I was on the road a great deal and away from my family. Thanks to Theresa, who had her hands full with the four M's, I was able to accomplish this mission.

It was amazing how the plan came together and created the first Institute at the Michigan Education Association's conference center in the spring of 1970. At that time, the nation's climate was not healthy for learning, excellence in education, or intellectual daring. The Institute's five-day training was in many ways a response to these challenges. The training staff had spent quality time getting acquainted and familiar with the design and their responsibilities. George opened the Institute with a dinner featuring a dynamic and provocative keynote address by Father Joe Devlin. Father Joe's keynote address introduced and explained in detail how racism was a significant factor in what was happening in the schools. Even though racism was discussed in the *Kerner Commission Report on the Causes, Events, and Aftermaths of the Civil Disorders of 1967* (released in 1968), it was not a household word in 1970. The Kerner Report shed light on the roots of racism and inequality in the U.S. That's why I think Father Joe's keynote was revolutionary. Not to mention he was a white Catholic priest speaking to a diverse audience.

During the week, there were two plenary sessions. One of the sessions featured Mario Fantini, a Ford Foundation program officer and a consultant to the Task Force on Urban Education. Mario's presentation built upon Father Joe's analysis of race as a key factor in educational impediments. He reinforced some of the specific changes that were necessary to improve the urban schools. The other session was led by David Spencer, the leader of the Decentralization and Community Control Effort in New York City. David's presentation focused on breaking up the large school systems and giving more control to the community. As the week progressed, the teams became more intense in their deliberations. By the time they finished, they had developed very detailed action plans that could be developed in other cities.

We conducted daily evaluations that were coordinated by an experienced researcher. They provided daily feedback from each team, as well as from the different identity groups, e.g., educators, students, parents, and others. The overall final evaluation was very positive and provided lots of feedback on how we should conduct the next Institute. We received only one scathing critique of the Institute which came from a white male school administrator who sent it directly to Dr. Sam Lambert, NEA Executive Secretary. Dr. Lambert forwarded it to George for a response. I was so proud of how George handled the matter. In George's letter, he addressed every concern the school administrator raised by educating him on why my efforts were necessary and justified. He was able to do this because I had prepared the plan and program by dotting every "i" and crossing every "t." In other words, I had my *sh$t* together! This experience reinforced my belief that you always cover your *a$$* and leave no stone unturned.

Overall, our first year of the Special Project on Urban Education (or Project Urban as we began to call it) was highly successful. We tripled our budget from $82,000 to $240,000. This allowed us to hire two additional staff in year two. In addition, I gained the support of two organizations within the NEA family, the National Council of Urban Education Associations (NCUEA) and National Council of Urban Executives (NCUE). Both organizations lobbied for the increase in our budget; they saw us as working for their members and for improvements in urban education.

Prior to the second year of Project Urban, George became the Director of the Center for Human Relations. He took over where Samuel Etheridge left off when he was promoted as the first Black NEA Cabinet member. I joined George in the Center as a staff member. We decided to move Project Urban into the Center because it increased our overall budget and gave greater access to staff resources. I continued to spend a great deal of time in the field following up with the teams who participated in the first Institute and began working on the second. We decided to hold the second Institute at a Hyatt Hotel in Des Moines, Iowa. NEA President George Fisher, a native of Iowa, was a huge supporter of our work. Seven teams from Des Moines and Waterloo, Iowa; Minneapolis, Minnesota; Little Rock, Arkansas; Wichita, Kansas; Lawton, Oklahoma; and University City, Missouri were selected to participate in the Institute. Several were not the typical big urban centers but had strong local associations and the same type and level of urban problems.

In terms of staffing, I recruited additional staff from the Center for Human Relations, including F.J. Johnson, a Black man; Lance Lujan, a Native American (Kiowa tribe); and Tomas Villerral, a Mexican American. After tripling the budget, George also hired Delyte Frost, a white woman, and Fred Husmann, a white man, to work on Project Urban. They were also a part of my team. Bill Moore and I maintained our roles as lead trainers. We made a few staff changes and altered the design based on the feedback we received from the first Institute. In addition, Jane Power, who assisted with the Task Force Report, attended the Institute and wrote the final report. We also added several State Affiliate staff to serve as documenters who were assigned to each of the teams. They observed and took notes about each team's efforts, which were incorporated into the final report.

In addition, the staff training teams recorded their planning meetings. We also arranged to take photos and videotape some of the sessions. We used these materials to create a 25-minute film that featured the Waterloo team and a 10-minute filmstrip which presented an overview of the entire process. These were used to make presentations to potential sites for the third Institute and to show the teams when we conducted follow-up meetings. We also had a newsletter which shared what the teams were doing and held a one-day debriefing and assessment of the team's activities. Representatives were invited to the session which was held in the NEA Midwest Regional Office in Chicago. Highlights from this second Institute included:

1. The Waterloo team had a Black woman who was blind, which meant we had to do a few things to make sure she would be able to fully participate. In addition, the team was asked by their school board to work with the school administration to carry through the team's plan of action. The school board also approved the creation of a Human Relations Director and allotted $85,000 of district funds for desegregation efforts.

2. The team from Little Rock was from the Little Rock Central High School area and they continued to actively function for three years after the Institute. Two members of their team were selected to be on a district-wide council to help develop a proposal for Emer-

gency Assistance in Desegregation.

3. Members of the Minneapolis team helped develop an instrument to assess what type of human relations training for both current teachers and those preparing for a teaching career.

4. Several members of the Wichita team participated in a week-long Human Relations Institute. This four-year old initiative was housed at Wichita State University. Phyllis Burgess, a university member of the second Urban Institute, served as the administrator. She invited me to be the Dean of the program. Several other facilitators from the Urban Institute were invited to be a part of the staff team: Kate, Larry, Lance, and Delyte.

The third Institute took place in the Southwest. Teams were invited from the following cities: Albuquerque and Los Cruces, New Mexico; Colorado Springs and Pueblo, Colorado; Phoenix and Tucson, Arizona. The Western Skies Hotel in Albuquerque was selected as the Institute site. Once again, activity began with preparatory work at each team site. Lance and Tomas joined me in the pre-work and were a great addition as they brought greater ethnic and cultural insights. There were several other additions to the staff training team. I wanted to have a team that reflected the area and that participants would be working with. Consequently, I brought on board three Hispanic and two Native American consultants. As in the previous Institutes, I shared with George all the plans and had his approval to hire each of the consultants, which included a Black woman and a white woman, a Native American man, and two Hispanic men and a woman.

The staff was the most diverse we had had. The top of the structure had Bill Moore as the overall Dean, me as Director, and a white woman as the Director of Research. At the next level, the Deans were two white women, a Black woman, a Black man, a Native American man, and a Hispanic man. At the team facilitator level, we had two white men, one Black man, two Black women, one white woman, one Hispanic woman, three Hispanic men, and two Native American men.

Prior to leaving DC, George, Tomas, Lance, and I learned our proposed budget for consultants would not be approved. We were not informed about the budget cut. To resolve this matter, we met with Dr. Lambert, NEA Executive Director. In the meeting, we advocated reinstating the budget to ensure minority consultants would be paid. We discussed how their absence would impact the Institute. Dr. Lambert agreed and we left with an understanding everything was okay. When the staff arrived in Albuquerque three days prior to our staff planning for the third Institute, I received a call from George indicating the consultants' budget had been cut. I was very disturbed. I called the entire team together to see if we could come up with a plan. All the consultants were there except two of the Native American men. We arrived at a compromise where each consultant would receive a reduced fee to ensure everyone was paid. Later, I met with the two Native American men, one of whom was a highly respected leader. He was very upset and expressed his strong resentment, "Once again promises have been broken." He spoke eloquently about the historic pattern of "Broken Promises." They were unwilling to accept the compromise of a reduced fee. The next morning, the team met and announced as a group they were unable to accept a compromise. So we decided to postpone the Institute and tell the six teams before they arrived. When I told George, he understood everything that happened and supported our decision.

When I returned home, I met with George at his home to discuss how we should address the postponement of the Institute given the fact a blistering letter was sent to Dr. Lambert from a very irate white male Executive Director of a local association. In his letter, the Executive Director expressed his anger and embarrassment for the time lost in preparing for the Institute. He wanted someone to be held accountable. I was afraid that I was going to be the one to take the hit and lose my job. By the time we finished working on a strategy, I felt a little better. Again, the one thing I knew was I had covered all the bases. I had all the necessary documentation and had kept George informed at every step.

On Monday morning when I arrived at the office, I was greeted with a huge surprise. Every one of the NEA staff members who had been a part of the Institute had arrived and indicated they were there to support me. By late that afternoon, George informed me that everything had been resolved and I was not to blame. I didn't even inquire because I was relieved I wasn't being blamed or fired. The third and final Institute was eventually rescheduled and held without my participation. This experience reinforced my belief in the power of relationships, making sure you have done everything by the book, and being willing to fight for the critical things you value.

CHAPTER 9 REFLECTION QUESTIONS

———————————

1. Individual: What does "Black Excellence" mean to you?

2. Individual: Think about an effort you were involved in that created change. What was your level of commitment? What were the successes and failures you experienced? What role did your values, attention to detail, and relationships play in your successes and failures?

3. Group Discussion: As a group, share your stories and insights. Each person would have 3–5 minutes to share their responses with the group. As a group, list some of the similarities and differences highlighted in the sharing session. Also, discuss one or two lessons each person has learned.

NEA Special Project: The Project Urban Upswing

"Not everything that is faced can be changed.
But nothing can be changed until it is faced."

—JAMES BALDWIN, a change agent, a novelist, a writer,
a playwright, a poet, an essayist, and a civil rights activist

———————————

The longer I worked at the NEA, the more I faced issues that I believed needed large-scale change in education and society. I also realized I couldn't change everything. However, I did learn that by working with others, we could face what needed to be changed by designing and implementing programs that created educational reform.

Project Urban Upswing, the NEA's second major effort which I designed, began when former NEA President George D. Fisher declared that the organized teaching profession could not leave the problems of urban education to the federal government, state education agencies, or local school systems in late 1969. As proof of NEA's willingness to put its money where its mouth was, NEA President Fisher asked for and received a commitment of resources to fund Project Urban Upswing. The basic concept underlying Project Urban Upswing was "involvement" which meant finding ways to give parents, teachers, students, and the community-at-large a voice in shaping decisions on educational policy that had mainly been restricted to a board of education and a few top-level administrators. It was extremely popular in the 1960s and 1970s when "participatory democracy" was a battle-cry in national as well as local politics. This was a period of time which brought conclusive evidence that traditional models of school governance had failed to meet the distinctive educational needs of minority and poor children. The report, *Schools of the Urban Crisis*, produced by the Task Force on Urban Education, was used as the guide for shaping the Project.

In September 1970, the Indianapolis Public Schools and the NEA embarked on an experimental, cooperative venture to upgrade the quality of education. Indianapolis was chosen as the site because it met the following criteria:

- A competent, sensitive, knowledgeable superintendent of schools who had made a public stand on educational reform.
- A Board of Education with demonstrated concern.
- A strong local urban teachers' organization, affiliated with the NEA.
- A city with little-known leadership potential that could be developed.
- A city with the imminent potential for a social explosion, but which had, for some reason, not yet exploded.

There were three additional factors for selecting the city as a site. First, Indianapolis participated in the first Institute in Battle Creek; 2) Reverend Landum Shields, a Black man, served as a member of the Urban Institute team and was the current president of the School Board; and 3) Indianapolis was my birthplace and home to many family members, friends, and colleagues I could easily tap for expertise and resources. Remember, RELATIONSHIPS are everything. They are some of your greatest assets.

There were four phases to the Project Urban Upswing: Phase 1—Inventory, Phase 2—Program Development, Phase 3—Program Implementation, and Phase 4—Evaluation.

The main purpose of Phase 1—Inventory was to determine the status of education in Indianapolis. Strengths and weaknesses of all major areas of school operations were identified. After the areas were identified, a determination was made about procedures and instruments that would be used in the inventory process. Examples of areas selected for evaluation were curriculum, instructional practices and performances, physical facilities, instructional supplies and equipment, staff organization and utilization, staff development, leadership functions, process of decision-making, community resources, financial support, human relations, and public relations.

Phase 2—Program Development included a search for urban education best practices from other cities that could be adapted to Indianapolis schools. Major research findings in education, psychology, and sociology were included in the program development process. Program development focused on the retention of strengths found in the current school operation, and in the elimination of weaknesses through corrective action of new programs which held greater promise of success.

In Phase 3—Program Implementation, the School Board was held responsible for overseeing and approving all programs. It took into consideration the available local, private, and public resources.

Phase 4—Evaluation became an integral and continuous process throughout the effort because it provided feedback to those engaged in program development and implementation. Programs were reviewed, expanded, or eliminated according to findings in the evaluation process.

The NEA Executive Committee became involved in the project. Executive officers of the Indianapolis School Board and the NEA provided leadership for the project. They included Dr. Stanley Campbell, Indianapolis Superintendent, and George Jones, Director of the NEA Center for Human Relations. George assigned Fred Husmann, a white man, as the project officer. As the project lead, I supervised Fred while I was also leading the second Institute. He worked out of an office the school system provided. We later moved the project headquarters to Cold Spring Manor, a building located on the current Marian University campus, which gave us space to hold meetings, workshops, and other activities.

A project planning committee was established and became responsible for developing plans, identifying and procuring consultants and resources, and preparing recommendations to the policy boards. The committee consisted of three representatives of the schools, the NEA project officer, and a representative from each of the following organizations: Indianapolis Education Association, Indiana State Teachers Association, Indianapolis Parent-Teacher Association, the Mayor's office, Indianapolis Consortium for Higher Education, and the Lighted Schoolhouse Program. There was a Community Liaison Group organized to help achieve widespread community involvement. Community organizations which had an interest in the project were invited by the Project Planning Committee to assign a liaison person to the group. Finally, a National Advisory Council was established. Its members were recognized leaders in education and related fields.

Project Urban Upswing was designed to extend over a three to five-year period. It was clearly understood that this would be an evolving project. During its first full year, it was determined that the best way to conduct Phase 1—Inventory was to establish a pilot effort. Ten elementary schools were selected to represent the total school system regarding size of school, racial composition, and socio-economic factors of the school community. A steering committee was formed in each school consisting of a parent or community representative, a teacher, and the principal to select a task force to complete the inventory. The task force consisted of representatives from the individual school staff, the parent organization, the student body, and the community. The task force was utilized to review the school and determine its strengths and weaknesses. It also had responsibility for making the school inventory which consisted of gathering information, reviewing the data about the school, and making recommendations for improvement. In developing the inventory, we decided to focus on elementary schools. As we navigated this process, cooperation among the school staff and individuals from Indiana University, the Indianapolis Consortium for Higher Education, and other organizations and agencies in the community emerged. The necessity for combining the resources of the school system, the local universities, and others to help solve the educational problems of urban school systems was apparent and became a model.

There were a few ups and downs with Project Urban Upswing. For instance, many of the participants in the initial phase were skeptical, especially the teachers who had to play a major role in the inventory phase. However, they began to feel it was worthwhile once they saw how their ideas would be incorporated in the process. Also, some of the parents and community members began to feel more positive when they saw how their input was included and their issues would be addressed. Problems emerged when some of the administrators did not take the project seriously. Personality conflicts between the superintendent and the school board president arose. In addition, the Indianapolis Board of School Commissioners voted four to two to discontinue its participation in June 1971. The members of the Indianapolis Education Association, along with citizens, expressed their disappointment in the decision. Their actions were effective, which caused the Board to reconsider its decision and to continue the project for another year.

In November 1971, the NEA Executive Committee selected a team to evaluate the project. Their task was to describe the process which the project sought to use, to report the findings of the team, and to make recommendations for NEA action. After a very thorough examination which included many interviews, the team determined the concept, on which Urban Upswing is based, was sound in January 1972. However, they also stated that under the present school administration, it would not work in Indianapolis because administrators actively resisted changes initiated by citizens, students, and teachers. As a result of their recommendations, Project Urban Upswing was discontinued and ended in June 1972.

Below are some of the Indianapolis Urban Upswing Project's accomplishments:

- The high level of cooperation between the different education organizations.
- The active involvement of the different community organizations.
- The quality of data produced from the 10 pilot schools through the inventory phase.
- The tremendous contributions by Indiana University and the Indianapolis Consortium for Higher Education.
- The securing of the Cold Spring Manor for the project's headquarters.
- The leadership skill development of the teachers, administrators, parents, and community members.
- The overall level and quality of community involvement.
- Lessons learned about what is required to build and maintain a collaborative effort.

Although the project ended in Indianapolis, the team recommended that the NEA seriously consider using it in another city. The concept of Project Urban Upswing held and continues to hold great promise for changing school systems. That potential can be realized in a system where everyone, including the administration and board of education, has the vision necessary to understand what can be done and the willingness to change its own behavior. In such a setting, the project can succeed and result in true educational reform.

Project Urban Upswing taught me how to organize and carry out complex, comprehensive, and collaborative projects with a diverse staff and numerous stakeholders for a project that lasted almost two years. All these experiences far exceeded what I learned as a teacher and a counselor. Even though there were some good results, I was disappointed that it ended far too soon. One of the key lessons I learned was how critical it is to plan for and manage the personalities of and relationship dynamics between key leaders in a long-term change effort. I carried this lesson and others into my future change endeavors.

CHAPTER 10 REFLECTION QUESTIONS

<hr>

1. Individual: What does writer and civil rights activist James Baldwin's quote mean to you?

    "Not everything that is faced can be changed. But nothing can be changed until it is faced."

2. Individual: Think back to a time in history or your life when efforts were made to change large institutional systems. For example, the movements that focused on Black, Indigenous, and people of color's (BIPOC) civil rights, women, and the Lesbian, Gay, Bisexual, Transgender, Queer and/or Questioning, Intersex, and Asexual (LGBTQIA) communities. What are some of the challenges facing change agents?

3. Group Discussion: As a group, identify actions that change agents could take to address today's current issues.

    Each person would have 3–5 minutes to share their responses with the group. As a group, list some of the similarities and differences highlighted in the sharing session. Also, discuss one or two lessons each person has learned.

CHAPTER 11

Trying to Create Change in a Racially Tense School District

*"The country is in deep trouble. We've forgotten
that a rich life consists fundamentally of serving others,
trying to leave the world a little better than you found it.
We need the courage to question the powers that be."*

—DR. CORNEL E. WEST, a change agent, a philosopher,
a political activist, a social critic, and an author

———————————

Because of the success of my work with Project Urban, I was asked to work with the school district in Aliquippa, Pennsylvania. It's been 54 years since I experienced what happened during my Project Urban assignment. Unfortunately, the racially tense experience I had has become an epidemic in many of the school districts in the United States today. Almost every week, the news or social media document racially tense situations. I ask myself what's it going to take to change what's happening. We need to do what Dr. West has urged: to find the courage to question the powers that be. We also need to take positive action to create a safe, equitable, and just world where no one is harmed.

Aliquippa was a steel-producing town of approximately

30,000 residents. Blacks represented 25 percent of the population, but due to the history of racial conflict, that percentage was shrinking. In May 1970, the schools were closed for the second time in three weeks due to racial conflict. After reopening, fights broke out in the high school and tensions increased and finally spilled over into the community with an incident at a local tavern setting off rock throwing, shooting, and destruction of a local store.

Upon a request from the Pennsylvania State Education Association (PSEA) and the NEA Regional Office, Dave Bork and I were assigned to help the school district resolve the conflict. This assignment turned out to be the most racially intense I had done thus far in my career. Dave was a white male who held a joint position with the NEA Classroom Teachers Association and the National Training Laboratory. When we arrived, we were informed I would meet with a group of Black students and later with a group of Black parents. At the same time, Dave would meet with white students and parents. The President of the Aliquippa Teachers Association (ATA) arranged for both of us to meet afterwards with all the school principals, selected faculty from the junior and senior high schools, and the ATA Executive Board. In addition, we met with the school superintendent and his three assistants, the mayor, and the School Board.

After Dave and I met with the groups, we compared notes, which revealed several facts as well as feelings that illustrated a history of racial problems in Aliquippa, the home of the Jones and Laughlin Steel Corporation. Since the early 1900s when Blacks first came to work in the steel mills, they resided in a geographically distinct part of town known as "the hill" or "Plan 11." In my meetings with Black students and parents, they stressed they had never been made to feel a part of the town, even after decades of living here. The Black students, for example, reported that when they learned how the selection process for a May queen worked, the school changed the procedure so no Black students could be chosen. It was incidents like this that led them to say, "We are just disgusted and are tired. We want to be a part of the school, and not just as members of sports teams."

On the other hand, white students expressed fear and anger and informed us they were not going to be pushed around anymore by the Blacks. One white student stated, "My father and I both have guns, and we will shoot any nigger who causes trouble." Both the white and Black students felt there was a double standard in dealing with discipline in the schools. The Black parents blamed it all on a breakdown of school discipline. White parents felt that the high school principal was bending over backwards to accommodate Black students. Black parents expressed a great amount of frustration because their children encountered the same situations they had when they were in school.

The teachers and administrators likewise highlighted inconsistency in school policy. One administrator remarked that the root of the problem was Blacks had never been allowed to be a part of the community. They were physically and educationally segregated until entering high school, living up on "the hill;" almost all had attended the all-Black elementary school. The school district's inability to achieve integration at the elementary school level had been cited in previous years as a cause for conflict at the high school level.

From the get-go, Aliquippa had an undeniable history of racial separation and conflict. Dave and I agreed that before they reopened the schools, they should utilize the support of trained facilitators and establish a task force with members who represented all segments of the Aliquippa community to discuss and develop a set of recommendations to address their dilemmas.

Throughout the day, Dave and I noticed white men driving around in pickup trucks with rifles on racks. They were on display for all to see. In the evening, Dave and I decided to drive closer to Pittsburgh to spend the night; we didn't feel comfortable staying in Aliquippa. The next morning, we made our recommendations to the School Board. We suggested they hold off on re-opening the school as the tension was just too strong. Also, there were many things which needed attention before a conducive climate could exist. We further recommended they design broad-based community involvement and use a problem-solving approach. We offered our assistance to help community members begin a systematic look at their problems and identify solutions. They asked a few questions and thanked us for coming. No decisions were made because they claimed three Board members were absent. In addition, they wanted to wait until they had received recommendations from the NAACP and the State Human Relations Commission. When I returned to the NEA, I sent a follow-up letter to the Board President that restated our recommendations.

A few days after we left, the schools reopened. As we predicted, it was short lived because racial tension exploded once again, causing the schools to close until the next academic year. During the summer, we learned the school district and community held several meetings to discuss changes. However, we were not invited to assist or participate. After completing our work, we concluded the following:

- Racial isolation existed in Aliquippa.
- There was plenty of evidence pointing to the school board's lack of participatory decision-making.
- There was inconsistency in administrative handling of school matters, especially discipline.
- The teachers and the ATA were part of the problem.
- Jones and Laughlin Steel Corporation did not support or participate in resolving or improving the racial climate in the town.
- Some genuine evidence of change or intention must be seen, or the community will remain polarized and continue to experience conflict and racial uprisings.

The experiences in Aliquippa were not atypical of what was happening in thousands of other school districts in the 1970s. This experience reinforced my concern for how difficult it is to change the generational patterns of racism faced by Blacks and other people of color. Even today, these same patterns are continuing to happen in numerous states in America, including Florida and Texas.

CHAPTER 11 REFLECTION QUESTIONS

————————————

1. Individual: Think about how racial dynamics, equity, and inclusion exist in today's school systems. Consider the racially intense environments that have been created by state governors and legislatures. Compare what you discover with what you have experienced and what has happened in the past 10 to 50 years.

2. Group Discussion: As a group, share your discoveries and insights. If you want to take a deeper dive, explore how the oppressive patterns that keep us from realizing true equity and inclusion for all people can be transformed.

   Each person would have 3–5 minutes to share their responses with the group. As a group, list some of the similarities and differences highlighted in the sharing session. Also, discuss one or two lessons each person has learned.

The National Training Laboratory of Applied Behavioral Science (NTL): A Major Influence on My NEA and Consulting Career

"It's essential to keep moving, learning and evolving for as long as you're here and this world keeps spinning."

—RASHEED OGUNLARU, a change agent, a life coach, a motivational speaker, an author, and a leadership, business, and executive coach

———————

Prior to joining the NEA, my educational experiences were traditional and structured. They prepared me to become a teacher and a counselor. In these roles, I learned how to establish relationships with my students and their parents, my colleagues and supervisors, and community members and stakeholders. I never understood the linkages between how people treated themselves and interacted with others, and the impact of their behavior on themselves and others, until I was introduced to the National Training Laboratory of Applied Behavioral Science (NTL). NTL is where I began to embrace lifelong learning. At 85, my intention is to continue learning and evolving.

In 1946, Dr. Kurt Lewin, the founder of modern social psychology, a pioneer in action research, and Director of Massachusetts Institute of Technology's Research Center for Group Dynamics, concluded that increased awareness of self and others could be accomplished through facilitated group dialogue in Training Groups (T-Groups) that advocate open-minded appreciation and inclusion of differences. Lewin found that T-Group participants who learned by experience provided high potential for diagnostic study, evaluation, and changing behaviors. His findings laid the foundation for NTL. In 1947, NTL was established in Bethel, Maine as a nonprofit organization committed to advancing Applied Behavioral Science (ABS) in the service of social justice, oppression-free societies, and healthy individuals, groups, and organizations. It was born out of a planning group funded by the U.S. Office of Naval Research and the NEA.

In addition to Lewin, three other scholars played a major role in the early days of NTL. They were Kenneth Benne, Leland Bradford, and Ronald ("Ron") Lippitt. Benne worked at Columbia University's Teachers College. Bradford served as the Director of Adult Education at the NEA. Lippitt, one of Lewin's students and colleagues, was a faculty member at my alma mater, the University of Michigan. NTL leaned heavily on the support of the NEA and operated as a quasi-independent organization.

NTL was a major influence during my career at the NEA and as a consultant. My NTL involvement began in February 1969. It was one of the most significant experiences I had in my first year at the NEA. At the time, the NEA provided NTL with office space and offered scholarships to NEA staff who wanted to attend their programs. George suggested Linda and I attend their basic Human Interaction Lab which was a two-week residential lab held in Zion, Illinois. It gave me an opportunity to explore who I was and how I related to others. It was a very intense program going from morning to late night with breaks for meals. Most of the time, I was in a small T-group of 12 participants and two NTL trainers. The overall group was predominately white with only one other Black male participant. Linda was in a different T-group with the other Black man. I became more aware of how white people related to me as a Black man when we were in the small group. Trained facilitators challenged us to express our feelings on different topics and situations.

Over the next two years, I attended two other NTL programs both in Bethel, Maine, sometimes called the "NTL Mecca." The second program was a four-week Educational Change Consultants Training Lab which I took during the summer of 1969. Once again, there were only a few Black participants. This lab focused on change concepts, skills, and activities. The participants were also placed in small T-groups which met each day in the evening. These sessions were not as intense as what I experienced in Zion. It did provide an opportunity for me to increase my awareness of how I related to whites and how they related to me.

The next summer, my NEA colleagues Larry Billups and Bob Harmon and I participated in a two-week Conflict Utilization Training Lab. The focus of this program was on how to respond and react to simulated conflict situations. We were grouped in teams of 10. In our teams, we developed conflict situations drawing on real life experiences that the rest of the lab community had to deal with directly and effectively. One of the highlights of the lab was our entire group planned and carried out a conflict situation that involved the entire NTL community. There were about six other labs at the time. The conflict centered around the issue of the lack of minority involvement in the NTL community. Some of the Black people challenged NTL about the lack of Black representation in the organization. The trainers were excellent and included NEA's Samuel Ethridge; Gordon Lippitt, Ron's brother who was on the faculty at George Washington University; and Mark Chesler, a University of Michigan faculty member who would later serve on my doctoral committee.

Throughout my NEA career, I was able to establish strong relationships with NTL staff because our offices were in the same building, which facilitated our getting to know and trust one another. I was invited to serve on the staff of several training contracts. One of the most enjoyable experiences was training individuals in a drug awareness program. I felt good helping them to make change in their clients' lives. As a result, I was invited to become an NTL member in 1973. Over the years, I served as a staff member on several programs such as Human Interaction Labs, the Management Work Conference, and the Senior Level Management Conference. The Human Interaction Labs allowed me to travel to Bethel in the summers. The Management Work and Senior Level Management Conferences were held in resorts for corporate clients. These experiences allowed me to build relationships with senior-level managers.

Upon leaving the NEA and establishing my own consulting firm, John F. Leeke Associates, Inc. in 1985, I attended the Myers-Briggs Type Indicator (MBTI) training. The MBTI is an assessment tool that is designed to identify a person's personality type, strengths, and preferences. It was developed by Isabel Myers and her mother, Katherine Briggs. They based their work on Dr. Carl Jung's theory of personality types. The MBTI tool was first published in 1962. Today, it is one of the most widely used and recognized personality tools in the world. After spending two weeks in the MBTI training, I became certified to administer the tool which I utilized in my consultant work for 30 years.

NTL partnered with American University (AU) to create the AU Master of Science in Organization Development program under the leadership of NTL President Edie Seashore and AU Professor Morley Segal. The first cohort began in 1980. In the 1990s, I mentored several graduate students who were enrolled in the program. As a mentor, I met with them and discussed their class projects and future career plans. Some later became NTL members. I am certain what they learned has proven to be as transformative at the personal and professional level as what I learned during my 40+ years of NTL involvement. It's all about doing the work!

CHAPTER 12 REFLECTION QUESTIONS

———————————

1. Individual: Think about organizations you have been a part of that have shaped your career. What were some of the significant experiences and relationships you developed? What skills did you obtain? Have you played any leadership roles in these organizations?

2. Individual: If you played a leadership role in an organization, what leadership model(s) did you use and/or witness? Which ones do you think would help to create change within an organization, community, or society?

3. Group Discussion: As a group, share your experiences. Each person would have 3–5 minutes to share their responses with the group. As a group, list some of the similarities and differences highlighted in the sharing session. Also, discuss one or two lessons each person has learned.

CHAPTER 13

Life in the Center
for Human Relations

"Ignorance and prejudice are the handmaidens of propaganda.
Our mission, therefore, is to confront ignorance with knowledge,
bigotry with tolerance, and isolation with the outstretched hand
of generosity. Racism can, will, and must be defeated."

—KOFI ANNAN, a Ghanaian diplomat who served as the seventh Secretary-
General of the United Nations, Nobel Peace Prize recipient, and a change agent

––––––––––––––––

The only place in the NEA that addressed the eradication
of racism was the Center for Human Relations. The Center
for Human Relations (CHR, which later became the Teacher
Rights Unit) was launched in response to the racial unrest and
a recommendation of a special task force on human rights
in 1968. Sam Ethridge was named the Director. Sam hired
numerous minority professionals and support staff. His hiring decisions were a major contribution to the NEA's diversity. Two years later, George Jones became the Director, and I
joined the team. That's when I had the opportunity to work
with wonderful and talented colleagues including Deborah
Byard Campbell (now Kirby), Delyte Frost, Fred Husmann,

F.J. Johnson, Earl Jones, Lance Lujan, Anna Marquez, Javetta Richardson, and Tomas Villerral. Our mission and work were a direct response to Kofi Annan's call to action to defeat racism and other forms of oppression.

We engaged in a variety of activities to advance equality and protect the civil rights of members. The CHR sponsored annual national conferences on civil and human rights that were attended by leaders in education, religion, civil rights, government, and other key areas. Studies were made on the desegregation progress, the displacement of minority educators, personnel policies, urban field studies, the treatment of minorities in textbooks, curriculum guides for ethnic studies, minority pupil dropouts, unfair treatment of minority teachers, and related subjects. Local associations used this information to begin addressing some of the issues in their local communities. NEA members and other stakeholders attended workshops and seminars on voter registration, student rights, racism, preparing for desegregation, displacement of minority educators, and personnel policies. In addition, the staff assisted local and state affiliates in conducting human relations activities. We operated as the CHR until 1972 when it became the Teacher Rights Unit.

During my CHR tenure, the two major initiatives that impacted my career were the Minority Involvement Program and the preparation of the *Education & Racism: An Action Manual*. The first initiative, the Minority Involvement Program, was established during the administration of NEA President Don Morrison who wanted to increase the active participation of minority teachers in 1970. The CHR team was charged with the goal of significantly increasing the number of minority delegates at the 1971 NEA Annual Meeting in Philadelphia. In the past, minority members attended the annual meetings, but did not have voting status as delegates. Our job was to create a pathway for minority delegates, which entailed identifying and training them at the local level. Most often, when inquiries were made at the local level about Hispanic, Native American, and Asian members, the typical response was "we don't have any." We knew this was not true because we had data on the teachers' racial and ethnic identities in the local school systems. So first, our role was to help local affiliates find minority teachers in their systems and sign them up as members. After they became members, we were able to train them to become delegates. At the same time, the minority members of the NEA formed ethnic-specific caucuses (Asian Caucus, Black Caucus, Hispanic Caucus, and Native American Caucus). In addition, the NEA established the Minority Affairs Committee. Our role as staff was to assist these entities in their work during and after the annual meetings.

Anna, Lance, and Tomas worked on signing up large numbers of Hispanic and Native American educators to attend the regional minority workshops. Deborah, F.J., Earl, Javetta, and I worked to increase the number of Black educators to attend the workshops. We used the workshops to educate the minority educators on how the NEA and local affiliates functioned. We also addressed how they could become active in their local affiliates and serve as delegates at the annual meeting. Weekend workshops were well attended. Through our training efforts, we achieved our goal, resulting in the largest number of minority delegates who had ever attended an annual meeting. Our success truly made a difference and was very fulfilling. This experience gave us an opportunity to meet and support many new friends who became leaders at the local, state, and national levels. This program continues even today.

Education & Racism: An Action Manual was born out of a partnership between the Michigan Education Association's (MEA) Human Relations Division, the NEA Teacher Rights Unit (formerly CHR), and the New Perspectives on Race, Inc., a Detroit-based organization launched in response to the 1968 riots. The MEA was represented by Dan Austin, the NEA by me, and New Perspectives on Race by Dr. Pat Bidol and Dick Weber. We worked together to develop a manual that addressed institutional racism, which we identified as the most crucial issue confronting the American education system. It was intended to provide information, program ideas, and encouragement to state and local associations that were attempting to meet the challenge of coping positively with the issues of institutional racism and equal educational opportunity. The manual defined racism as "racial prejudice (the belief that one's own race is superior to another race) combined with the power to enforce this bias throughout the institutions and culture of a society." This definition was taken from *Developing New Perspectives on Race: An Innovative Multi-Media Social Studies Curriculum in Race Relations for the Secondary Level*. Dr. Pat Bidol was the principal developer.

In creating the manual, we utilized President Lyndon Johnson's National Advisory Commission on Civil Disorders and Robert Terry's book *For Whites Only* as resources. It was published in 1973 and covered racism and its manifestations in education, anti-racism activities, racial checklists and inventories, and group dynamics tools. The manual also had an extensive bibliography. It became a groundbreaking publication that was made available to the NEA state and local affiliates as well as other educational organizations.

My time in the CHR/Teacher Rights Unit was one of the best times in my NEA tenure because it helped me realize the type of work I was meant to do. During this period, the NEA Staff Organization (NEASO) secured the right to bargain with the NEA. The first strike took place in 1970. Naturally, I joined it and served as one of the strike coordinators. One of my responsibilities was to give the daily message to the members after we held our meetings in the Metropolitan A.M.E. Church's main sanctuary. The historic church was located across the street from the NEA. In preparation for my daily message, I listened to the NEASO president and lead negotiator. I incorporated their main messages into my rallying charge. In many ways, it felt like former President Barack Obama's "Fired up! Ready to go!" charge that he used in his campaign rallies. After a few days, the strike was settled. Through our efforts, NEASO negotiated salary increases and better working conditions.

As a CHR/Teacher Rights Unit staffer, I continued managing the Urban Institutes and Urban Upswing. Lance and

Tomas were also working with me on the Urban Institutes. In our work together with Anna, we tackled very challenging projects and met and impacted the lives of many educators. Through it all, I deepened my relationships with them. As we traveled and trained educators, I learned about their lives and cultures. They expanded my perspective on what America's melting pot was all about and helped me understand the importance of speaking multiple languages, specifically Spanish. As a result, I was able to expand my own family's perspective on America's diversity and require my children to take at least two years of Spanish in junior and senior high school. Theresa and I also planned a trip to Puerto Rico to give our children an opportunity to immerse themselves in a Spanish-speaking environment.

Education & Racism: An Action Manual *was born out of a
partnership between the Michigan Education Association
(representative Dan Austin), Human Relations Division,
the NEA Teacher Rights Unit (representative John Leeke),
and the New Perspectives on Race, Inc. (representatives
Dr. Pat Bidol and Dick Weber)*

CHAPTER 13 REFLECTION QUESTIONS

1. Individual: What actions have you taken to understand different cultures and to establish relationships with diverse people? What's your understanding of, and beliefs surrounding, racism? What have you done in your life to help dismantle racism in your workplace, schools, government, and community?

2. Group Discussion: As a group, share your experiences. Each person would have 3–5 minutes to share their responses with the group. As a group, list some of the similarities and differences highlighted in the sharing session. Also, discuss one or two lessons each person has learned.

The Rise of a Strategic Change Architect: My Move to NEA's Instruction and Professional Development Unit

"If we don't figure out a way to create equity, real equity, of opportunity and access, to good schools, housing, health care, and decent paying jobs, we are not going to survive as a productive and healthy society."

—TIM WISE, a change agent, an author, an activist, and a speaker on the topic of race

———————

When I look back at the time I spent at the NEA, I am amazed at the amount of experience I acquired and relationships I built during the period of 1968 to 1985. Those efforts were directed at creating what Tim Wise calls "real equity of opportunity and access" in society. My relationships and experiences were instrumental in my rise as a strategic change architect. A strategic change architect is a person who shifts the direction of an organization, through timely planning and critical analysis, that improve conditions for all. In this role, I was able to master the ability to learn while leading and then teach and train others.

Two years before I joined the Instruction and Professional Development (IPD) Unit, several of my NEA colleagues and I began talking about pursuing a doctorate. Earning a doctorate was not an academic endeavor I had planned. In fact, I had decided my master's degree was more than enough. My plate was full being a husband to a wife who was getting her college degree, a father to four children, and a traveling NEA staffer. Although I was busy, I still made room to explore a doctoral group commitment. The relationships I had with my colleagues and our group approach to using our current work convinced me to pursue the degree. Adopting this approach allowed me to stay open to new ideas and opportunities.

In my conversations with my NEA colleagues, Anna, a Latina; Lance, a Native American man; Ellwood Erickson, a white man; Delyte, a white woman; Kate, a white woman; and Larry, a Black man, we talked about our individual goals. We discovered we had one common goal: combating institutional racism, culturalism, ethnicism, and sexism. We turned our common goal, Combating Institutional Racism, Culturalism, Ethnicism, and Sexism, into an acronym for our group name, CIRCES. Delyte identified a doctoral program at the Union Graduate School, an outgrowth of the Union for Experimenting Colleges and Universities located in Yellow Springs, Ohio. Union was formed in 1964 as a consortium that included 10 liberal arts colleges. Its goal was to provide innovative higher education alternatives to working adults. Today, it is known as the Union Institute & University. The current president is Dr. Karen Schuster Webb, the wife of my now deceased long-term friend Wallace (Wally) Webb. Wally's mother and my mother were close childhood friends. I am the godfather of his daughter, Ramona.

We submitted a group application in the fall of 1972 even though Union did not accept group applications. Since Union's charter claimed it was an alternative and innovative institution, we decided to challenge its values with an in-person appeal. After presenting our case, the committee, under the leadership of Dr. Roy P. Fairfield, the co-creator and first dean of the experiential doctoral program, recommended we be admitted as both individuals and a group. We were well on our way to becoming strategic change architects. To my knowledge, we remain the first and only group accepted into the doctoral program.

We began our doctoral studies in July of 1973 at a month-long residential Colloquium in Northfield, Massachusetts. Prior to attending the Colloquium, Deborah Byard Campbell (now Kirby), a Black woman, replaced Anna who decided to make some major personal and professional life changes. Deborah was another NEA Teacher Rights Unit staff member who had worked with all the members of CIRCES on NEA projects.

In the midst of working at the NEA and completing my early doctoral work, I began having conversations with Lance and Tomas about the lack of diversity in most NEA Units. We put on our strategic change architect hats and agreed that it was time for us to address this issue by making changes internally. I explored career opportunities in the IPD Unit. Lance selected the Government Relations Unit because it was the best way he could help address issues faced by the Native American community. Tomas chose to use his skills as a natural organizer in the Field Services Unit.

While I was in the Center for Human Relations (CHR), I was named to a cross-unit committee to explore the development of a teacher in-service program that would be delivered to teachers in the local associations. Dr. Dave Darland, the Director of IPD, a white man, was the committee chair. The committee met four times during the year. I developed a relationship with Dave and learned about a staff position in IPD. IPD was a unit that was the result of a merger in 1971 of former departments: Center for the Study of Instruction; Teacher Education and Professional Standards; Department of Adult Education; and Department of Educational Technology. The job announcement piqued my interest because it would help me bring diversity to the unit as its first Black male professional staffer. It would also be a promotion with an increase in salary. Most of the IPD managerial and professional program staff were white men with doctorates. Although a doctorate was not a requirement, it was highly desired. The hiring committee selected me for the position in March of 1974.

When I arrived in 1974, there were three women of color, Jessie Muse, a Black woman who worked in the Department of Educational Technology (DET); Florence Fan, a Chinese woman who worked in the DET; and Enyd Medas, from British Guinea, who worked in Teacher Education and Professional Standards (TEPS). These Departments were part of the merger in 1971 that resulted in the formation of the IPD Unit. Later, there were other people of color who joined the staff including Carmel Sandoval, a Hispanic man; Roy Fuentes, a Hispanic man; Javetta, a Black woman who had been in Human and Civil Rights (Center for Human Relations was changed to HCR); Al-Tony Gilmore, a Black man; Larry, a Black man who had been a manager in Field Services; and Sharon Robinson, a Black woman who was in HCR and became the Director of IPD. Roy and Larry were my managers at different times.

Most of the staff had very little experience working in the field with local teacher associations. I had a wealth of experience from my days in Project Urban and CHR. In addition, I brought my NTL experience and the ability to facilitate small groups. I was asked by one of the managers to conduct a training session on consulting skills for the staff. It was well received, but there was one comment from a white man who spoke to me after the session. He said, "John, you handle the English language so well." I am sure his intent was to compliment me, but he was unaware that his comment was condescending. His comment represents one of the many microaggressions that people of color face daily. At that moment, I chose not to confront him. Instead, I gave him grace and chalked it up to his ignorance. One of the things I learned over my life is you can't take on every slight. If you do, you'll wear yourself out! You have to play the long game with white supremacy.

THE MODELS OF
A TEACHING IN-SERVICE PROGRAM

My assignment was to develop a teacher in-service program. My research started with gathering data about what NEA members felt they were not getting in the traditional in-service programs provided in their school systems. Their feedback indicated they needed help in learning how to vary their teaching styles to meet students' different learning needs. They would often report that their method classes in undergraduate school didn't go far enough. Based on their feedback, I began searching for something that would address this need. I came across a textbook, *Models of Teaching*, by Dr. Bruce Joyce and Dr. Marsha Weil, professors at Columbia University. After reading the book, I reached out to them and set up a meeting in New York City. After much discussion, they offered to work with me to design a program using seven models which we felt would represent a variety of teaching strategies: Concept Attainment; Concept Formation; Inquiry Training; Jurisprudential; Role Playing; Simulation; and Synectics.

After meeting with them, I decided to design a 15-week program that would meet the requirement for in-service credit. I set about presenting the theory and rationale for each model, a way to demonstrate the model, and a procedure for practicing the model. I began to build a notebook that presented each teaching strategy in three sections: (1) the theory section which included readings, discussion guides, and a rationale of the model; (2) the demonstration section which enabled the teachers to observe the model and identify its distinctive features and the teaching skills which make it work; and (3) the peer teaching section which involved practice teaching exercises. One of the program's unique, and at the time groundbreaking, aspects was that each participant would be videotaped during a demonstration lesson and then participate in a review and critique.

Once done, the next step was to identify a site to pilot test the program in a place where I had developed a strong relationship with leaders and staff. After reviewing the program prospective, the Des Moines Education Association agreed to participate. They identified 10 teachers. I requested a racially diverse group. In a show of support, the school system provided a classroom for the trainings. We met every Wednesday after school for 15 weeks, with each session lasting three hours. That meant I would travel from Washington to Des Moines every Tuesday evening. Wednesday mornings would find me prepping for the trainings. I would return Thursday morning or go on to another assignment.

Throughout the training period, I developed a wonderful relationship with the co-authors of *Models of Teachings,* Bruce and Marsha. I continued to rely on them for expertise advice. As a result, Bruce invited me to join his instructional team at the National Teacher Corps summer training program which was held in Richmond, Virginia the following summer. In addition, he agreed to fund two of the teachers from the pilot in-service program to be a part of the team. This marked the beginning of my long-term involvement with

National Teacher Corps.

Once the pilot was over, I identified five other sites. In the next round of trainings, I conducted the program in a slightly modified version in several locations and facilitated train-the-trainer sessions. One of the most successful efforts took place in the Huntingdon area school district in Pennsylvania. With the assistance of my colleague Dr. Bill Gaskins, I trained four classroom teachers who then delivered the in-service program for at least three more years. In 1978, a seven-page article was written about the effort in the Pennsylvania State Education Association's *Pennsylvania School Journal.* I also presented the program to several other states, but unfortunately the local associations were not able to fund it.

MITIGATING RACISM

After working a couple of years in the IPD Unit, I started working on the Mitigating Racism project which allowed me to utilize a great deal of the expertise I developed on racism during my doctoral studies. Terry Herdon, who was the NEA Executive Director and the former Executive Director of the Michigan Education Association, wrote a concept paper entitled "Mitigating Racism." Terry's paper was written as a response to a report from the Human Relations Committee. In his paper, he wrote, "Racism may be the result of the projection of racist institutional decision-makers or may be something wholly apart from personal prejudice." He went on to say, "Finally, we come to the definition which must be the object of our program: the racism which is a core problem in human relations and that is racial chauvinism." By this definition, racism is a mode of social behavior which may be practiced by any individual. Terry proposed the NEA commission the development of a diagnostic manual patterned after *Profiles of Excellence*, but directed toward an appraisal of the adequacy of a school district's capacity to serve its racially, culturally, and ethnically diverse population.

It was almost by accident that I received the opportunity to work on this assignment. At the time, Howard Belton, a colleague who was recruited by Terry from the Michigan Education Association, was serving as the Director of Human Resources and the Acting Director of the IPD Unit. Terry had shared with Howard his thoughts regarding the need to do something significant on racism. Much of the work on racism-related issues had always been the purview of the Human and Civil Rights Division. Terry considered hiring a consultant to do the work. Howard shared the paper and some of Terry's concerns. Because of my doctoral work on racism, I convinced Howard that I could do the job. After discussions with Terry and the development of a working paper that included a team of three colleagues, I was given the assignment. The team consisted of Dr. Mark Chesler, Dr. Gloria Fauth, and Dr. James "Jim" Tanner.

Dr. Mark Chesler was a professor at the University of Michigan. We had met in the summer of 1969 when I was a participant in an NTL program and Mark was an NTL trainer. He later served as an adjunct faculty member on my doctoral committee. We also collaborated on bringing to the Human and Civil Rights Division a major body of work on school desegregation developed at the University of Michigan. Dr. Gloria Fauth, a Flint school system colleague, and I had worked together on a major change effort in 1967 and 1968. Dr. James "Jim" Tanner was the Associate Superintendent in the Cleveland Public Schools. I met Jim while working with the National Teacher Corps. Jim and I were part of a team that prepared a monograph for Teacher Corps, *Planning for Institutionalization: The Continuation of New Programs and Practices*.

As a team, we spent about six months preparing a draft paper. Our approach began with the understanding that there was racial inequality in education. We introduced the term "disprivileged" which means denied privileges. We used the word to describe victims of inequality in education, as well as the educationally disadvantaged, deprived, and oppressed. We chose the term because it implies that benefits are actively denied to some participants in the system of education which is evident in every index of public educational effort, including the allocation of public funds; the location and quality of facilities; and the enforcement of practices. Schools are structured and operated in a manner that reinforces economic and racial inequality. This promotes the advantages of the white majority, while restricting them for those of the minority races, as well as the economically disadvantaged. Despite America's pronouncements about the importance of education, it has not matched its ideological commitment with action or investment of critical resources in educational affairs.

Our purpose was to build a process on how to recognize the substance and manifestations of racial inequality in education, and how to eradicate it, or at least substantially reduce it. Our concern was with all aspects of the school system: its philosophy, structure, curriculum (what is taught and how), whom it employs, and how it expands its resources. We wanted the paper to be informative and suggest concrete and specific ways of gathering and interpreting evidence about racial inequality in a school or a school system.

We operated from the concept that institutional racism most accurately identifies the source of racial inequality in schooling. By institutional racism, we meant the creation or perpetuation of advantages or privileges for one racial group with the exclusions and deprivations for other racial groups who participate in or are served by the institution. It requires the exercise of power by groups (based on race) within the institution to advance or maintain their advantages or privileges. This definition stresses behaviors and outcomes, rather than attitudes and intentions. It also stresses the location of racism in institutional power structures rather than in the isolated behaviors of individuals. It suggests the existence of a conscious or implicit ideology justifying racially inequitable arrangements. Finally, it calls for vigorous action to create change.

We identified seven areas for data gathering and analysis: (1) Governance and Administration; (2) Personnel and Staffing; (3) Curriculum and Instruction; (4) School Facilities; (5) Student Services; (6) School/Community Relations; and (7) Commitment to Equal Opportunity and Affirmative Action. A major method of obtaining diagnostic information was through the examination of formal documents and records. A second procedure for diagnosis was participant observation, one of the most natural and simple ways of gathering information. Surveys, questionnaires, or interviews represented the third procedure. The fourth procedure included a combination of all three with a checklist. The checklist captured a summary of the procedures and the respondents' formal documents and records, observations, and opinions. In using the checklist, we were able to document the existence of inequality. Examples and suggestions as to how to use the variety of data-gathering approaches were included. We also provided questions to discuss in doing the analysis. We believed our detailed approach was the best way to equip those who would use the data to convince others of the outcomes and to secure commitment to change.

When we completed our final draft, I submitted our work to my Director, Dr. Sharon Robinson, a Black woman, who delivered it to the Executive Director. The team felt we had done some of our best work because our document was thorough and practical in working toward eradicating racism in schools. After my follow-up meeting with Sharon, I was angry, frustrated, and deeply disappointed with her feedback. I didn't expect it or the outcome. It was difficult to accept that our team's work was good, but too detailed and would be too much for local associations to manage. We were asked to significantly reduce the document. In response to the feedback, I challenged Sharon by saying I didn't feel she had really represented our work to the Executive Director, or he didn't really want a strong, powerful piece of work. After meeting with my team, I realized we could do what we were asked without compromising the quality and substance of our work. We worked to produce a more streamlined document that was accepted and published as the NEA's first so-called *Profiles of Excellence*. It was titled *How to Establish Racial Equity in Schools*, and ultimately became the model for what the NEA called *Profiles of Excellence*.

How to Establish Racial Equality in Schools is the first publication in The NEA *Profiles of Excellence* series of guides that helped NEA affiliates access the quality of specific educational programs and policies in their school districts. They were designed to get teachers involved in the process of determining what is educational excellence and in planning and implementing change to achieve excellence. After *How to Establish Racial Equality in Schools* was established in 1980, I traveled and trained affiliates on how to implement it. I also helped other NEA IPD staff who were assigned to work on additional profiles such as bilingual education.

This experience taught me three great lessons that I carried with me throughout my career: 1) no matter what feedback I receive on my work, I will do my best to remain open to constructive criticism and compromise; 2) ensure my work represents the highest integrity and quality I can deliver; and 3) do good work no matter what. Learning these lessons also gave me a framework for the leadership coaching and mentoring I would later do as a consultant.

KU KLUX KLAN PROJECT

In 1980, Ronald Reagan and George H. W. Bush were elected U.S. president and vice president. That same year, I was still the only Black male staff person with significant expertise and experience working on racism in IPD when I was assigned to work with the Connecticut Education Association (CEA) and The Council on Interracial Books for Children. We came together to prepare materials about the Ku Klux Klan (KKK), Neo-Nazis, and other extremist groups for classroom use. The KKK is a white supremacist terrorist hate group that commits violent crimes (that often go unprosecuted) against African Americans, immigrants, leftists, people who self-identify as LGBTQ (later became LGBTQIA), Catholics, Muslims, atheists, and more. Like the KKK, Neo-Nazis are also a white terrorist hate group based on Nazi ideology.

The CEA's need for these materials was in direct response to a Klan rally that was held earlier that year. After the rally, the CEA appointed a classroom teacher Special Study Task Force on the KKK to put together an informational and instructional kit for teachers dealing with the threat of the KKK. Since 1966, the Council on Interracial Books for Children had prepared and disseminated print and audiovisual materials for teachers and others to combat racism and sexism, and to develop pluralism, the positive concept of valuing and recognizing all groups, in schools and society. These three groups joined forces and combined resources in 1981 to create an informational and instructional kit entitled *VIOLENCE, THE*

KU KLUX KLAN AND THE STRUGGLE FOR EQUAL-ITY. The kit was published in 1981 with lesson plans that informed teachers about the KKK and provided instructional procedures and resources for classroom discussion. The lesson plans were critical to helping teachers paint a true picture of this white domestic terrorist hate group. The kit included a wide range of topics such as the KKK today; the birth of the KKK; the death of Reconstruction; the beginnings of white supremacy; the KKK in the 1920s; the civil rights era; the struggle for racial equality; reflection of an ex-Klansman; the myth vs. reality, part one: social perceptions; the myth vs. reality, part two: the process of scapegoating; and countering the KKK. Today's educator can even find the publication on Amazon for just $6.29. Given the current racial climate and the resurgence of the KKK in America, I highly recommend it.

After the publication was released, I joined a team of workshop facilitators who trained NEA affiliates at conferences in Illinois, Indiana, Michigan, Minnesota, Ohio, and other states. In Minneapolis, the publication was featured in the St. Paul Pioneer Press. One of the issues the educational toolkit discussed was the KKK's recruitment of students at schools, on playgrounds, and in public marketplaces. For example, the KKK ran newspaper ads that read, "If you are between the ages of 10 and 17, join the Klan Youth Corps." Flyers also urged students to enroll. The main rallying charge was that white students "had it with Blacks." That kit and our training sparked interest from a local radio station, and I was invited to appear on the station's talk show. I also spoke about the issues raised in the toolkit at panel discussions and other events.

While doing this work, it never crossed my mind that I was putting myself and my family in harm's way. I did not have any direct experience with the KKK while growing up in DC and spending my summers and later attending college in Terre Haute. This project was my deep dive into the inner workings of one of America's most dangerous domestic terrorist organizations. As a result, I gained a greater understanding of the KKK's influence and contributions to institutional racism. Had the internet been available, Google and I would have become the best of friends!

NATIONAL COUNCIL FOR ACCREDITATION OF TEACHER EDUCATION (NCATE, NOW KNOWN AS THE COUNCIL FOR THE ACCREDITATION OF EDUCATOR PREPARATION)

Another assignment I worked on was as the NEA's main liaison with the National Council for Accreditation of Teacher Education (NCATE) which was established as a professional accreditor of teacher education programs in U.S. colleges and universities in 1954. Five national education groups were instrumental in the creation of NCATE: the American Association of Colleges for Teacher Education (AACTE), the Council of Chief State Officers (CCSO), the National Association of State Directors of Teacher Education and Certification (NAS-

DTEC), the National School Boards Association (NSBA), and the NEA. It consisted of a coalition of 33 member organizations of teachers, teacher educators, content specialists, and local and state policy makers. In 2014, NCATE and the Teacher Education Accreditation Council (TEAC) merged with the Council for the Accreditation of Educator Preparation (CAEP).

In my role as the NEA liaison to NCATE, I kept the NEA president apprised of current issues and activities and briefed him/her on NCATE issues before meetings, especially when he/she served as the Council chair. As a result of our NCATE regular meetings, we established close working relationships that gave me a bird's eye view into the ins and outs of a national organization. I gained insights as to how leaders of major organizations navigated conflicts and chaos, reached consensus, and collaborated and compromised on critical decisions. I also witnessed a wide array of leadership styles that helped me later in my career as a consultant with corporate executives. These real-time experiences were my on-the-job training in organizational change. I was literally building and flying the organizational change airplane at the same time.

During my tenure, I made significant contributions to a major review and revision of the NCATE standards. Through a series of group discussions, I shared my knowledge of multicultural, multiracial, and diversity issues and training expertise. My contributions helped to create new standards that directly addressed the issue of under-representation including the need for colleges and universities to increase the number of instructors of color as well as provide curriculum that accurately discussed the contributions and lived experiences of people of color. I believed these standards were essential for holding the academic institutions accountable and preparing future teachers. Once the training program was finalized, I traveled as a member of the training team. We conducted on-site trainings for visiting teams and monitored accreditation efforts. After I left the NEA, the NCATE Director hired me to work as a consultant for several years.

OHIO EDUCATION ASSOCIATION

While still on staff at the NEA, I worked with the Ohio Education Association (OEA) to develop a plan for how it would address the numerous recommendations from *A Nation at Risk: The Imperative for Educational Reform*. *A Nation at Risk: The Imperative for Educational Reform* was published in 1983 by the U.S. National Commission on Excellence in Education. It is considered a landmark event in modern American educational history. The report contributed to the ever-growing assertion that American schools were failing, and it touched off a wave of local, state, and federal reform efforts. In addition, I assisted in developing and conducting workshops for the leaders and members of their organization.

POLITICAL ACTION WORK

Political action is one of the best ways I have found to initiate and support change at a national, state, and local level. In the 1970s, the NEA became very active in political action. It approved procedures for endorsing presidential candidates in 1974. Four years later, the organization endorsed Jimmy Carter for President. Staff members in the Government Relations and Field Services divisions were assigned organizing duties during the campaign. Due to my organizing experience, I was assigned to work in Field Services on the 1984 Presidential campaign for Walter Mondale and Geraldine Ferraro. That assignment allowed me to bring my political beliefs to work and strengthen my relationship with my colleague Mort Mondale, Walter Mondale's brother. Mort and I shared a belief in equality and worked with local teachers together in the IPD Unit.

The Mondale-Ferraro campaign took me to a rural area near Champaign, Illinois, where I helped organize local teachers for several months. I met with teachers at the end of the school day, attended staff meetings in Chicago with other NEA and Illinois Education Association (IEA) staff members, and made telephones calls in the evenings from my hotel room. While calling teachers on behalf of the IEA, I learned quite a bit about folks in the Midwest. Many of the teachers I spoke with were women; I expected them to be both liberal-leaning and happy to see a woman finally nominated as a vice presidential candidate for a major party. When I asked them if they would support the Democratic party's candidates, their reactions and responses surprised me. Many of their comments were negative. One woman said, "No way will I vote for a Democrat." Another warned me that "the country is not ready for a woman." Others admonished me and said, "I am voting the way my husband votes. How dare the NEA tell me who to vote for." I was shocked and caught off guard just as I would be more than 30 years later when I volunteered for Hillary Clinton's Presidential campaign in 2015 and 2016.

How to Establish Racial Equality in Schools *is the first publication in The NEA* Profiles of Excellence *series of guides that helped NEA affiliates access the quality of specific educational programs and policies in their school districts (housed at the Library of Congress)*

VIOLENCE, THE KU KLUX KLAN AND
THE STRUGGLE FOR EQUALITY,
*an informational and instructional kit with lesson plans
that informed teachers about the KKK and provided
instructional procedures and resources for classroom discussion
(housed at the Library of Congress)*

253

CHAPTER 14 REFLECTION QUESTIONS

———————————

1. Individual: Take a moment to read Tim Wise's quote out loud to yourself:

   "If we don't figure out a way to create equity, real equity, of opportunity and access, to good schools, housing, health care, and decent paying jobs, we are not going to survive as a productive and healthy society."

   What opportunities have you had to change conditions around education, housing, health care, and employment?

2. Group Discussion: As a group, share your experiences and discuss what equity means in education, housing, health care, and employment. Give each person 3–5 minutes to share their individual response with the group. As a group, list some of the similarities and differences highlighted in the sharing session. Also, discuss one or two lessons each person has learned.

The Pursuit of the Doctorate

"Education is the passport to the future,
for tomorrow belongs to those who prepare for it today."

—MALCOLM X, a change agent, a Muslim minister,
and a human rights activist

————————————

My family valued education in the same way Malcolm X expressed his belief that "education is the passport to the future." Although my parents only attended several years of college, they wanted me to obtain as much education as possible. I followed in the footsteps of my aunts Mabel, Paulyne, and Jane who earned undergraduate and graduate degrees. Growing up, I only knew one African American man who had earned a Ph.D., Dr. John Lydia, a friend and neighbor of my grandmother Eunice. Other than Dr. Lydia, I didn't have any role models or connections to people of color who had earned a Ph.D.

Looking back, I was also following in the footsteps of one of my heroes, Dr. W.E.B. Du Bois, the first African American to receive a Ph.D. in History from Harvard University in

1895. Throughout my intellectually challenging Ph.D. journey, I read several of Dr. Du Bois's books. His book *The Souls of Black Folks* opened my eyes to the history and experiences of Black people I hadn't learned about in elementary school, high school, college, or graduate school. Being able to dedicate time to study, reflect, and make connections to what I experienced in my life and work as a teacher, counselor, and NEA staffer to the history and experiences of Black people and other people of color was a great deal more than I anticipated. My Ph.D. journey was one of my greatest personal growth experiences.

The journey taken with my CIRCES colleagues was filled with many ups and downs as well as twists and turns. We challenged each other on how we showed up in our individual identities by race and gender. Naturally, our conversations were often heated and necessary all at the same time. Because we had strong relationships with each other, we were able to be vulnerable and open as we struggled to understand and appreciate each person's concerns.

During the first year, Ellwood decided to leave the program. I think he had difficulty dealing with many of the issues centered around how white men were at the root of the problems women and minorities were facing. In addition, he was the only CIRCES member who had not worked in Teacher Rights Unit. As a result, I believed he lacked experience working on issues of race and gender. Lance left during the second year. He no longer had the desire and wanted to focus his time and energy in a direction in which he could make a greater contribution to his people. The remaining five continued to pursue the work as a group until we came to a critical juncture.

I never anticipated the amount of time it would take to manage the communication and administrative side of working with four other peer members and a large doctoral committee during the first two years. Our official Union committee consisted of two Union core faculty members, five adjunct faculty members, and five peer members. The five peer members were doctoral students who entered the program with us in 1973. We were committed to the development of change intervention techniques which could be applied within organizations and institutions for creating alternative behavioral systems that would aid in combatting racism, sexism, culturalism, and ethnicism.

At the start of our third year in 1975, we met with Elsie Cross, a group facilitator. That meeting changed the trajectory of our group effort. Elsie pointed out that we were doing great work and doing the work as a group was holding us up. Most of our peers who entered the program had finished their degree. We were beginning to incur more expenses. She recommended we disband the group and focus on our individual doctoral projects. Her insights made sense to me because I had reached a point where I simply wanted to complete the degree. We accepted her recommendation and decided to restructure ourselves. The next was to inform our two Union core advisors. They accepted our decision and were very supportive. They couldn't understand why we hadn't done it sooner.

Each of us began preparing our individual plan of study.

My new doctoral committee included Dr. Andress Taylor, a core advisor; adjunct faculty members Dr. Mark Chesler and Dr. Reginald Wilson; and peer group members Dr. Argentine Craig and Dr. Peter Kramer. With their support, I became very focused and committed to completing the requirements for my doctorate in Organizational Behavior. It helped me to arrive at the following objectives:

- To acquire in-depth knowledge about institutional racism and its impact on both the victim as well as the oppressor.
- To explore what happens to a Black man who is consciously combatting institutional white racism in a racist organization(s).
- To examine a collaborative approach to combatting institutional racism.
- To produce, in lieu of a more traditional dissertation, a publishable manual containing concepts, activities, strategies, and behaviors to assist others in combatting institutional racism.

As doctoral students who were no longer a part of a group effort, we had to meet the requirements for: 1) attendance at a residential colloquium; 2) the development of a portfolio that includes formal education degrees, workshops, training experiences, seminars attended, and other work-related activities that contributed to our study; 3) an internship; and 4) a dissertation-like document called the Project Demonstrating Excellence (PDE). We chose to attend the Northfield Colloquium as our residential requirement. Each day, we spent six to nine hours discussing our beliefs about race and sex bias issues. This was a major accomplishment for a group of men and women who were Black, Native American, and white to grapple with many controversial issues and remain intact. Once again, I learned the power of having collegial relationships with my colleagues.

My development of a portfolio was a chronology of events associated with my learning strategy. My learning strategy consisted of four major areas:

- A series of evolutionary activities which occurred over the span of my doctoral pursuit: book readings, articles, reports, and CIRCES activities, trainings, and other activities
- My personal analysis of the impact of the critical events
- My internship
- My PDE

The chronology of events captured my work product during the first four years of my Ph.D. studies. It included the many meetings of CIRCES that dealt with administrative details and Sunday seminars. The Sunday seminars were explorations of specific topics with invited experts as well as discussions of books led by one of the members. It also included the many activities I led, assisted, and participated in that dealt with racism, sexism, group relations, and other related topics. Having the chronology of events helped me see how much I had grown personally and professionally. It also served as a reminder of how valuable this learning experience had become.

My personal analysis of the impact of the critical events produced two aha moments, the first of which happened while reading Chancellor Williams's book *The Destruction of Black Civilization*. Reading Williams's book helped me to confirm that my African ancestors created the first great civilizations of the world. Having this information empowered me. It also helped me comprehend the historical factors I was up against in dealing with racism and why the western world went to great lengths to erase, downplay, ignore, and misinterpret African and U.S. Black history and contributions. Unfortunately, it hasn't worked because I know in my heart I am a son of Africa, the cradle of civilization.

My second aha moment occurred when Elsie Cross, a Black woman who served as an advisor and facilitator to CIRCES, intervened and helped us look at some of the difficulties we encountered as we tried to process our working relationship as a group. Because Elsie was able to share both the perspective of a woman and a Black person, she exposed the racist and sexist dynamics present in the group itself. For me, having a Black woman point out sexist behavior I was participating in helped me own my part in maintaining a form of oppression. It also deepened my commitment to doing the work to change my beliefs and behavior. Witnessing Elsie point out the racist behavior of other group members helped me feel like everyone in the group was being held accountable. Having her support made a big difference in how we individually and collectively moved forward in our Ph.D. program and work.

My internship was unusual in that rather than involve a specific project within an institution, the focus of my internship was to monitor a white woman (Kate) working on an anti-racist project in a major organization, as a way of evaluating the progress and quality of that work. This form of monitoring is rooted in the concept that since racism is a white problem, sustained and beneficial to whites, then whites must assume greater responsibility for actions to eradicate racism. Therefore, whites must initiate anti-racist actions that are directed primarily at white behaviors and institutional arrangements. Because whites rationally can't be expected to do this completely on their own, people of color must be involved. In this internship, as a person of color, I took on the role of monitoring, in which I was expected to model behaviors and skills that would result in a stronger anti-racist outcome.

Because I was the monitor and not the person coordinating the project, I had to refrain from taking control of the effort. It increased my insight into what it takes for a person of color to be critical in a helpful manner to a white person who is trying to be anti-racist. It proved that people of color can support whites' efforts to combat racism in a way that cleared up time and space for people of color to work on combatting racism and other prejudices within communities of color.

The title of my PDE was *Notebook on Combatting Racism: A Practical Tool for Organizational Specialists and Trainers*. The Notebook laid out a set of beliefs, assumptions, and concepts which could be translated into behaviors, skills, activities, and programs to combat racism. The format was taken from the outline of *Handbook for Group Facilitators* by John E. Jones and J. William Pfeiffer, which is highly respected, and I thought would strengthen my work. The Notebook was organized into five major sections. The intention was to help users gain knowledge, information, and conceptual frameworks and was supported through specially designed lectures, instruments, activities, and additional resources. All of it could be used to address racism and other forms of oppression. One of the unique features of the Notebook was that it made an effort to speak to specific behaviors of minority and/or majority group individuals as they implemented suggested actions.

The first section of the Notebook presented theoretical pieces that discussed the four major concepts underlying the rest of the material: Defining Racism, Need for Historical Perspective, Minority Collusion, and Minority Monitoring. This section was meant for background reading and study in preparation for working with individuals and groups within organizations. It could also be used for preparing lectures within a training effort. Today, I think this section would help people living and working in Florida or other states that have enacted legislation and government policies attacking affirmative action and creating racist environments because advocates could use the information to support their arguments for changing the legislation and policies.

The second section presented a collection of lecturettes which were short, succinct statements that could be used as an introduction or as summary materials by organizational consultants, trainers, and workshop leaders. The three topics included Dynamics of Institutional White Racism, Minority-Majority Collaboration, and Minority Survival Axioms. They could also be reproduced as handouts to reinforce what was discussed in a previous training or workshop activity.

The third section presented a collection of items which could be used to gather data, analyze certain aspects, and draw tentative conclusions about racist policies and practices that individuals and/or organizations used. The intent was to use the results from such instrumentation to further plan and select appropriate alternatives. The five topics included Forces in Society Affecting Equality of Opportunity, Organizational Diagnosis for Implications of Eradicating Institutional White Racism, Inventory of Reactions to Organizational Anti-Racists Reform, Behaviors for Combatting Racism Scale, and Classroom Teaching Behavior Assessment.

The fourth section presented a selection of structured activities which could be used primarily with small groups aimed at examining a specific set of ideas. Suggestions were provided for individuals to use their racial identity as a lens to analyze issues. The four topics were Exploring Institutional Racism Through Synectics, Agree-Disagree: Examining Racial Beliefs and Attitudes, Constructing a Non-Racist Organization, and Analyzing Racism Vignettes.

The PDE's final section was dedicated to Resources which included a selected bibliography, suggested project ideas, and training designs. The five topics were A Training Design:

Group Relations Workshop, A Training Design: Racism and Sexism in Management, An Organizational Proposal: Increasing Minority Involvement, An Organizational Proposal: Organizational Development: Racism and School Systems—A Beginning Diagnosis, and Bibliography.

DYNAMICS OF INSTITUTIONAL WHITE RACISM AND THE USE OF DISCRETIONARY POWER

When I wrote my PDE in 1977, I included a segment on the "Dynamics of Institutional White Racism" that addressed discretionary power. Institutional white racism occurs when the outcome of the use or access to power by whites subordinates others or distributes benefits differently based on race. Discretionary power is a process that exists in every institution. There is no institution in which the use of discretionary power is more evident than the judicial system. This system interprets and enforces the laws which govern the land. Laws are written standards of conduct that are developed from the values and beliefs of the people. Historically, only white people's values and beliefs have been considered when establishing the standards of conduct. However, the laws govern all people. Until very recently, people of color have had little or no involvement in determining these laws. Institutional white racism, discretionary power, and their impact on people of color continue to be misunderstood today as I am writing this in 2024.

Police departments are responsible for protecting all citizens and enforcing the laws. Their role and responsibilities give them an enormous amount of power over the lives of the people they serve. In 1977, most police departments were under white male leadership and consisted of white male officers. At this time, the number of white officers in urban areas was disproportionate to the number of people of color they served. The absence of large numbers of officers of color working in these areas was due to systemic discriminatory hiring practices and the result of an unequal education system that viewed people of color as unqualified. This illustrates how two institutions, the police department and education system, have contributed to a racist outcome in the judicial system.

Most of the interactions white police officers had with people of color included a high level of mistrust that contributed to unwarranted police brutality and harassment. Officers brought their personal bias and beliefs into these interactions and their use of discretionary power. All these things influence how they conduct investigations, make arrests, book, and interrogate. In numerous cases, they treated people of color differently. All these factors play a role in what officers shared in their testimony about the arrest at trial.

Once an individual was arrested, they may have experienced an arraignment, a bond setting, a plea bargaining, and the setting of a trial date. The key players in this process who exercised discretionary power included judges, bail bondsmen, investigators, clerks, and other personnel. They were almost always white.

An arraignment is a procedure where the accused is brought before the court to plead to the criminal charge against them in the indictment (written accusation) or information. At an arraignment, a judge had the power to determine if probable cause existed for the accused. The judge had the power to make a lot of decisions about the way a person traveled through the judicial system, including whether they would be tried, detained, eligible for bail, and assigned a public defender.

The accused has a right to pursue a bond. However, the bail bondsman, who is in private practice, could decide to post or refuse bond. In 1977 and today, if the accused was unable to post bond through their own lack of resources or because of a bondsman's refusal, they would remain in custody. This limited their access to legal counsel prior to trial. It also exposed them to well-documented inhumane treatment in overcrowded prisons. These factors increased the prospect of the accused pleading guilty to a lesser charge—or even pleading guilty to avoid remaining in custody for an even longer period, and losing employment, income, and other rights such as custodial. Not having income to pay for a proper defense created even more hardship.

Trial by a jury of one's peers is the next step in the process. Historically, people of color were systematically excluded from serving as jurors. White local government officials used arbitrary requirements such as voter registration and English literacy exams to deny their right to serve. At trial, if the defendant was denied bail, had inadequate legal counsel, and appeared in court wearing a prison uniform, they were extremely vulnerable to implicit bias. Because white people have an inherent belief in white superiority and Black inferiority, it takes very little to convince them that a Black person is guilty.

Once a person was found guilty and sentenced, the type of correctional facility they were assigned to affected how they experienced incarceration. The differences that existed in the correctional facilities were significant. Individuals who were convicted of "white collar" crime were incarcerated in facilities that are often referred to as "country clubs." Those individuals were typically white. More people of color were convicted of robbery, assault, murder, and drugs, and assigned to state and federal prisons. Examination of inmates in penal institutions revealed there were fewer people of color in the "country club" prisons. Finally, prison personnel, like the personnel in other institutions, were predominately white.

Parole and release are the final aspects of the legal system. Parole boards decide whether a person can be released from their sentence early based on factors such as "good behavior" and threat to society. Historically, these boards were composed of political appointees and resulted in all-white boards. They had the power to grant or deny parole as well as to set parole conditions. Upon parole, the person of color returned to society with a prison record and the same unequal educational preparation they started with when they entered prison. Their new reality often limited their opportunities. The likelihood of them returning to prison was three times as great as a white person.

After reviewing these processes, it is clear that the use of individual discretionary power contributes to institutional racism to the detriment of people of color. When individual prejudice is supported by structures, policies, and practices within the broader system, the results become detrimental for people of color.

If the system operates based on the belief that white is right, then fairness becomes inaccessible to people of color. Institutional racism victimizes people of color and gives whites a false sense of superiority which makes it extremely difficult for them to accept the reality of racism. If it continues, America's future will be extremely depressing and disheartening. And if we look at 2024, we may already be there.

THE FINAL YEAR OF
MY DOCTORAL STUDIES

Fortunately for me, the NEA offered a sabbatical leave that allowed me to take a year off to complete my PDE while receiving half of my salary. My sabbatical year began in September 1976. My children were in elementary and junior high school. After helping them get ready for school each morning, I would spend the next six hours writing my PDE. My mother helped type my first draft. This schedule helped me produce a draft for my doctoral committee to review in December. Their feedback arrived a month later. I had no problem incorporating their minor changes over the next month. In June, I presented my PDE to my doctoral committee and received their final approval.

The Union did not hold formal graduation ceremonies. Instead, students designed their own celebration called a Terminar. I held my Terminar for family, friends, and colleagues at my home on a wonderful, bright, sunny Saturday in June. I was pleased my five-year journey was finally over. I will never forget how thrilled and proud my father was. He showed up in a colorful yellow sport jacket and was going around informing everyone that he was the father of the Ph.D.

One of my favorite memories from that day is captured in a photograph hanging in my home office. It features three of my CIRCES members, core faculty member, adjunct faculty members, and peers. It marked CIRCES's third doctoral degree. Delyte finished with a PDE about power in March 1976. Later that year, Kate finished with a PDE centering around her intervention with the Girl Scouts of America on racism. Deborah completed her PDE focused on Black women in leadership in 1978. Larry was the last to finish and his PDE was focused on organizational management in 1979.

John F. Leeke and his parents, John L. and Frederica Leeke, at his doctoral celebration

John F. and Theresa Leeke with George Jones at his doctoral celebration

John F. Leeke and George Jones at his doctoral celebration

Members of John F. Leeke's doctoral committee.
Standing (L–R): Dr. Mark Chesler, Dr. Lawrence Billups,
Dr. John F. Leeke, Dr. Andress Taylor, Dr. Kate Kirkum,
Dr. Argentine Craig, and Dr. Peter Kramer.
Seated (L–R): Dr. Delyte Frost and Dr. Reginald Wilson.

CHAPTER 15 REFLECTION QUESTIONS

---

1. Individual: What is your reaction to the passage below?

    Institutional racism victimizes people of color and gives whites a false sense of superiority which makes it extremely difficult for them to accept the reality of racism. If it continues, America's future will be extremely depressing and disheartening. And if we look at 2024, we may already be there.

2. Group Discussion: As a group, share your viewpoint and discuss what institutional racism is. Give each person 3–5 minutes to share their individual response with the group. As a group, list some of the similarities and differences highlighted in the sharing session. Also, discuss one or two lessons each person has learned.

STANDING IN MY OWN SHOES UNAPOLOGETICALLY AS I MOVE FULL FORCE TOWARDS GREATER SERVICE, GREATER PROGRESS

(1985–2015)

CHAPTER 16

Establishing John F. Leeke Associates, Inc.

"Oh, he's ready. Gonna make a move, yeah.
Oh, he's ready. And makin' moves, yeah."

—An excerpt from "Gonna Fly Now," the theme song of the movie
Rocky by BILL CONTI, a composer and conductor

———————

Becoming a full-time entrepreneur was never a consideration or a dream. As you may recall in previous chapters, I did not have a career plan or strategy. Nothing was written down. My career opportunities happened as I was living my life. I always thought I would work full-time for an organization. Part-time consulting opportunities knocked on the front door of my life. I accepted them and focused on doing the work. Over time, the part-time consulting expanded and the relationships I had with clients and partners deepened while I continued to work for the NEA.

After working 17 years for the NEA, I realized I needed more freedom to determine the focus of my work, the clients I served, and the fees I generated. Also, my consulting practice and client base had generated more income than my salary and previous part-time work. These factors convinced me I was ready to leave the NEA and establish my own firm. After I talked to my wife Theresa and received her support, I had everything I needed. I was ready to make a big move like the one composer and conductor Bill Conti wrote about when he penned "Gonna Fly Now."

In September 1985, I launched John F. Leeke Associates, Inc. I did not have a mission statement or a business plan. I hadn't read a bunch of how-to books or taken a single course. I didn't think about getting a coach or a business mentor. Looking back, I now realize I was following in my ancestors' entrepreneurial footsteps. The two entrepreneurs that come to mind are my grandmother Eunice Ann Thomas Roberts, a tailor, and my grandfather James Ebard Leak, a barber shop and after-hours club owner. Like them, I was ready and willing to assume full control over my destiny and income.

Becoming a full-time entrepreneur is more than just waking up and wearing the title. For me, it's about being deliberate and structured, and this started years before I left the NEA with making sure the income I generated from my consulting efforts was properly reported to the IRS. That meant I needed to establish a relationship with a tax accountant. Fortunately for me, I was able to hire Art Belton who was referred by one of my Elsie Y. Cross Associates (EYCA) colleagues, Brenda Dancil-Jones, and her husband, Norman "Rocky" Jones. Art became my long-time tax accountant and business advisor.

Art and I had several conversations that helped me create the accounting and legal framework for my business. With his help, I was able to file my articles of incorporation for a limited liability corporation (LLC). Following his advice, I was able to file my personal and LLC taxes and increase my exemptions for a home office, supplies, and equipment. In addition, he recommended that my LLC hire and pay me a salary with a fringe benefit package that included health and life insurance as well as a pension plan. We also included professional development trainings such as the NTL Myers-Briggs Type Indicators certification program and Building and Utilizing Simulations.

By the time I announced my resignation in February 1985, several of my NEA colleagues had expressed concern about my decision. They knew our family was in the midst of paying private high school and college tuition for our four children. Michael, Madelyn, and Mark were already in college. Matthew was in his final months of high school. Their concerns were genuine. They were afraid my decision was too risky. They had seen others leave the security of a traditional career with a dependable salary, benefits, and retirement, and fail. To my credit, I had explored my options and factored in many of their concerns with the support of Art who was also a successful entrepreneur. I also had conversations with the NEA's Human Resources Division.

What I didn't share with everyone was that my decision to resign was not the first time I had considered going out on my own. During my sabbatical year, I did some consulting and saw it could be beneficial. Two years later, I requested a leave of absence from the NEA. During that year, I worked with

EYCA as well as several other clients. It was so successful I asked for a second year but was denied. After much discussion with Theresa, who had reservations, I returned to the NEA and continued to think about what conditions would be necessary to arrive at a different decision. The conditions were many of the same as my colleagues had raised when I finally left.

During that next year, I continued doing some consulting work, strategically using my leave to work with my clients. I was able to do so because the NEA staff union had negotiated several leave clauses that worked to my advantage. In addition, my work ethic and reputation as one of the most competent staffers who served above and beyond what was asked, along with the positive relationships I had with several managers and support staff, gave me the flexibility to lay the foundation for full-time entrepreneurship. Again, I didn't have a master plan. I was making decisions as the opportunities presented themselves. Operating in this fashion expanded my capacity to have patience, trust, and faith in the process of being an entrepreneur.

Even with my careful use of leave, challenges began to arise. My manager informed me that he was being moved to a different position and his replacement had been directed to "bring me in line." There had been questions from higher-ups about my leave patterns. Based on this information, I began to put together a plan as to what I needed to do in preparation for leaving and my timeline. Now I had to have a plan! I consulted Human Resources about my retirement status and the amount of sick and vacation leave I had left. I explored with Elsie the amount of work I could do in her firm along with outside consulting work. We agreed I would work full-time for EYCA. Once I presented all the information to Theresa, she felt confident that we would be okay. I made my announcement to my director and manager in February. I set May 15, 1985 as my official date of resignation.

CLIENT RELATIONSHIPS

My consulting began while I was pursuing my doctorate and working in the NEA Center for Human Relations. My colleagues Delyte, Kate, and I formed a consulting group called Resources for Change (RFC). Our work focused on race, gender, and school unrest. RFC's first client was the Indiana State Department of Education's Human Rights Division. I was contacted by a college classmate who worked for the agency. He was given the assignment to help the large school districts in addressing their racial issues. He contracted with RFC to conduct a weekend workshop for school administrators. Afterwards, we were contacted by three districts to work on change efforts that would improve race issues. We subsequently did a major year-long project in the South Bend School Cooperation and several workshops in Fort Wayne and Evansville.

In my early days, some of my bigger clients included the U.S. Department of Agriculture's (USDA) Graduate School, the Montgomery County Public Schools, Bell Laboratories (was a part of AT&T), the National Teacher Corps, and the

National School Boards Association. These client relationships spanned a period of five years or more. They started with a relationship with a key person or a referral and were developed on an engagement-by-engagement basis. Working with these clients gave me a great deal of comfort and helped me believe and trust I would have work after leaving the NEA.

USDA Graduate School

On a return airline trip from an NEA assignment, I struck up a conversation with my seatmate during dinner in first class. (At the time, my contract dictated that any time I flew over three hours, I could exercise the option to fly first class.) He was the manager of the USDA Graduate Programs. As we talked, I shared where I worked and what I did. He told me his agency had very few minority trainers for their programs which served government employees. At the end of the flight, we scheduled a meeting to explore how we could work together. That meeting resulted in a week-long management training course that covered team building, project planning, giving feedback, and communication skills. During the course, several Black participants came up to me to express how pleased they were to have a Black instructor. I was honored to receive such praise. This training opened the door to more week-long trainings for USDA over the next few years. At the end of each training, my performance was evaluated by the participants. My performance was rated outstanding and often included written comments that impressed the USDA Graduate School team. All of it created a welcoming climate for me to explore greater opportunities.

One of those opportunities included a groundbreaking joint proposal I made with my colleague Patti Wilson, a white woman, who was one of only a few women instructors. We proposed they offer a three-day program, Racism and Sexism. We were already doing this work and kept hearing about issues of race and gender in our week-long trainings. Seeing the need, we believed the USDA Graduate School could benefit from the program. After we made our proposal, the training director was on board and approved it. Our program became a regular offering in the USDA Graduate School catalogue. That program, and our growing platform, paved the way for additional work.

When the training director received a request from one of the agency's clients, the Building Services Contract Association International, he asked Patti and I to meet with them. The Building Services Contract Association International members had large government contracts throughout the world. Most of the owners and managers were white men. At this point, we stepped into the role of representing the USDA Graduate School and delivered the first-ever workshop on Race and Gender at their annual national conference. Our workshop was so successful we were invited to deliver it at two more annual national conferences. We were able to establish relationships with several member companies. In addition, I was appointed by Joan Wallace, the Secretary of the USDA Graduate Board, to serve a three-year term as the trainer representative.

Montgomery County, Maryland Public Schools' (MCPS) Division of Training for Support Staff

My colleague Delyte was working as a consultant for Montgomery County, Maryland Public Schools (MCPS). MCPS was actively looking for minorities to deliver some of their training. She recommended me which began a long-term client relationship. My trainings focused on how to communicate, counsel, and evaluate staff. I later designed several new programs on how to navigate a diverse workforce and became a consultant to the transportation, maintenance, and cafeteria workers divisions. I coached division leaders and trained their staff.

Bell Laboratories (Bell Labs)

Bell Labs became my first corporate client. As a result of a lawsuit, Bell Labs was required to conduct affirmative action programs. They were seeking trainers and reached out to see if I was available to conduct the One-Day Awareness program. I conducted the program in many of their locations across the country, mainly in New Jersey.

National Teacher Corps

My relationship with the National Teacher Corps started with an invitation from Dr. Bruce Joyce who led the instruction segment of a four-week summer Corp Member Training Institute in Richmond, Virginia. I joined the team as an instructor. The following year, the Institute was held at Florida State University in Tallahassee, Florida. Dr. Jack Gant, a Black man who was the Dean of the School of Education at Florida State University, led the Institute. I knew Jack from NTL and from his participation in NCATE and AACTE. He served as a mentor to me. He would later become one of the members of the EYCA Network. He knew I had experience in all four of the Institute's training modules: Instruction, Multi-Culture, Organizational Development, and Community Involvement. He invited me to be a member of the Institute staff. This invitation also provided an opportunity for me to take two of my sons, Michael and Mark, to spend a week on a university campus. They were able to live in a dormitory, eat in the cafeteria, swim in the pool, and be on their own most of the day. They had a ball.

While I was on sabbatical the next year, John Savage, a white man who wore many hats for the National Teacher Corps, asked me to join the Institute team in San Diego, California. In this role, I was assigned to Dunbar High School, a predominately Black institution in Baltimore, Maryland, to conduct research on normal school activity, problems that occurred, and the behavior of and interaction between students, teachers, administrators, and community members for one week. John used my research to write Distant Drum, a case study that was used by National Teacher Corps members to discuss, analyze, and plan how to address issues in schools located in urban settings.

Later that year and into the next, I was asked to join a team that produced a monograph entitled *Planning for In-*

stitutionalization: The Continuation of New Programs and Practices. The team members were Roger Pankratz, James Tanner, and Bill Moore. This was the first time I was able to witness and actively participate in an organization's decision to institutionalize the changes that were made and lay the foundation to continue making changes.

National School Boards Association

Jerry Floyd, an NEA member who I worked with previously, was hired by the National School Boards Association (NSBA). He reached out to me to be a part of a team that designed and delivered several three-day workshops on racism. Having the opportunity to work with school board members was powerful because they are elected by citizens to represent their community's voice in public education. As a citizen-based governing board, they have knowledge of the community's resources and needs and are the policy-makers closest to students. They have also been used as a tool for perpetuating white supremacy and allowing white people to stop racial progress in public schools. Today, school board elections are even more important given the policies that are anti-critical race theory, question and ban the teaching of African American history, and restrict LGBTQ content in books and classes and bathroom and pronoun use. When I think back to the NSBA workshops with school board members, I hope our work together helped them become more aware of the implications of racism in public education and incorporate what they learned into their policy decisions.

MOST SIGNIFICANT AND MEMORABLE CLIENT EXPERIENCES

After leaving the NEA, I continued making changes in the lives of many individuals and organizations. Like many consultants, I turned my former employer into a client. That relationship allowed me to work with the NEA and its affiliates such as the California Teachers Association, Connecticut Education Association, Maryland State Education Association, Michigan Education Association, Ohio Education Association, and Pennsylvania Education Association. I liked having the NEA as a client because I had access to the executive leadership and could leverage my access, previous NEA experience, and freedom to address a wider range of issues to help transform the organization from the inside out.

I also worked with Booz-Allen & Hamilton, Consumer Product Safety Commission, DC Government, EYCA and Associates, Federal Aviation Administration, Girl Scouts of the USA, Junior Achievement, Leadership Washington, Maryland National Capitol Park and Planning Commission, National Teacher Corps, New York State Department of Social Services, U.S. Office of Education, York City, Pennsylvania Public Schools, and York County, Pennsylvania School of Technology. All my client work was rewarding. However, there were several client relationships that deepened my awareness and understanding of race, gender, and sexual orientation; expanded my subject matter expertise in coaching; and increased my leadership and managerial skills. They included the NEA

Affiliate Services Division, Michigan Education Association, Ohio Education Association, York City, Pennsylvania Schools, NEA Dialogue on Social Justice and LGBTQ (later became LGBTQIA) Issues, NEA Affirmative Action UniServe Intern Program for Women and Ethnic Minorities (discussed in a later chapter), and EYCA (discussed in a later chapter).

NEA Affiliate Services Capacity Building Division

In 1988, I met Deloris Rozier, an NEA Organizational Specialist in the Pacific Region, during the second year of my work with NEA Affirmative Action UniServe Intern Program for Women and Ethnic Minorities (NEA Intern Program). From 1988 to 1995, Deloris held several managerial positions at the NEA. In 1995, she became the Director of the NEA Affiliate Services Capacity Building Division and contracted me to work with and coach her managers as a group and individually. Three of the key assignments I was involved in transformed how the organization provided services to its members. They included:

- Facilitation skills for the training section.
- Planning and implementation of the National Council of Urban Education Associations (NCUEA) annual conference (Rocio Inclan).
- Crisis management assistance with the Las Vegas Education Association (Vade Bolton).

The training section of the division was responsible for

training state and national staff. It did not yet have a facilitations skills training course. Deloris knew how valuable it would be because she witnessed its impact in the NEA Intern Program. She assigned me to work with Tamara Hamilton, a former NEA intern, on designing one. In creating the course, I leaned heavily on Roger M. Schwarz's book *The Skill Facilitator: Practical Wisdom for Developing Effective Groups*. We pilot-tested a five-day program that included the opportunity to practice facilitating a small group and receiving feedback. In the pilot, attention was paid to having a diverse participant population. We also built in scenarios with race and gender issues. The pilot was very successful and became one of the programs in the training division's catalogue of offerings for UniServ, state, and national staff. In addition to creating this program, I was also a part of a diverse four-person training team and conducted several trainings for the UniServ, state, and national staff.

Deloris also requested I work with Rocio Inclan, Manager for National Council of Urban Education Associations (NCUEA), in planning and implementing the NCUEA annual conference. In hiring me, the team was able to tap into my previous experience in planning NEA conferences, as well as my Urban Institute and NCUEA work and relationships. One of the highlights was meeting and getting to know keynote speaker Carl Upchurch, the author of *Convicted in the Womb: One Man's Journey from Prisoner to Peacemaker*. I spent several hours talking to him about his experience both in prison and as a returning citizen. It was powerful because our conversation reminded me of my previous work experience at the Indiana State Penal Farm.

In addition to training, I was able to engage in conflict management consulting. I liked conflict management consulting because it helped the parties communicate and collaborate better. I had an opportunity to utilize my training when Deloris asked me to work with Vade Bolton, the former manager of the NEA Training Division, to help resolve conflict between the Las Vegas Education Association's president and executive board. We met with them separately and had them identify their issues. After these meetings, Vade and I met to discuss each party's priorities and next steps. When we brought them into one room, we shared their priorities and helped them understand their challenges, agree on how to resolve them, and work more collaboratively.

Michigan Education Association (MEA)

In 1997, the Michigan Education Association (MEA) staff and member leaders were raising questions about racially charged issues such as advancement and bias. At the time, Julius Maddox, a Black man, served as the MEA President. Several of the key managers were also Black. Their leadership and support made my job easier in conducting three-day training workshops for the entire management and professional staff on the topic of managing and participating in a diverse work environment. I tapped my EYCA network to build a four-member training team that was diverse by race and gender.

My consulting role was unique in that I wore many hats that involved logistics, managing a training team, facilitating the trainings, and coaching MEA staff. My MEA work was the most comprehensive client project I had undertaken because it involved me working with numerous leaders including the president, executive director, key managers, and union leaders. They were all members of the MEA Diversity Training Committee. Before the training began, I met with them to determine their training needs, identify any labor and management issues that needed to be resolved, and to finalize the training agreement.

Before we could schedule the trainings, we needed to make sure every participant had access. That meant I worked with Bob Marshall, MEA Director of Labor Relations, and his staff on logistics. This called for a great deal of coordination. For example, workshops could only be conducted during normal work hours and off-site. Any union staff member that didn't live in the Lansing headquarters area would stay in the training hotel free of charge. Due to the large number of staff (almost 800) and the fact that they were only able to do one workshop a month, it took three years to complete. In addition to delivering the training, I met monthly with the MEA Diversity Training Committee that was formed to oversee the effort. This created a series of coaching relationships with several managers. As a coach, I helped staff expand their capacity to manage an increasingly diverse workforce.

Near the completion of the training with virtually 800 employees, Bob Marshall shared his perspectives on the training's impact with the staff. He told them the training had increased their awareness of:

- How they could hurt each other by thoughtless and insensitive words or actions.
- How people of color could be ignored and put down with racial jokes.
- How women, who have much to contribute to a discussion or decision, were often excluded from the decision table.
- How managers, sometimes by words or deeds, intimidated those they supervise.
- How support staff often felt undervalued and left out of the mainstream of organizational activity.
- How each of them from time to time failed to tell the truth about the organization or each other or what has been done to them or others.

Bob's comments were important because as a white male manager who represented the dominant culture, he was able to see the benefits of the work and endorse it. After the training was completed, I maintained a consulting and coaching relationship with MEA that allowed me to utilize my knowledge and skills in organizational development. This client relationship was a financially rewarding and fulfilling experience that became a model for how I worked with NEA affiliates and other clients.

Ohio Education Association (OEA)

I had a similar experience with Ohio Education Association (OEA). They had a smaller staff, but they included their support staff members, and their sessions were spread out more overtime. I maintained a much longer consultative relationship with this organization. Beside the staff diversity training, I engaged in some troubleshooting for several regional staff managers and assisted with a major organizational project over a two-year period. I also developed a strong coaching relationship with Dennis Reardon, a white man who was serving as the OEA Executive Director, and Pat Foster-Brooks, a Black woman who was serving as Vice President and later became the first Black woman OEA President. These coaching relationships were confidential. My NEA colleague Deloris Rozier, a Black woman, and I coached Pat for three years. The relationship we established has continued throughout our retirement.

My OEA experience had some unique learning opportunities. My coaching relationship with Dennis represented the first time I coached a white Executive Director who trusted me to support him in his management of an organization that was undergoing significant change. To establish a strong foundation, I made sure we met outside of the office for dinner in a relaxed environment. I believe this approach created a comfort zone that helped Dennis share his frustrations about running an association and managing relationships with elected leaders. My coaching also involved helping him effectively manage his relationship with Pat and support her efforts in getting elected to serve as the first Black woman OEA President.

When Deloris and I coached Pat, our collaboration was strengthened through our shared values, principles, and concepts. As a result, we were able to help Pat navigate moving from one leadership position to the top position in the organization. In doing so, she had to manage some of the typical racial issues that most minorities must cope with as they progress in predominately white organizations. By supporting leadership development in this way, we helped OEA create true institutional change.

York City, Pennsylvania Schools

My work with York City schools developed out of my relationship with Clinton Gibbs, a Black man who was an NEA intern. Clinton worked as an UniServ Director in York. He had been working with the local teacher organization and the school district to address issues of race in the schools. He had also been working with the Challenge of Change Committee, a cooperative effort between the Board of Directors of the York City Schools, the Administrators, and the York City Education Association. During the two years he worked with the Committee, he kept me informed about their progress. At the Committee's request, he invited me to make a presentation on how I could help them. My presentation highlighted the successful approaches I had taken with other organizations. Afterwards, they asked me to come back and work with a smaller group to design a plan for training administrators, teachers, and support staff on diversity. We designed and held a three-day diversity training workshop in February 2004.

Two years later, the Board hired me to provide diversity training for all staff in the school district. I conducted a total of 14 sessions; each session had approximately 25 to 30 participants. They included administrators; teachers from elementary, middle, and high school; counselors; and support staff. The participants were diverse in race and gender. The sessions were scheduled with lunch during the school day to accommodate the teachers' work schedule. The school districts hired substitute teachers to handle the teachers' classes.

I utilized a three-person team that included myself and a combination of a white man or woman and either a Black woman or Hispanic woman. My team members were colleagues that had worked with me on other similar projects. We conducted two-day follow-up sessions that were scheduled approximately three to six weeks after each training. They were held for three hours each day and designed to work with small groups of participants at the high schools, middle schools, and elementary schools. In addition, I consulted with the school principals and several central office administrators.

My work in York City paved the way for my contract with the York County School of Technology. The School of Technology specialized in providing education to students who were interested in pursuing careers in auto mechanics, culinary science, cosmetology, and other trades. The school administrator was aware of my work and requested a diversity training for the faculty. It was like the training I led for York

City. Instead of three consecutive days, I spread each normal three-day training over three weeks. In addition, rather than using a team, I conducted the sessions alone.

NEA Dialogue on Social Justice and LGBTQ Issues

The NEA Office of the President interviewed and awarded me a contract to help NEA members achieve an initiative that was approved during the 2012 NEA Annual Representative Assembly. It called for the NEA to re-affirm its commitment to promoting social justice, equality of educational opportunity for every student, and professional status for every educator by:

- Holding a special dialogue on social issues facing ethnic minority members, students, and communities of color.
- Addressing diversity in Association leadership and active engagement of ethnic minority leaders at all levels.
- Developing recommendations for ensuring equitable education opportunities for students of color.
- Partnering with progressive organizations to address today's civil rights issues.
- Holding a dialogue on the unique issues of LGBTQ students and educators.

A committee was established to oversee this effort. I worked with the co-chairs, Becky Pringle, a member of the NEA Executive Committee and now NEA President, and Pat Foster-Brooks, the past OEA President. The committee also included staff from the NEA President's office, the NEA Executive Director's office, and the Director and Assistant Director of the Human and Civil Rights Division.

My colleague Dr. Susan Gallant and I planned and facilitated two dialogue weekend sessions: (1) a Dialogue on Social Issues on December 7–8, 2012; and (2) a Dialogue on LGBTQ Issues on May 4–5, 2013. Both were in Washington and utilized a Provocateur Fishbowl process which was new to me. This process brought together a group of experts who presented information, thoughts, and feelings for the purpose of stirring up further discussion and action. The Social Justice session had the following provocateurs:

- James Ferg-Cadima, Regional Council for the Mexican American Legal Defense and Education Fund
- David J. Johns, Policy and Research Director for Obama for America
- Stacy R. Long, Director of Public Policy and Government Affairs at the National Gay and Lesbian Task Force
- Karen Narasaki, former President and Executive Director of the Asian American Justice Center
- Ahniwake Rose, Executive Director of the National Indian Education Association

The Provocateurs for the LGBTQ session were:

- Mara Keisling, Executive Director of the National Center for Transgender Equality
- Darren Phelps, National Executive Director of Pride at Work

- Marty Rouse, National Field Director for the Human Rights Campaign
- Adam Tenner, Executive Director of Metro Teen AIDS

Susan and I led the fishbowl sessions. In a fishbowl session, there is an inner circle of chairs and an outer circle. The people who sat on the inside were a part of the fishbowl. As they discuss a topic, those on outside observed. We included an open chair to allow participants to ask questions. At the end of the sessions, participants returned to small discussion groups to reflect and develop lists of what they had heard and how they could use the information. Participants developed a two-minute non-verbal public service announcement that represented the results of the two-day Social Justice Dialogue session. As a result of the Social Justice Dialogue session, Educators for Social Justice, a group of 51 educators who were NEA leaders and representatives from national civil rights organizations, was formed. These dialogue sessions reconnected me to the work I was engaged in during the 1970s and 1980s. After working in the field for over 40 years, I found it disturbing that some of the same issues I had worked on remained unresolved.

CHAPTER 16 REFLECTION QUESTIONS

---

1. Individual: Are you an entrepreneur or have you used an entrepreneurial approach in your career? Who did you seek advice and support from? What relationships and resources did you acquire to navigate your business or entrepreneurial career experience?

2. Group Discussion: Give each person 3–5 minutes to share their individual response with the group. As a group, list some of the similarities and differences highlighted in the sharing session. Also, discuss one or two lessons each person has learned.

DEI Innovator Elsie Y. Cross and the EYCA Story

"Most people in this society are not willing to look at the systemic issues. We almost always put the burden on the victim rather than on the perpetuation of a system that helped create the victim. But if you can get to the systemic level, you get to the source. Our work is based on the fundamental belief that racism and sexism are deeply rooted in our culture. We have never resolved these problems because people are not given an opportunity to talk about these issues in a safe environment."

—ELSIE Y. CROSS, a change agent and
President and CEO of Elsie Y. Cross Associates, Inc.

Source: The *Los Angeles Times Magazine* article
"Elsie Cross vs. The Suits" by J.P. White, August 9, 1992

———————————

When the *Los Angeles Times Magazine* interviewed Elsie Yancy Cross in 1992, I never imagined her words would accurately describe what is happening today in 2024. Elsie's words remind me why we were able to work together with our colleagues as change agents committed to dismantling all forms of oppression. They also fill my heart with gratitude for being able to know and work with her for over 40 years.

Elsie, a Philadelphia native, was the daughter of funeral homeowner, Daniel Yancy, and Mary Skidmore Yancy. Elsie was a force of nature. A powerhouse. A trailblazer. The Madame C.J. Walker of the diversity industry. Today, she would be known as a diversity, equity, and inclusion (DEI) innovator. Elsie launched her consulting firm, Elsie Y. Cross Associates, Inc. (EYCA), with a dream and her life experience, intelligence, savvy, and willingness to include others in 1977. Her passion and commitment to changing organizations and society to recognize, accept, and fully utilize everyone, regardless of their age, ethnicity, gender, national origin, race, religion, or sexual orientation, was at the core of everything she did as President and CEO.

She was a product of the Philadelphia public school system and graduated from Girls High School in 1946. In 1949, she earned a Bachelor of Science degree from Temple University. Almost 20 years later, she returned to Temple and completed two master's degrees in business administration and educational psychology in 1967.

She began her career teaching at William Penn High School for Girls, Germantown High School, and Olney High School. Elsie quickly became active in the Philadelphia Teacher's Union, where she served on the contract negotiating committee and became Vice President of the Philadelphia Federation of Teachers. She later worked as an administrator in the Philadelphia school district's Office of Inter-group and Integration.

She also wrote *Managing Diversity—The Courage to*

Lead in 2000; published *The Language Guide*; and founded *The Diversity Factor*, a quarterly e-journal, which was recognized as a leading source of information for people facing the deeper issues of diversity. She co-edited a second book, *The Diversity Factor: Capturing the Competitive Advantage of a Changing Workforce*, with Margaret Blackburn White.

As a thought leader, she served as the NTL Board Chair and taught a leadership class at the University of Pennsylvania's Wharton Executive Education Center. She was a sought-after speaker frequently interviewed by national publications and radio and television programs and contributed to President William J. Clinton's Initiative on Race.

Elsie received numerous awards and recognitions. One of her most cherished was the prestigious Trailblazers Award. She received it along with the poet Dr. Maya Angelou. She died of a heart attack on December 7, 2009, and was survived by her son, Barry Cross, Jr.; grandson, Barry Cross, III; granddaughter, Alexandra; stepson, Kevin Cross; and family members.

MEETING ELSIE

I first met Elsie in 1970 while I was conducting a conference for the NEA Center for Human Relations in Harpers Ferry, West Virginia. The conference involved teams of students, teachers, school administrators, parents, and a few activists who had been identified by the U.S. Justice Department. The teams came from school districts in the Northeast. Elsie was a member of the Philadelphia team.

Over the next few years, our paths would overlap in our work with NTL and Bell Laboratories. Elsie's NTL involvement began when her school district sent her to a nine-week summer institute at their Bethel, Maine site. She was involved in the effort that challenged NTL to include more Blacks in their programs and which was ultimately successful; thanks to the work she and cohorts did, more Blacks had opportunities to participate in trainings.

In 1972, she left the school system to become an independent consultant. Bell Laboratories was one of her first clients for whom she launched the Men and Women in the Work Environment Program. It was designed in response to a $30 million lawsuit against AT&T for discrimination against women. During this same period, I worked as a contract trainer for Bell Laboratories conducting One-Day Affirmative Action Workshops.

Later, when my NEA colleagues and I were pursuing our doctorates, Elsie became our group facilitator and gave Kate, Delyte, and me much needed advice while we worked on our degrees and formed Resources for Change, a consulting group that focused on racism and sexism. She told us, "You need to finish your doctorate work and then let's get serious about the work you have been doing that will make a real difference." That intervention led us to focus and finish our program with Union Institute.

Elsie's tenacious drive and passion greatly impacted me, especially when I watched her create a safe container for white male leaders to be vulnerable and reveal their beliefs about race. She was able to gain their trust which created strong client relationships. I found her efforts helpful as I continued to develop my ability to do the same. Working with her helped me transition from a full-time employee to a full-time entrepreneur. It also opened the door for me to create wealth that gave my family greater opportunities.

WHAT IS EYCA?

I wound up working for more than 40 years with her and EYCA, an organizational development consulting firm that specialized in helping Fortune 100 companies manage diversity. EYCA was a diversity, equity, and inclusion (DEI) innovator before these terms were commonly used in society. In short, we were trailblazers in the field.

My EYCA colleagues became my second family. When Elsie launched the firm, she formed a diverse senior management team that consisted of four colleagues, including myself, Delyte (a white woman), Kate (a white woman), and Joseph Potts (a white man), the Executive Director of NTL. We all held doctorates except Elsie. She was known for building strong and knowledgeable teams.

As CEO, Elsie generally made initial contact with the potential client. When we first started, all our organizational and corporate clients had white men in key leadership positions. We were successful because of Elsie's amazing talent in relating to and building relationships with white male leaders. She laid the foundation so the rest of us could conduct individual and group interviews, gather data, facilitate workshops, and do follow-ups.

Eventually, the firm began to take on more consultants which led to the formation of the EYCA Network, our strongest asset. The Network consisted of men and women of different racial, ethnic, and cultural identities as well as different sexual orientations and religious beliefs. Members lived all over the United States and were independent contractors. Using this model helped the firm avoid having a huge overhead expense of salary and benefits. It did, however, allow the firm to compensate its members handsomely. I thought this was a savvy business decision and used it in my own firm.

Most of the Network members had advanced degrees and were also NTL members. They came to the firm possessing, and were committed to:

- Increasing their understanding of the history and so-cial-political realities of oppression and discrimination.
- Studying the principles and practices of organizational development and change.
- Committed to academic and experiential learning about how adults learn.
- Working to understand their own attitudes and behaviors toward people who are different by race, gender, sexual orientation, and physical ability.

As we took on more clients and expanded our services, our Network increased. In response to our growth, we developed an orientation training program for new members that taught them our philosophy and approach. We paired them with senior staff mentors who shared the same race and gender identity. When new members worked with clients for the first time in a workshop setting, they served as co-trainers with their senior staff mentors. All these efforts maintained the integrity of our firm.

HOW EYCA SERVED CLIENTS AS A DEI INNOVATOR

We only took on clients who were willing to make a long-range commitment of several years. Additionally, EYCA required that the work start with the CEO and senior management team because we believed real change started from the top. In our work, we used the strategy of Managing Diversity which referred to addressing issues of racism, sexism, heterosexism, and other forms of discrimination embodied in an organization's policies and practices. Implementing this strategy helped us work with clients to identify the type of culture they wanted that would benefit all people. We adopted the "culture-change process" developed by John Kotter and Chris Argyris, organizational development theorists, in our work. This innovative process was pioneering. No other firms were using it at the time. Nowadays, it is embedded in diversity and inclusion.

In our client work, we introduced the Managing and Working in a Diverse Workforce Environment model for strategic change. The strategic change we had in mind was to integrate concepts of fairness and equity with the business goals of organizations. As we did the work, we remained flexible enough to refine our process. Our refinement led to the Managing Diversity Intervention Model. It had three overlapping and recurring processes: Start Up, Capacity Building, and Institutionalization.

Start Up included five steps:
- Step 1: Problem Identification
- Step 2: Data Collection
- Step 3: Analysis and Diagnosis
- Step 4: Education and Awareness
- Step 5: Organizing and Implementing

Capacity Building included on-going consultation, development of internal capacity, metrics, and organizational culture review. Institutionalization was the final process that included the building and maintaining of the new culture. As a result of our work, we laid the foundation for today's diversity professionals including Chief Diversity Officers, internal diversity committees, identity groups, and external diversity advisory boards.

EYCA CLIENTS

EYCA worked with companies in the communications, education, finance, manufacturing, petrochemical, and pharmaceutical industries. We also worked with several nonprofit organizations and universities. In 1981, EYCA began working with a petrochemical company; Elsie had met the manager at an NTL Management Work Conference where she was the Dean (team leader). They held several exploratory meetings, and by early 1982, EYCA was hired to deliver our Managing and Working in Diverse Work Group Situations Program. Due to the amount of work scheduled for the first full year, I requested and was approved for a one-year leave without pay from the NEA so I could engage in this work.

Elsie, Delyte, and I began conducting pre-workshop interviews with individual managers who were white and mostly men. We also interviewed participants who were women and people of color. In our interviews with women and people of color, we coached them on how to discuss the reality of their positions and the racial and sexual discriminatory issues they encountered and treatment they received from white managers. Having their participation contributed to the success of the workshops.

The workshops were staffed by four EYCA members: Elsie, Delyte or Kate, Joseph, and me. Following the workshops, we conducted post-workshop interviews. The process was very intensive, and the participants significantly increased their awareness and understanding of the issues. In response to the workshops, the petrochemical company established a management committee. Other groups were established including a sensing and feedback group, a woman's group, and several luncheon groups. Several one-day follow-up sessions resulted. As a result of the momentum, the employees began to assume greater responsibilities for the change process. This contract lasted approximately two to three years.

A second major client was a pharmaceutical company. This intervention built on what had taken place in the previous intervention with the petrochemical company. Some aspects were refined and added too. The most significant addition was the introduction of the Cultural Change Process which was named "Synergy through Diversity." It included an intensive five-day culture change workshop for the management group. Many specific action plans were created, including: 1) conducting champion training; 2) starting same race and gender and cross race and gender support groups to discuss how to cope and develop strategies for effective informal relationships; 3) designing an assessment tool for measuring behavior in concert with the new culture; 4) demonstrating sensitivity to work, personal, and family life issues; and 5) ensuring the inclusion of white women and people of color in key developmental positions.

As the firm grew, Elsie hired some staff that worked out of an office in the Germantown section of Philadelphia. She had always been very supportive of her family. She employed one of her sisters, a brother, and a nephew. Later, her son, Barry, prepared himself to eventually become a member of the Network. As EYCA grew, several members of the Network, including Carol Brantley and Daisy Rios, took on staff responsibilities in addition to continuing in their project management, workshop dean, and workshop team member roles. As a result, the firm was able to expand and seek more clients.

MY EYCA EXPERIENCE

I, like my colleagues, wore many hats. As a consultant, I was a senior management team member, a project manager of several clients, a dean of numerous workshop staff teams, a trainer, and a member of many staff teams. Conducting workshops was my most fulfilling role. What was most eye-opening in these workshops was observing many participants share their new awareness. Their insights included the way women and people of color were discriminated against, passed over, not acknowledged for their suggestions, and underutilized. It was encouraging to hear white participants reflect on what they heard, witnessed, or experienced when they were growing up. Often what they heard were expressions of prejudice and bias toward people of color. Many of the older whites would initially say they didn't have any early experiences with people of color but would then remember they had a Black nanny. Whites were enlightened when they heard stories from participants of color about their childhood and how they learned to successfully navigate the white world.

In addition to what participants shared, I would sometimes offer my own experiences to help white participants gain a true understanding. For instance, I told them what it was like to travel first class as a Black man who frequently encountered white flight attendants that often assumed I was flying coach. In an effort to cope with their bias, I always dressed appropriately in a suit or a jacket. Like many Black people, I was taught to dress my best to ensure I was treated appropriately.

This was not the case for my white colleague who would often travel wearing jeans and shoes without socks. How we were treated was different because there was, and remains, two sets of rules for whites and people of color.

Another example I used was being mistakenly identified when I arrived at a client's office. A white employee came to escort me. She saw a white man sitting near me, looked directly at him, and announced "Dr. Leeke." The white man responded, "No." Hearing his response, she became very apologetic when she realized I was in fact Dr. Leeke. These examples represent a few of the microaggressions I, and other people of color, experienced and shared. Our sharing made a significant impact because it helped white participants understand the daily microaggressions faced by people of color.

One thing that has been significant throughout my work life has been the role of a team. I value this aspect of work and life. Teamwork was front and center in EYCA. We spent thousands of hours in meetings where we struggled with every issue, concept, strategy, internal dynamics, and conflicts as we grew as a firm. It was not easy because we were strong, smart, highly skilled, and independent individuals. We learned to listen to each other and disagree with a willingness to compromise. We used Myers-Briggs Type Indicator to understand each other's strengths and weaknesses. All of it created a community of care that supported us, especially when we were triggered in our workshops. In addition, we each had our own self-care practices. Mine included finding alone time to reflect and recharge. My alone time was often spent swimming and exercising in gyms. I used my travel time to decompress before arriving home and seeing my family. My trips with colleagues and solo trips were spent thinking and talking about my family's current activities. All of it helped me free my mind from the deep work I was involved in.

I cherish the relationships that were born out of our teamwork and continue to maintain them today. Some of my strongest relationships were with women of color: Carol Brantley, a Black woman; Toni Dunton-Butler, a Black woman; Brenda Dancil-Jones, a Black woman; Barbara Riley, a Black woman; Rita Andrews, a Black woman; Shirley Fletcher, a Black woman of Jamaican descent; Daisy Rios, a Puerto Rican woman; and Celia Young, a Chinese woman. Because we traveled together, we had many opportunities to talk about our life struggles and successes, families, and societal issues. Our conversations forged a strong bond and helped me understand what they faced as women of color, wives, mothers, and significant others. I am certain it helped me in my relationship with Theresa and my children. We all interacted and got to know our families.

I was able to establish relationships with men of color in a similar manner. However, the EYCA model of diverse workshop staff teams only allowed for one man of color to conduct workshops in team settings. Although my interaction was limited because of the model, I became close friends with Dr. Chip Henderson, a Black man, while working on a program that focused on Black men. Our relationship confirmed my ongoing belief in the power and strength of Black men. We got to know each other's families, explored other work opportunities, and engaged in conversations about the issues of the day. Our relationship was the springboard to cultivating other relationships with Black men, including Jamie Washington, Curt Waller, Norman Jones, Douglas Fletcher, Jack Gant, Barry Cross, Rich Huntley, Nelson Hewitt, Ollie Malone, and Fred Bryant. In addition, I was able to do the same thing with Guillermo Cuellar, a Colombian man, and Elfi Martinez, a Puerto Rican man.

I developed similar relationships with white women and men. My relationships with Delyte and Kate were the longest as we worked together at the NEA and during our doctoral program. The relationships with other white women and men, including Michael Burkart, Lynda Detterman, Tom Finn, Susan Gallant, Bill Gregory, Dan Holden, Mark Kaplan, Suzanne Kaplan, Judith Leibowitz, Denise Matteucci, Rob Neal, Joseph Potts, Bo Razak, Duncan Spellman, Lynda Stolzman, Duane Wade, Patty Wilson, and Nancy Zane, were just as deep and long-lasting. Like with my brothers and sisters of color, they enhanced my awareness and understanding of issues between whites and people of color as well as women and men.

Finally, because in EYCA there was a strong commitment to dealing with LGBTQ issues and there were gay, lesbian, and bi-sexual members of the organization, I was able to significantly increase my awareness and understanding of how their lives were different from mine as a heterogenous man.

Celebration was a core value of EYCA. We made a conscious effort to acknowledge and celebrate our wins and efforts.

One of the big celebrations happened when Elsie arranged for the entire Network and office staff to spend an expense-paid weekend in St. John, a Caribbean Island. Our spouses and life partners were also included in the trip. During the weekend, we did some work on our rebranding and future directions as a firm. Most of the time was spent relaxing and celebrating.

WORKING WITH
A PHARMACEUTICAL COMPANY

My work with the pharmaceutical company was unique because it had three Black men in senior management positions in the 1980s. Elsie thought I would be a good fit as a project manager. During my tenure as project manager, a Black man held the position of vice president of research and development and later became president. In addition, the director of finance and the director of human resources were Black men. My first assignment was to shepherd the company through the EYCA managing diversity intervention process. I served as the workshop dean and a member of most of the workshop teams that moved through the entire organization. The workshops began with the top leadership and concluded with workers in the factory operations. This was truly a rewarding experience because it showed how a group of Black men could work together successfully. In the midst of these efforts, the company transitioned in name and focus. I leveraged my organizational development and management experience to help them navigate these changes.

WORKING WITH A FINANCIAL
SERVICES CORPORATION

The financial services corporation was one of my most re-warding long-term client relationships. It was one of EYCA's first major clients. We worked with them through several mergers. Our organizational development and management experience helped them navigate these changes. We also brought our Managing Diversity Intervention Model to them which introduced three-day awareness workshops. During the workshops, the participants reflected on when they first became aware of their racial identity and how they related to other racial groups. These sessions were often very emotional. Many of the white participants recalled what and when they had learned about Black people. To give them a sense of what white people learned at an early age, we shared a quote from Lillian Smith's book, *Killers of the Dream*: "I learned it is possible to be a Christian and a white southerner simultane-ously; to be a gentlewoman and an arrogant callous creature in the same moment; to pray at night and ride a Jim Crow car the next morning and to feel comfortable doing both." This quote was the catalyst for deepening the discussion. Several white participants told stories about their relatives who were Ku Klux Klan members and witnesses to lynchings of Black people. The Black participants also shared their separate but equal experiences when they were forced to drink from dif-ferent water fountains and could not stay in hotels when they traveled. It's worth noting that these discussions probably offered participants their first public conversation about race in a diverse group. If these conversations were happening nowadays, they would be a perfect fit for the work Michele Norris, a Black journalist and author of *Our Hidden Conversations: What Americans Really Think About Race and Identity*, is doing with The Race Card Project she launched in 2010.

After a couple of years, we recognized that the people of color spent the bulk of their time educating their white colleagues during the workshops. We realized the corporation needed to have the opportunity to focus on their issues. After gathering and analyzing our data, we recommended workshop experiences for people of color. During the five-day workshop series, we used some of the material from my Ph.D.'s Project Demonstrating Excellence. Each workshop was staffed with a Black man, a Hispanic man, a Black woman, and a Hispanic or Asian woman. Participants were Asian, Black, Hispanic, and biracial. During these workshops, participants examined the topics of who am I, interpersonal and intrapersonal relationships, minority collusion, collaboration, and how to use power.

Some of the most emotional conversations occurred when we discussed the issue of color. I will always remember several conversations where Black women talked about the impact of colorism; a term believed to be first coined by author Alice Walker. According to *Merriam-Webster Dictionary*, colorism is defined as "prejudice or discrimination especially within a racial or ethnic group favoring people with lighter skin over those with darker skin." It is not racism although there is a clear relationship. The dark-skinned Black women shared what it was like to be dark even in their own family dynamics. That was countered by several light-skinned Black women who spoke about being resented for their complexion. Biracial women commented on the issues they faced, including mistreatment due to their hair texture and style. The dynamic between the relationship of the men of color with the women of color was also a hot topic. Throughout the workshops, participants explored issues they had never discussed before. It was painful for everyone involved. The level of vulnerability expressed created a lot of tears, new understandings, and heartfelt apologies. In the evenings, the workshop staff would debrief and have their own emotional session. These workshops were different than the diversity-focused workshops because in these, one could address topics like colorism and how it impacted people in their familial relationships that were never discussed in the presence of white people. Due to our EYCA relationships, we were able to bring topics like colorism into our full Network sessions. This is what made the EYCA experience so powerful and rewarding.

DEVELOPING A CORPORATE AFRICAN AMERICAN MEN'S PROGRAM

The work I am discussing in this section refers to an African American men's program that was based on the unique challenges they faced in corporate America. The African American senior managers that I worked with repeatedly encountered unseen barriers: lack of direct performance feedback, effective socialization, role ambiguity in relationships, and unseen organizational standards even though they were recruited as top talent, based on academic skills and significant prior experience. These factors were not enough for African American men to achieve individual and collective success. In recognition of these factors, the corporation's leadership demonstrated its commitment to the advancement of Black men in senior management by launching the African American Men's Program. A group of 15 high-performing, high-potential African American men and their managers participated in the program. The men were selected based on a track record of success as well as their assessed potential to take on greater levels of responsibility. Their managers, who were both white and people of color, were involved because they played a key role in their advancement. The highest level African American male executive sponsored the program. We reported to him directly.

In developing the African American Men's Program, I partnered with Chip, another Black man. We received assistance from Barbara, a Black woman who was the client project manager; Delyte, a white woman; and Michael, a white man. The purpose of the program was to ensure meaningful development and retention of African American men within the organization. This effort also continued the building and institutionalization of an inclusive culture.

We utilized information from two of the corporation's studies, Company Exit Interviews of African American Male

Managers and Senior Leaders Interview Study, to design the program. These studies revealed three key factors that differentiated and determined the success of African American men at the company. They included:

- Creating a high expectation of success within the African American men and those who work with them.
- Creating the ability to form career-enhancing relationships with mutual trust across identity groups.
- Increased ability to access critical developmental assignments.

The program consisted of eight objectives:

- Identifying and managing barriers to success.
- Increasing the ability to identify and navigate political climate in situations and in the organization.
- Increasing participants' confidence, competence, and credibility.
- Understanding how to use power.
- Increasing participants' capacity to manage conflict and dialogue with managers and peers.
- Identifying and managing discrimination as a barrier to success.
- Building alliances and support within and across all identity groups.
- Increasing participants' ability to manage their own career.

The seven key program elements were:
- Self-assessments
- Defining and examining keys to success
- Building trustful relationships across identity groups
- Simulations
- Individual, small, and large group exploration and discussion
- Intense feedback sessions
- Designing and implementing action steps

Chip and I supplemented our own lived experiences with several resources, most notably Price M. Cobb and Judith L. Turnock's book, *Cracking the Corporate Code: The Revealing Success Stories of 32 African-American Executives*, and David A. Thomas and John J. Gabarro's book, *Breaking Through: The Making of Minority Executives in Corporate America*.

Barbara suggested we use the Leadership Circle Profile™ to help the men examine their productive or unproductive style of leadership. The Leadership Style Profile™ is a 360-degree profile that measures the two primary leadership domains: Creative Competencies and Reactive Tendencies. Creative Competencies measures how one achieves results, brings out the best in others, leads with vision, enhances one's own development, acts with integrity and courage, and improves organizational systems. Reactive Tendencies are leadership styles emphasizing caution over creating results, self-protection over productive engagement, and aggression over building alignment. These self-limiting styles over-emphasize the focus on gaining the approval of others, protecting yourself, and gaining results through high-control tactics.

Each participant completed the profile and had his manager, and several peers and subordinates, complete the profile as well. Later, time was spent reviewing and discussing the results, which generated very valuable insights. This process helped to confirm some of the feedback they were getting from their participant colleagues. It also matched their own insights from information they were gaining in the workshop sessions. Because we saw how powerful the profiles were, Chip and I also completed ours and spent time reviewing and discussing our results.

Fourteen of the 15 men completed the program. Several received promotions during the program. Others received feedback indicating they were on the fast track to higher level positions. Some were impacted by the corporation's merger and began looking for new opportunities. The program ended with a wonderful celebration at a banquet where each participant received a certificate. I was excited and encouraged by what we had accomplished. We had met and worked with some incredible men and got to know some additional members of the organization. The supervisors gained valuable insights about how to manage the careers of others, especially Black men. As a result of the program's success, the corporation began exploring the possibility of having a similar program for women of color.

WORKING WITH
A MANUFACTURING COMPANY

Our work with a manufacturing company represented an example of what it takes to achieve substantial change. Because we were committed to long-term work with our clients, we never believed it was enough to solely facilitate workshops that helped to increase awareness of the need to change. Instead, we focused our efforts on identifying the policies and practices within an organization. We also introduced the concept of tracking to white managers. Tracking is observing what is happening and how it is impacting the goals and objectives of the desired change. It was one of the core diversity skills EYCA wanted its clients to have.

The company's management and diversity committee were committed to increasing women and people of color in the company. They recruited highly qualified individuals from top colleges and universities who had 4.0 or higher GPAs and were very active in school activities. After bringing in two recruited classes, they noticed none of the women and people of color were in the company's top performance rankings as they thought would happen. Utilizing the tracking skill helped them recognize the company needed to do more to support women and people of color to integrate into the company's unique culture.

Next, the company's management and diversity team examined development and promotional practices. After two years, they noted that very few women and people of color had achieved high performance ranking; some had left the company. We suggested they interview members from the two classes of new employees. They found new employees had received very little mentoring or development and had been assigned non-challenging work. Given this information, we suggested interviewing their white managers.

The interview results were illuminating. The white managers said they wanted their employees to be successful. They assigned them tasks they knew they could do, but weren't difficult, challenging, or ones that would demonstrate their capacity to perform at higher levels. In evaluating the results, they discovered they had a ranking system that gave high scores for more challenging work. This was similar to the scoring system used in gymnastic and swimming competitions where high scores are awarded based on the degree of difficulty. As we went deeper in the interviews, the managers began to admit they didn't feel comfortable with the women and people of color. They wanted them to be successful but didn't realize they harbored uncertainty that women and people of color could do top-level work. This is what we would call "implicit bias" today. In addition, some of the white male managers were not comfortable relating to the women because they were afraid they would be accused of sexual harassment. They also said they didn't know how to relate to the people of color.

As a result, we began working more with the managers in one-on-one and group sessions to help them shift their mindset and behavior. In a year or two, we witnessed positive changes such as new employees receiving more mentoring and challenging assignments from their managers, which resulted in higher rankings and more promotions.

This work required a much greater depth of exploration and capacity to understand oppression, listen deeply, and probe unconscious biases. To be successful, you must recognize that you consciously choose your mindset and behavior. Your understanding of oppression is a journey. Start with small steps and a willingness to listen and learn from people who are different from you. Check out the reflection questions at the end of this chapter and the resources at the end of this book for more information.

Elsie Y. Cross, Delyte Frost, and Carol Brantley at EYCA celebration in St. John in the U.S. Virgin Islands

John Leeke with his EYCA colleagues
Dr. Shirley Fletcher and Dr. Daisy Rios

CHAPTER 17 REFLECTION QUESTIONS

1. Individual: What is your understanding of oppression and how it shows up in the workplace and everyday life? What has been your experience with oppression (provide details)? What did you learn from reading this chapter that has expanded your understanding? Did you experience any aha moments?

2. Group Discussion: Give each person 3–5 minutes to share their individual response with the group. As a group, list some of the similarities and differences highlighted in the sharing session. Also, discuss one or two lessons each person has learned.

CHAPTER 18

The Story of the NEA Affirmative Action UniServ Intern Program for Women and Ethnic Minorities

"I knew that God was calling me to have an impact in a much bigger arena. The internship provided me the self-knowledge, support, and skills to fulfill God's purpose for my life."

—BRYANT WARREN, a change agent, a member of the Intern Class of 2004, and UniServ Director at the Illinois Education Association

———————————

The NEA Affirmative Action UniServ Intern Program for Women and Ethnic Minorities (NEA Intern Program) is my most singular greatest career accomplishment as a consultant because it gave me an opportunity to share my knowledge and skills with a community of professionals committed to change. It also allowed me to fulfill one of my life purposes and to help others fulfill theirs.

The NEA Intern Program was about change: (1) changing the makeup of the UniServ program with greater inclusion of women and people of color; (2) significant change in the lives of individuals selected for the program; and (3) change in the preparation of the staff who serve the members of the NEA.

The UniServ program was established in 1970 as the national staffing effort that served the NEA's membership. In my work, I directly altered the lives of over 300 NEA members. They were able to impact other lives and continue to impact many more. The program had longevity and lasted 27 years. I was with the program the entire time.

HOW THE NEA INTERN PROGRAM BEGAN

Less than a year after I left the NEA and established my own organizational development and training firm, I received a call from Patricia Orange, a white woman who served as the NEA's Director of Human Resources. Pat asked if I would come in to talk with her and Vinnie Kiernan, a white man who was the NEA Mid-Atlantic Regional Director. In the meeting, they explained that the minority NEA members had complained about the lack of women and people of color in the UniServ program for several years. The NEA finally addressed this issue as an affirmative action concern at the 1986 NEA Representative Assembly. In response, the NEA Board of Directors told the Executive Director, Terry Herdon, to develop a program that addressed the issue.

Pat and Vinnie asked if I would be interested in helping to design such a program. They knew I had done a great deal of work on race, gender, and diversity issues, and was very familiar with how the NEA and its affiliates worked. After several weeks, I returned with an affirmative action plan to address the increase in the number of white women and people of color. The plan was submitted and approved by Terry and the NEA Executive Committee. Shortly afterwards, I was contracted to begin implementing the plan that would create the NEA Intern Program.

PREPARATION FOR THE NEA INTERN PROGRAM'S FIRST CLASS IN SUMMER 1987

I approached the preparation process with a high degree of intention, trust in my insight and experience, a knowledge of what it takes to educate adults, and respect for the UniServ staff and their work. I started by arranging and conducting a two-day focus group with selected national and state staff who had the responsibility of selecting, hiring, and managing current professional staff. They helped to outline the responsibilities of the UniServ staff position as well as the desired skills, knowledge, and prior experiences. They shared their thoughts about the kind of preparation that was required to compete for jobs. The group confirmed many of the thoughts I had; these became part of the initial plan. The focus group also served as a sounding board and a source of active participants in the plan's implementation. With the results of the focus group, I developed the training as well as an internship component that would prepare prospective candidates to be hired as UniServ staff. I also began a plan for announcing the program and a process for selecting potential intern candidates.

Garfield Bright, a Black man who was a staff member of

the NEA's Field Service Division, was assigned to work with me on logistics. We had to identify a facility to conduct the initial four-week summer intensive training in the DC area. We also had to select trainers, managers, and subject matter experts.

Selecting the site was an interesting endeavor. I had experience in conducting many residential trainings and knew that an intensive four-week experience with adults required a special type of facility. I recommended Garfield check out the Adult Education facility at the University of Maryland. I had participated in some training events there and thought it would be a good site. Unfortunately, I must not have been clear to focus on just the Adult Education facility and why. We needed a different type of location with a retreat setting, hotel rooms, a dining facility, and meeting rooms in the same building. He contacted the main campus in College Park instead. When we met with the university representative, I knew right away the campus offerings would never work because they were planning to house our participants in dormitory rooms. Getting to and from the dormitories, classrooms, and the cafeteria in hot, humid July weather was a recipe for disaster. After conferring with Garfield, we informed the representative this would not meet our needs; in any case, the Adult Education facility was not available. At this point, I suggested we explore the 4-H Center in Chevy Chase, Maryland. While it wasn't perfect, it met most of the criteria and it did work out reasonably well for our first year.

For the next 26 years, we held the training in different hotels in the DC metropolitan area. Our best site was the Bolder

Center, a retreat center with a campus setting and several buildings in Montgomery County, Maryland. It had been a Catholic religious order seminary. One of the buildings had hotel rooms, a cafeteria, and an activity center. Another building served as the training facility with different-size meeting rooms, the latest multimedia equipment, and an on-site tech team.

The four-week training program consisted of five modules: Organizing, Bargaining, Arbitration, Organizational Development, and Diversity. These modules were developed based on suggestions from the focus group members. They were very clear about potential staff people needing to know how to organize, bargain, and arbitrate. This was fundamental union work. Based on my NEA experience and doctoral work, I believed the organizational development and diversity modules were critical. Diversity concepts were woven throughout the training with special attention during the final week. We devoted an entire day to addressing diversity by having them explore their race and gender identities. They drew pictures of themselves and illustrated who they were in their everyday lives. They shared and discussed their drawings with the group. I also introduced them to the Dimensions of Diversity, a model Kate and I developed when we were at the NEA and expanded it during our doctoral work. The Dimensions of Diversity model gives a roadmap on how to explore and understand the complexities of race and gender. In addition, I believed the training should focus on attitudes, knowledge, and skills of diversity.

In selecting the training staff, we needed trainers who

were both subject matter experts and were capable of delivering training in organizing, bargaining, and arbitrating. With the help of some of the focus group members and other state and national staff, we selected diverse trainers and assembled training teams of two to four members for each module. I took responsibility for the organizational development and diversity module. I selected my colleague Dr. Bill Gaskins, a Black man who worked as a staff member of the Pennsylvania State Education Association, to serve as a co-trainer. Dr. Bill had a strong background in organizational development and was an excellent trainer.

In preparation for the first class, Bill and I spent several work sessions developing the weeklong design. We believed the interns should understand organizational development. We borrowed from the following theorists: (1) Cecil Bell, Wendell French, and Robert Zawachi and their book, *Organization Development: Theory, Practice, and Research*; (2) Peter Senge's book, *The Fifth Discipline: The Art & Practice of the Learning Organization*; and (3) William Bridges's book, *Managing Transitions: Making the Most of Change*. We also relied on the knowledge and expertise I gained while working on the Task Force on Urban Education, Urban Institutes, and Urban Upswing Project. We developed a case study to analyze and design plans for addressing the needed changes. It was built around a community. The teacher association's role was to make changes in its organization, school system, and broader community. The case study was later incorporated into the other three modules on organizing, bargaining, and arbitrating. This helped link all the modules together. Diversity issues were also included in the case study.

Every year, Bill and I would arrange to meet at a location of equal distance from our homes. We mainly met at the Hunt Valley Marriott just outside Baltimore. We would review our design and make any necessary changes and have lunch. Bill would arrive the day before the start of our week. We spent a lot of time together and shared stories about our families and other work assignments. Over the years, we included our wives on several trips connected to the program as well as attending some social events. We also took a cruise together. Unfortunately, Bill passed after a short illness on February 4, 2011. I had the honor of speaking at his memorial service at St. Paul's Episcopal Church in Harrisburg, Pennsylvania. At the time, Bill's death was the most difficult loss I had experienced other than my parents.

After the program was designed and the trainers were selected, we focused on promoting and recruiting. We developed information to announce the program that included objectives, who the program was for, applicant requirements, expectations of the interns, what the training would consist of, and the time and financial commitments. An application and a system for interviewing were developed. Pat and Garfield promoted the program and application process. A team of NEA managers reviewed the applications, rated the applicants, and selected the candidates to be interviewed. Sixteen people were selected to participate in the first class of the NEA Intern Program. They were Black men and women and Hispanic and white women. Upon their arrival, the interns were told, "This is the first day of your new life and it will never be the same."

THE FIRST INTERN TRAINING EXPERIENCE

Several interns said the four-week training was like "being in bootcamp." The days were long, starting with a group break-fast at 8 a.m. Formal sessions began at 9:00 a.m. and ended around 9 p.m., with breaks for lunch and dinner. After the formal sessions ended, participants often had homework. They were given the weekends off to enjoy what the area had to offer.

One of the major aspects of the four-week training was the inclusion of the Myers-Briggs Type Indicator (MBTI), a well-researched personality instrument. It was introduced during the first week and referenced and utilized throughout the training. We shared the MBTI profiles of each intern and trainer. This information helped people understand their communication style, how they processed information, and how they made decisions. It also helped them develop an understanding of how to best interact with their colleagues. Many interns embraced the tool and used it throughout their careers.

I lived with the interns for the entire month. On the weekends, I went home to visit my family. I sat in on every module session and consulted with each week's training team. On several nights, we held fireside chats where we invited different individuals from NEA headquarters to present information about the different programs. One evening during the first week, one of the trainers invited the interns to his home for happy hour. We had a very powerful discussion about race, gender, and some of their interactions. It was like a T-group session at an NTL program. Since I had experience as a facilitator and had been observing them, I was able to step in and manage an emotionally intense conversation. Bill and I used this experience to organize a full-day session devoted to diversity in the final week.

I had many one-on-one conversations with the interns at mealtime and in the evenings. These conversations helped me better understand them and their family background and life experiences. During the final week, I invited them and Dr. Bill to my home for a spaghetti dinner. They had an opportunity to meet my wife and children. The social activities helped start a tradition of offering a weekly social outing that was organized by different training teams.

INTERNS GET ON-THE-JOB TRAINING

The next major phase of the program was a three-month paid on-the-job training (OJT) experience with a seasoned UniServ staffer and mentor at a local association. In preparation for the interns' OJT, the trainers observed them during the first three weeks of the four-week intensive training. We identified their strengths, weaknesses, and the areas they needed to experience during the OJT. They were evaluated at the end of each week. In addition, the program team began contacting potential mentors. Considerations were given to the race and gender of the mentor and what type of activities would be taking place during the intern's OJT assignment. The interns were assigned to the associations based on their continued development. The interns were informed of their assignment at the end of the third week of the training. During the fourth week, the intern contacted their mentor. The mentors were brought to the training site for a two-day briefing and the opportunity to meet their interns. The interns began their assignment the first week of September and ended just before Thanksgiving.

The NEA made a huge financial commitment to the Intern Program. The program budget provided the interns with their current salary for three months, transportation to and from the OJT site, two home visits, housing, food, and a rental car. The local association helped them find appropriate housing. Their school district arranged for a substitute staffer to cover their duties during the period they were away.

Once the interns completed their OJT, they returned to the training site with their mentors for a debriefing in December. They participated in a graduation ceremony and were awarded a certificate of completion. After graduation, they sought employment as UniServ staff, with no guarantee of getting a job. However, every effort to assist them was made. For example, we scheduled time for formal interviews with several State UniServ Managers and other hiring staff. We also encouraged the interns to get to know the managers during meals. Some interns were offered jobs; others received second interviews.

This first intern class (Class of 1987) was exceptional. Many of them could have been hired even before participating in the program. Fourteen out of the 16 were hired within three months. One individual decided not to seek employment. Two years later, she changed her mind and was hired. The other individual decided to return to teaching. Another worked for a year before resigning and returning to the classroom. Since their training, some have given back to the program by being involved as trainers and mentors. They also recommended potential interns. Through it all, I have maintained contact with all of them and followed their careers into retirement.

THE GROWTH OF THE INTERN PROGRAM

Significant change took place during the second year when Deloris Rozier, an Organization Specialist in the NEA Pacific Regional office, replaced my NEA partner Garfield who was re-assigned to a different effort. Deloris was highly regarded. John Hein, NEA Director of Field Services, thought she could bring a lot to the Intern Program. While working with her, I witnessed her promotion from Organization Specialist to an Assistant Regional Manager. She was later selected by Evelyn Temple, a Black woman who served as the Associate Executive Director, as the Director of Affiliate Capacity Building. In this position, she oversaw the largest number of staff and was responsible for the largest budget within the NEA. The NEA Intern Program's administrative team's major priority was to ensure buy-in and participation from other NEA divisions. Their efforts were successful and opened the door for the first class.

Fifteen people participated in the second and third intern classes. Only one man was selected to participate in the second intern class (Class of 1988). In the 27-year history of the Intern Program, we only experienced this once. Most of the second class were hired. One of the youngest interns later became the Director of Field Operations in a large state affiliate. The third intern class (Class of 1989) was even more successful because all 15 members were hired and have had long careers. Several went on to positions at the NEA and have served in different roles in the program. Two became director of the program. The third class started the tradition of naming themselves. Their name was "The Mighty Fine of '89."

The program's class size ranged from a high of 16 to a low of 9 over the course of 27 years. According to a report by the NEA, 244 participants were selected during the program's first 20 years. Out of the 244 participants, 202 completed the program and were hired. As a result of the program's success, we were able to help increase the number of state affiliates that hired diverse interns including a blind woman. She was a member of the Class of 2000. With the support of her service dog and a few adjustments we made, she successfully completed the program and her OJT. She was later hired and had a long career. At the national level, the program produced 27 national NEA staffers. Seven became NEA managers.

Each of the 27 classes were unique. Check out some of their names: Class of 1992, "Too Legit to Quit"; Class of 1993, "Flashes of Brilliance"; Class of 1994, "Through the Window of Change: Prepared—Positive—Proud"; Class of 2000, "Magnificent Millennium"; Class of 2010, "Thinkers to the 12th Power"; and Class of 2011, "Literal Living Legends."

They also designed a class shirt with a statement that reflected a saying from their month-long training. It began with the
Class of 1987. They selected a phrase I would often say, "Here's
Another Piece." The Class of 1988's shirt featured one of my
sayings, "Just a Quickie." The Class of 1990 also chose my
saying, "Another Caveat." In 1991, the interns selected "Para-
digm Pioneers." "We Diversify—Integrity—Dignity" decorated the Class of 1996's shirt. The t-shirt for the Class of 2011
was more like an affirmation: "Yes, We Did Ascertain That
We Are the Best." In addition, many of the classes produced a
class song and published newsletters to stay connected.

The Intern Program created a unique culture that included
many long-lasting friendships. The interns knew they shared
a very special connection. This connection forged a bond of
support in their professional career and personal life. They
attended weddings and other celebrations and supported each
other in times of great joy, illness, and the death of loved ones.
They understood the importance of giving back and the saying, "For whom much is given, much is expected." As a result,
they recruited other interns and mentored them. Whenever
they attended NEA meetings or training sessions, they met
with each other. They organized the first reunion celebration
during the program's fifth anniversary. They also celebrated
the 10th year and 25th year anniversary. During the 25th anniversary in 2011, we traveled to Miami, Florida. The reunion
theme was "25 years of Class and Distinction." Every class
was represented. Several classes had as many as 10 in attendance. In addition, NEA staff, program trainers and mentors,

and others attended. The classes honored me with a special plaque for my 25 years of care, dedication, and commitment to the Intern Program. That moment caught me off guard and filled me with tremendous joy, humility, and fulfillment.

After 25 years, there was a 60% increase of women who applied and secured staff positions throughout the NEA system of local and state affiliates. People of color experienced a 40% to 45% increase in securing staff positions. The overall success rate of the program's graduates was approximately 85% of whom were hired into state, local, and national positions throughout the program's history.

PROGRAM CHANGES

Each year, a debriefing session was held to review, discuss, and consider changes. One of the early changes happened when we developed an administrative team to replace my role of working one-on-one with each intern. Each administrative team member was assigned three to four interns. This model provided interns with more personal attention throughout the program. We also realized the interns needed more than the knowledge and skills we were training them in. We began helping them with writing, making presentations, upgrading their professional appearance, resume preparation, and interviewing skills. We also spent time observing them in different work-related settings and provided individual feedback for improvement.

Our approach focused on the total person. We recognized the importance of their well-being and paid close attention to their health and mental states. As a result, many of the interns began to carve out some time for exercising. Informal walking groups, workout time in the hotel exercise rooms, and changes in eating habits took place. We were also able to work with hotel staff on presenting a varied and balanced menu. Our efforts helped them transform their presentation skills and professional appearance, as well as increased their confidence.

Leadership roles changed as the program grew. During the first 15 years, I spent the entire four weeks at the site as the training director. As time passed and the administrative team took on more responsibilities, I spent less time at the site, though I was always there to conduct the final week of training. Deloris's role also changed as she handed off the overall directorship of the program to our colleague, Dr. Deborah "Debbie" Byard (Campbell) Kirby. Debbie would later hand it off to Nas Afi, a member of the Intern Class of 1989. Years later, Nas handed the baton to her Intern classmate Dan Hand. Dan handled the virtual transition of some of the program's components in 2015 and led the program until it ended in 2017.

INTERN PROGRAM BECOMES A CATALYST FOR OTHER NEA PROGRAMS

UniServ Professional Development Program

Several years after the Intern Program began, white male NEA members questioned and challenged why they didn't have the opportunity to be in the program. Each year at the NEA annual meeting, the NEA Executive Committee and Board of Directories told them white men held the majority of UniServ positions and without this affirmative effort there would be very little change. Data was provided to show the improvement in the hiring of women and minorities was almost exclusively due to the Intern Program. However, eventually it was decided to establish the UniServ Professional Development Program (UPDP), which was open to all.

From October 1999 to July 2003, the UPDP program trained two classes per year in the fall and summer. In its first few years, the UPDP classes were attended by mostly white participants. The program was reduced to a two-week intensive training that used the Intern Program's five modules and some of its trainers. That summer, UPDP participants were able to interact with the Intern Program participants during the Star Power simulation (described below), at meals, and in informal settings because they were trained in the same location.

Star Power is a simulation game of an organization or system in which leaders are given unlimited powers to make and change the rules. R. Gary Shirts of Simulation Training Systems created the face-to-face, non-computer-based game in 1969. I used it in every aspect of my work in my firm and with EYCA. I also incorporated it into the Intern Program's last week of training devoted to organizational development and diversity. During the game, participants progress from one level of society to another by acquiring wealth through trading with other participants. Once the society is established, the group with the most wealth is given the right to make the rules for the game. The power group generally makes the rules which maintain or increase its power, and which those being governed consider to be unfair. This generally results in some sort of rebellion by the other members of the society.

Star Power teaches: 1) to change behavior, it may be necessary to change the system in which the behavior occurs; 2) few people are likely to participate in an endeavor if they feel powerless; 3) if rules do not have legitimacy, they will not be obeyed; 4) what seems fair to those in power is not likely to seem fair to those who are out of power; and 5) persons who are promoted rarely remember those they leave behind. The UPDP program also used Star Power throughout its duration.

In addition, the UPDP program added the concept "whole person development" to its training curriculum. It was introduced by a former intern, Tamara Hamilton, who had become a staff member of the NEA Training Division in Affiliate Capacity. It also had an administrative team headed by Al Perez, one of the NEA managers in the division. They performed the same functions as the Intern Program's administrative team.

The George Meany Program

The AFL-CIO had a two-year initiative held at their training site in Maryland called the George Meany Program. This program provided the opportunity for some of the interns who did not have a college degree to attain one. The Intern Program had accepted individuals who were in Educational Support Positions in their former life. When they completed the Intern

Program, they sometimes had more difficulty getting hired because some associations required a college degree. As a result, Deloris was able to negotiate an agreement with the George Meany Program to accept members of the NEA staff and interns into their program. One of my memorable highlights was attending the graduation ceremony of the first interns who completed the program. This was a very meaningful accomplishment for them and increased their earning potential.

State Interns Programs

NEA affiliates in California, Illinois, Michigan, and Ohio created their own intern programs modelled after the NEA Intern Program. Their motivation for creating these programs was to fill positions held by an increasing number of retirees, to demonstrate their commitment to affirmative action, and to recruit women and people of color for UniServ-level positions. Each of the states had key leaders who had supported and valued the NEA Intern Program. These leaders also invested resources in their states to increase the number of women and people of color. They included:

- California Teachers Association: Carolyn Doggett, Executive Director; James Clark, Deputy Director; and Robert Stenhouse, Human Resources Manager
- Illinois Education Association: Clayton MarQuardt, Executive Director; and Alice Vandersteen, UniServ Field Coordinator
- Michigan Education Association: Chuck Anderson,

Executive Director; and Robert K. Marshall, Director of Labor Relations
- Ohio Education Association: Dennis Reardon, Executive Director; and Sandy Schwellinger, Assistant Director of Member Services

PROGRAM IMPACT ON INTERNS

I asked several former interns to share how the Intern Program changed their lives. They included Nas I. Afi, Eric B. Beck, Demetrice Davis, Candace Lilyquist, and Bryant Warren. Their reflections are contained below.

Nas I. Afi, a Black woman, Class of 1989, Organizational Specialist, NEA

I came to the NEA UniServ Intern Program the summer of 1989. How overwhelming it seemed with its high-powered staff and superstar participants. Participants in my class were seasoned leaders in their local associations: local presidents or other offices. I came into the program with only the experience of being a local association representative. I wasn't sure how I would fare in such an experienced and esteemed group. I was nervous to say the least.

The program as designed, gave me skills in organizing people, negotiating contracts, advocating for members through grievances and arbitrations, and building an effective organization. The trainers and training teams were dynamic and very diverse in gender, race, personality, and style. That was a plus for me in the learning.

The program was intense with long hours and tedious work, but somehow the core staff made the journey an honor and pleasure for each of us to be there. Every day was exciting and held revelations that took our skills to the next level, uncovered hidden talents, and increased our knowledge base in a most rewarding way. Dr. John's work on organization health and effectiveness was a highlight of the program. He made us think deeply about people and relationships that either help or hinder organizations. He made us examine who we are and everything in our background that shaped our communications, interactions, values, goals, and on and on. Dr. John was an awesome teacher and mentor. He has had a profound impact on my life in a most unforgettable way! I learned from him how to use my gifts to make a difference in the world. I learned how to mentor and help others.

Thirty years later, I still remember the experiences from being a member of the Intern Class of 1989. I am still proud to proclaim it as a highlight of my life. I am still grateful to all the trainers, but in a very deep way to Dr. John, Delores Rozier, and Dr. Deborah Kirby for helping me transform my life. I am proud to claim their success in me, as I was fortunate to be able to coordinate the program, the training and field mentoring experience, for six years once on staff at the NEA. I could never fill their shoes, but they instilled in me what I believe was the right stuff to do for other interns what the program did for me. Their mantra and charge was "to reach back to bring along others, to lift up others!" I never forgot the charge and still strive to live it.

Eric B. Beck, a Black man, Class of 2004, UniServ Director, Alabama Education Association

In September 2004, during my field training, I wrote: "I feel that presently I am experiencing personal and professional "application" to the "growth" that I experienced in Virginia. I am using many of the lessons—especially the harder ones for me—in my daily interactions with my colleagues, members, school board and community."

In October 2004, nearing the end of my field training, I wrote: "Personally, I am working through a great many things. I feel the tools that I acquired in Virginia and Mobile will be invaluable to me making it through this time in one piece. Professionally, I am about to take the next step into a life I could not have dreamed about a few months ago. I am ready."

In September 2020, as the senior UniServ Director in my state, I wrote: "Without question, the NEA

UniServ Intern Program for Women and Ethnic Minorities provided me the foundation upon which my family, professional, academic and business structures presently stand. I am blessed to have had the trials of the 'Throughput.'"

Demetrice Davis, a Black woman, Class of 2001, Education Policy and Practice Consultant, Ohio Education Association

Marlene Fong, the UniServ Field Organizer for my local association referred me to the NEA UniServ Intern Program while I was a building rep for the San Diego Education Association. From the interview process to the program graduation and throughout my career, the one word that resonates with me when I think of the Intern Program is EXCELLENCE.

The classroom training was the best personal and professional development that I ever experienced. The learning activities were challenging, realistic, experiential, and adult centered. The interaction and engagement with other interns and the in-the-moment feedback from the trainers built a bridge to successfully completing the program.

The field experience with a mentor with the intent of placing us in a location unlike our hometown enriched me personally and professionally on a day-to-day basis. I learned something new every day, from how to watch for deer, to the use of hunting season as a bargaining chip when negotiating the school calendar.

When it was time to find a job, I was surrounded by a network of mentors planning for my success. I received feedback from each interview until I successfully landed my current job of 18 years. The success was only possible through my continued connection and networking with mentors and other former interns.

In addition to the important economic benefit of securing a well-paying job, going into and through the Intern Program has led to opportunities that I had not envisioned prior to the Intern Program. I have traveled across the United States, met U.S. Presidents, State Governors, and help lead my organization during the COVID-19 pandemic by designing virtual initiatives to keep our members connected and informed while providing excellent programing.

Candace Lilyquist, a white woman, Class of 1998, Organization Specialist, NEA

The NEA Affirmative Action Intern Program changed my life. I have been interested in helping others since early childhood. With maturity, that internal sensibility morphed into an interest in advocacy. After more than eight years in the classroom, peppered with local association activism, I was selected to be a candidate in the program. The whole world started opening even as I submitted the application. There were significant questions about world view and cultural diversity. I started learning from the feedback peers gave me about the answers I prepared. The intensity was significant from the start. Dr. Leeke began to remove the scales from our eyes. He led us through a series of activities that helped us reveal our experience with race, justice, and many forms of diversity in people. We learned how everything works in organizations. We learned how to identify where people were and to take them from that space to higher understanding. We were able to diagram groups, organizations, and communities' ways of interacting. All this work was done through a racial equity lens, long before this terminology hit the main streets.

Dr. Leeke stayed with us through the work, both formally and informally. Dr. Leeke kept building our understandings and weaving attitudes, skills, and knowledge for individuals, the group, and the whole program. He would appear at the back of the room and observe us as we worked. He took meals with us from time to time sharing stories of the past and teasing out our ideas of the future. He worked to build connections and relationships. Even though we did not know it, he knew we would need this knowledge and skill as we advanced in the work.

From the NEA Affirmative Action Intern Program, Dr. Leeke has maintained a 20-year relationship with me and other students too. He trained us, he offered follow-up conversations, and he even led a Star Power event during my grad school class. Many students went through the NEA Program in its 25-year existence. Dr. Leeke opened new worlds for them. So, they in turn could also open new understandings for public school employees, their students, and the communities we all live in.

Bryant Warren, a Black man, Class of 2004, UniServ Director, Illinois Education Association

One of the greatest factors that has determined the trajectory of my life's journey was acceptance into the NEA Affirmative Action Internship Program for Women and Minorities a/k/a "The Intern Program" in July of 2004. At the time, I was going through a painful transition. My marriage ended in divorce earlier that year and I was struggling with being separated from my three-year-old daughter. It was also during this time that I was yearning for a new direction for my life. After teaching industrial technology in the suburbs of Chicago for eight years I was feeling a call to something more. I knew that God was calling me to have an impact in a much bigger arena. The internship provided me the self-knowledge, support, and skills to fulfill God's purpose for my life.

The Intern Program increased my confidence by

giving me a greater understanding of self. My "aha" moment was learning I was an introvert after taking the Myers-Briggs questionnaire. This knowledge explained my preference for time alone to think and re-energize after long periods of socializing. Prior to this knowledge, I felt there was something wrong with me because I was more reclusive than others. Throughout my life I was often criticized for being withdrawn and for my world view. But the knowledge I gained about myself during the Intern Program led me to not only accept myself but feel pride in who God created me to be. It gave me a greater sense of self-worth to understand that my personality type gave me unique characteristics that were valuable to the work I was called to complete. I no longer felt like an outsider. The Intern Program provided a network of people that accepted and affirmed me.

The Intern Program connected me to a national network of friends and colleagues that reached far beyond my South Side of Chicago origins. Many of the people I have met have developed into friends and mentors that will last my lifetime. These relationships have benefited me personally and professionally. Since 2004, there has not been a major event in my life in which I did not have the support of my intern colleagues. When I faced a major tragedy in 2011, intern alumni from around the country flew into town to support me. Professionally, the intern network has provided me with mentors that have opened new opportunities, celebrated my successes, and provided feedback when necessary. I love the intern network! The Intern Program also gave me a new set of unique skills.

I have always had a passion for advocacy and fighting for social justice. The Intern Program provided me with the skills and resources to fulfill my passion. Prior to the Intern Program I had no experience as a union representative. I worked in a school district that was predominately white and opportunities to serve in union leadership were not made available to me. It is the Intern Program that gave me the opportunity to learn skills in bargaining, organizing, organizational development, and advocacy. Utilizing my new skill set and the support of the intern network, I have served NEA and its statewide affiliates for over 16 years, and I look forward to many more.

Beyond my career, I have utilized the skills that I have honed over the last 16 years to benefit my own community. My passion for justice and racial equity still burns! On behalf of NEA members, I have organized strikes for fair contracts, advocated for better working conditions, and assisted with political campaigns for education-friendly candidates. But there was always a longing to assist my own people, Black people living in urban areas that did not have access to economic resources, quality public schools, or a fair justice system. Therefore, while serving as UniServ Di-

rector, I also volunteer as the Director of Social Justice for my church. My church is one of the largest churches in the south suburbs of Chicago with over 4,000 members. Utilizing the organizing skills I learned in the Intern Program and developed as a UniServ Director, I am educating, motivating, and mobilizing my community against the strongholds of racial injustice.

I am particularly grateful to Dr. John Leeke for creating such a powerful program that has significantly impacted my life! "Dr. John," as he is affectionately known among intern alumni, is an important piece of my network and development. While I was in the program, Dr. John challenged my thinking and taught me about the hurdles Black men face as a UniServ Director. Dr. John gave me a solid foundation in organizational development that I am still building on to this day. Thank you, Dr. John, for helping me to be all God had called me to be.

NEA INTERN 25TH ANNIVERSARY SONG

During the 25th year anniversary reunion in 2011, the intern alumni composed a song that I believe embodies the true meaning of what it was like for them to be a part of the program. When I heard them singing the song, memories of the work we accomplished together flooded my mind. I also felt a deep sense of gratitude and fulfillment.

NEA Intern 25th Anniversary Song

*In the beginning was an interview
It was the interview for all time
And when we got the call, no one knew
What a journey of a different kind.
To be an Intern...
All hearts were yearning,
To be an Intern...
So ready for learning,
To be an Intern...
"Passion for the Cause", still burning.*

*Intensive summer training
Working in the group, while working on me.
The A-Team took us deeper, helped us discover
Engaging heart and mind is the key.*

*NEA Interns...
Taught and mentored by the best
NEA Interns...
Until it's done, we won't rest
NEA Interns...
Bringing competence and zest!*

*Now we work hard out in the field
As UD's, program staff, and managers
We have achieved but never do we forget
It's still "all about the members"!*

We are the Interns...
We give our all
We are the Interns...
We'll go to the wall
We are the Interns...
Always standing tall!

It's our intent to keep on growing
And through 25 years, it's very clear
The program changed the face of all it touched
A testament, a legacy so dear.

CHAPTER 18 REFLECTION QUESTIONS

1. Individual: Have you had a group experience over the course of six months or more that impacted your life and career? What was it? Describe how it impacted your life and career.

2. Group Discussion: Give each person 3–5 minutes to share their individual response with the group. As a group, list some of the similarities and differences highlighted in the sharing session. Also, discuss one or two lessons each person has learned.

PART FOUR

THE FINAL ACT: LEAVING A LEGACY

CHAPTER 19

Life in Retirement

"What a privilege to be here on the planet to contribute your unique donation to mankind."

—**MORRIS DEES**, an American attorney, co-founder and former chief trial counsel for the Southern Poverty Law Center, and a change agent

———————————————

I value my retirement because it has given me the freedom to do what I want, when I want, and how I want. My freedom in retirement is a privilege that has expanded my capacity to serve and continue making contributions with the knowledge and experience I have acquired for the betterment of others.

Growing up, I didn't know much about retirement. I had no idea it would offer me the freedom and privilege I currently possess. The first person I saw retire in my family was my Aunt Mabel. After she retired from her teaching career, she moved from Elkhart, Indiana to live with my parents in Washington, DC. Her retirement was traditional, which meant permanently leaving the workforce. My Aunt Paulyne embraced the same approach when she retired from her nursing career. My parents applied a slightly different approach to their retirement from the Federal Government. At different times during their retirement, they chose to work in less strenuous jobs. My mother tapped into her secretarial skills and worked part-time for a news service. My father chose to use his driving skills as a seasonal delivery driver for Lee's Flowers, one of the oldest Black businesses in DC. I also witnessed family and friends retire from military service or a company.

I didn't have any clear role models for retirement as an entrepreneur. That meant I had to create my own idea of what my life in retirement would look like. I started with shifting my mindset to one rooted in the belief that retirement is the freedom to choose how I use my time. I also committed to continuous learning. Embracing this mindset and commitment allowed me to focus on service in my church, community, and alumni associations. I also focused on maintaining relationships, health, personal interests, use of technology, and travel.

PREPARING FOR FINANCIAL RETIREMENT

When I left the NEA, my tax accountant, Art, helped me map out my retirement as an entrepreneur. We set up an IRA account and a pension plan that would supplement my NEA retirement and social security benefits. I also started a stock trading account that I continue to use today. I waited until I was 66 years old to claim my full social security benefits. All these choices laid the financial foundation of my official retirement.

Five years before I officially retired, I recognized my involvement with EYCA was concluding due to a decrease in client contracts and activity caused by changes in the diversity industry. Companies began creating in-house diversity officers and staff. Most of EYCA's long-term clients adopted this approach. At the same time, the NEA Intern Program was nearing an end. In my own firm, I stopped seeking new clients and completed the work for existing clients. While I was finishing work on my last two clients in 2013, Art and I reviewed my long-term finances to determine when it would be best to retire and close John F. Leeke Associates, Inc. We decided I would retire at 71. Knowing I would soon function on a reduced income, I began to significantly reduce my debt by paying off credit cards. This effort helped me manage my monthly budget and expenses.

MY RELATIONSHIP WITH ST. JOSEPH CATHOLIC CHURCH

Theresa and I made the decision for our family to join St. Joseph Catholic Church in 1969 because it had a welcoming community that was predominately African American and like what we experienced at Christ the King Catholic Church in Flint, Michigan. Our family has continued to be active in the church like my grandparents Henry and Eunice Roberts were in their church communities in Terre Haute, Indiana. I feel proud of the role I have played in my church community. I derived a sense of satisfaction watching my children and godchildren and many others grow, develop, and make a way in the world. I loved attending their church performances, showing support, and helping them be the best they can be. I continue to spend time encouraging and affirming them because I believe in investing in our youth.

With my freedom of time as a retiree, I chose to deepen my service in my church, community, and alumni associations. Prior to retirement, I had always attended Mass and other services at St. Joseph Catholic Church, but due to the intense nature of my work, I had consciously chosen not to be involved in any of the ministries or organizations. I did, however, become a eucharistic minister and even took on a leadership role. I reorganized the ministry into teams, which allowed them to be more structured. After doing that, I turned over the leadership to another person but remained one of the eucharistic ministers. Also, during an earlier period, I accepted a position on the church parish council. The parish council serves as an advisor to the pastor. I served for a couple of years until it was disbanded.

The current pastor reinstituted the parish council in 2018. Since I was retired, I was able to serve as one of the 13 elected council members. At the first meeting, the council voted me in as their chairperson. Under my leadership, the council completed a new church directory, designated church volunteers to oversee activities for youth and young adults, organized and hosted Black History programs with youth and outside speakers, and planned the church's centennial activities. We also advised the pastor on navigating the coronavirus pandemic and meeting the Archdiocese of Washington's protocols.

St. Joseph Catholic Church is richly blessed with worshipers from around the world. Our diversity presents a unique attraction for membership and a more relaxed worship community. Over the past 10 years, we have experienced a significant increase in membership due primarily to an influx of people from Benin, Cameroon, Dominican Republic, Ethiopia, Ghana, Guyana, Haiti, Jamaica, Kenya, Mexico, Nigeria, the Philippines, and Trinidad. In 2017, a core group of people from the continent of Africa came together to form the St. Joseph Community of Africans and Friends (SJCAF). The SJCAF promotes African culture and social values in line with the Catholic faith among its members, friends, and the community at large.

I chose to join SJCAF when I recognized the demographics of the church were changing significantly because I wanted to ensure new members felt welcomed and had opportunities to be actively engaged. I also joined to provide further support to the Adeleye family. My wife, Theresa, met John Adeleye when he became a cantor in the early 1990s. As they worked together, she learned about his life in Nigeria and developed a friendship. When John decided to apply for his U.S. citizenship, he asked us to sponsor him. Several years later, we became friends with his wife, Bosede ("Bose"), and served as her sponsor too. As time progressed, John and Bose became extended family and asked us to be godparents to their children, John and Olusayo ("Sayo"). Although their youngest child, David, has different godparents, we also treat him as a godchild, primarily because he demands it.

When John Adeleye became president of SJCAF, I was elected to serve as treasurer. By serving as treasurer, I wanted to help build a strong foundation for the organization. I also wanted to share the lessons I have learned while being a church member and leader as well as an organizational development consultant. I am proud of the work and programs SJCAF has been involved in over the past several years. We formed an African choir that sings on the fourth Sunday of each month. During the Lenten season, we have worked with African youth to enact the Living Stations of the Cross on Good Friday. Except for a couple of years during the coronavirus pandemic, we held an annual anniversary dinner celebration. Our Harvest Thanksgiving Mass gives SJCAF members an opportunity to share aspects of their traditional harvest celebrations with the wider community. Each family is dressed in their traditional attire. They dance down the aisle as they offer gifts and are blessed by the priest. Their gifts include financial donations and canned foods that are placed in the church pantry for families in need. The African choir also sings throughout the Mass.

My SJCAF experience has given me a deeper appreciation for my African roots. While writing this book, my daughter and I decided to trace our family's DNA with African Ancestry, a Black-owned company founded by Dr. Rick Kittles and Gina Paige in 2003. African Ancestry is the world leader in tracing maternal and paternal lineages of African descent. It has the largest and most comprehensive database of over

30,000 indigenous African DNA samples. When I learned my family's DNA was traced back to the Yoruba people in Nigeria, I realized the Leeke and Adeleye families shared an even deeper connection. One Sunday after Mass, I told John about our shared connection. We both reflected on how our Yoruba ancestors brought us together at St. Joseph's Church. Our connection made it possible for my son Mike's wedding to include Nigerian attire worn by Theresa and me, and food prepared by Bose and John. Over the years, the Adeleye family has participated in our annual Kwanzaa celebration. We also attended their children's graduations and other family events including the 90th birthday celebration of Bose's mother and Sayo's wedding to her husband, Alexander.

I joined the Men's Ministry group in 2017. Its mission is to provide a space for the men of the church to engage in communal prayer, worship, sharing, reinforce learning about our Catholic faith, all while putting our faith into action. We strive to reinvigorate a tradition of faith formation for men of all ages. Our vision is to strengthen all our men in their Catholic faith and to explore how to be strong fathers, husbands, sons, brothers, and citizens, instilling humility and supporting the protectors of our community. Our intergenerational group included men aged 23 to 85 years old. Prior to the pandemic, we met every Saturday morning. Our meetings opened with prayer and a scripture reading from the Bible followed by a discussion. Members shared how the reading impacted them, gave personal updates about their life and challenges, and discussed current events. I often shared some of my life lessons from being married over 50 years and raising four children. We learned a lot about each other and were able to forge strong bonds. All our sharing helped us support and encourage each other. The group gave me a space to focus on my faith, deepen my prayer life, develop a habit of reading the Bible, and practice the presence of God during the Lenten and Advent seasons. This experience reconnected me to the teachings of the Catholic Church. It's something I truly value because I hadn't had any concentrated time to do it since grade school and high school. The group stopped meeting during the early days of the pandemic in 2020. Thankfully, the church offered daily Mass online which helped me continue to nurture my spiritual life. In 2022, the group resumed meeting in-person. Our membership doubled in 2023. That same year, I served on the planning committee for our first all-day retreat. During the retreat, I enjoyed the group's camaraderie. It felt like we were becoming brothers. I also deepened my understanding of, and appreciation for, the different parts of the Mass. The guest speaker inspired me to reflect and recommit to serving as a husband, father, and leader in the church.

POLITICAL ACTIVISM

Growing up, I always believed I had a responsibility to be civically engaged. My belief was crystalized into social action while working as a teacher in Flint, Michigan to improve the quality of life of Black people. It expanded into political activism when I began working for the NEA. During my NEA tenure, I was assigned to work on the Democratic presidential election campaign for Walter Mondale and Geraldine Ferraro. I served as a field organizer and helped the teacher union members get organized to work at the local levels in support of the Mondale and Ferraro campaign.

When former President Barack H. Obama launched his campaign in 2007, I read his books *Dreams from My Father* and *The Audacity of Hope* and listened to his speeches. I learned he was a committed community organizer, an effective communicator, a brilliant thinker, and a knowledgeable lawyer who had the ability to relate to all people. His life and diverse family background represented America. I felt his innovative ideas, energy, and deep commitment to equality and justice for all were the things America needed to move forward. He convinced me America was ready for a Black president. I joined his campaign in Prince George's County, Maryland to help make it happen. Working at the local level of the Obama campaign gave me an opportunity to make telephone calls and knock on doors in Maryland, Virginia, and Pennsylvania. I was also able to establish connections with my fellow volunteers. Many of us later volunteered on President Obama's re-election campaign and Anthony Brown's campaigns for Governor of the State of Maryland and the U.S. House of Representatives.

When I moved to Anne Arundel County, Maryland in 2016, I learned there was a small percentage of people of color who were serving as election judges. This fact motivated me to get involved and volunteer to participate in the election judge training and later work the primary and general presidential and state elections for the past four election cycles. In my county, I have been impressed by the way the county officials interacted with voters and ensured a fair and safe election that meets the needs of all people. This year, I am preparing to work the presidential general election cycle. I keep showing up each year because I am invested in making sure people of color are involved in the electoral process.

ONLINE ACTIVISM

Prior to retirement, I only used technology to support my business. My computer and I were best friends with email and Microsoft Word. I did not enter the digital world until the night of President Barack H. Obama's first inauguration on January 20, 2009. Throughout President Obama's campaign, I volunteered on the ground in my local community and in different states. The excitement I experienced from helping him win the election and the desire to stay informed about his administration's programs are the reasons I asked my son Matthew to help me join Facebook that night. After Matthew gave me my first Facebook tutorial, my life as a digital senior citizen began.

After I joined Facebook, I sent invitations to family, friends, and colleagues who were already members. Many, including my daughter, Madelyn (Ananda), who even wrote a book entitled *Digital Sisterhood*, were shocked. She even called me to see if I had actually been the person who sent the friend invitation. When I told her that I was online, she laughed and said, "President Obama has made you one dangerous digital senior citizen." She was right. In a short time, I saw how connected I could be with my Facebook friends. In an instant, I was reunited with classmates from high school and college, fraternity brothers, former colleagues and clients, NEA interns, church members, and neighbors. Facebook helped me create a community that represented all parts of my life.

After a day of being on Facebook, I joined millions of Americans in signing up for the Obama administration's WhiteHouse.gov daily updates. Getting these updates and watching YouTube videos of President Obama and his team fueled my passion for using technology to educate myself and my Facebook friends. It also introduced me to my favorite news websites such as *The Washington Post*, *The Atlantic Monthly*, and *MSNBC*. Having access to this information empowered me to start conversations with my diverse Facebook community of friends.

Months later, I realized my ability to communicate and share information with others had changed. My digital curiosity created a thirst in wanting to know more about these tools and how I could use them to leverage my online activism and interests. Since my children are tech savvy, I tapped them for in-house support and training. Mark and Matthew taught me how to use my smartphone, especially the camera. Madelyn (Ananda) showed me how to use Twitter, LinkedIn, and Pinterest. She also introduced me to my first blogging and social media conferences and events in the DC area. Naturally, I networked with her digital friends who became my friends too. Having these in-person and online experiences were pure joy for me. Being connected to them expanded my view of how I could use social media to speak about political and social justice issues, sports, and entertainment, including Shonda Rhimes's successful political television show, *Scandal*.

Watching *Scandal* taught me how to live tweet and post concise comments about the episodes, engage in post-episode conversations, and build a "Scandal Gladiator" community of Facebook friends. I even traveled to the 2013 Blogalicious Conference in Atlanta and participated in a *Scandal* viewing and live-tweeting with bloggers and influencers. All these experiences helped me hone the skills I used to live-tweet political debates and news television shows on *MSNBC*. I also used these skills to launch a Tumblr blog, *Dr. John: Change Agent, Change Advocate, and Change Influencer*, in 2011. My blog is devoted to sharing thoughts, opinions, and information, and raising questions about issues of race, diversity, and differences. It gives me the opportunity to serve as a motivator, stimulator, agitator, questioner, and hopefully an advocate for improving the quality of life for all regardless of who they are. My hope is that it educates, encourages, inspires, and influences others to take action and responsibility for ensuring the survival of our democracy in the U.S.A.

Some of my most meaningful blog posts discussed the mid-term and presidential elections. For example, I published a five-part podcast series that addressed the importance of voting, my voting story, and what it means to be a digital citizen in the weeks leading up to the 2018 midterm elections. Several years earlier, I used my blog to document my work as an Obama campaign volunteer with stories and photos from canvasing activities in Maryland, Pennsylvania, and Virginia. My blog also featured highlights from my work as a volunteer for Anthony Brown's campaigns for governor and congressman in Maryland.

Whenever I attended an in-person event I felt others would benefit from, I wrote about it. One example was when I conducted a seminar for the NEA Retired Organization (NEARO) in Washington, DC in 2014. This effort began as a result of one of my earlier blog posts, "Starting Discussions on Race." Someone from the NEARO newsletter read it and asked me to write an article. The article led to an invitation to participate in the NEARO Board's planning committee for a personal and interactive gathering. As the facilitator, I helped the members explore how to have meaningful conversations on race. I knew, and had worked with, everyone who attended the session.

I began the session by sharing a statement from U.S. Supreme Court Justice Sonia Sotomayor that was taken from her 58-page dissent after the U.S. Supreme Court upheld Michigan's constitutional amendment banning the consideration of race in public university admissions.

This refusal to accept the stark reality that race matters is regrettable. The way to stop discrimination on the basis of race is to speak openly and candidly on the subject of race, and to apply the Constitution with

*eyes open to the unfortunate effects of centuries of ra-
cial discrimination.*

I continued my introductory remarks by referring to a
quote from Dr. Maya Angelou: "It takes courage to be courageous." I challenged the participants to be courageous as they
began their conversations in small racially mixed groups of
six to seven people. Their conversations were intense, prob-
ing, and thoughtful. Some shared experiences they had when
they first encountered someone who was racially different.
Others shared what they felt when they were insulted or discriminated against because of their racial identity. They expressed that even though they had known one another for
many years, they were learning much more about each other
and at a much deeper level. The conversations went beyond
the assigned time frame which was encouraging.

A year later, my blog featured my participation in the
White House Conference on Aging. Visiting the White House
during President Obama's administration had been a wish of
mine that came true when my daughter received an invitation
to meet with Jason Goldman, the White House's first Chief
Digital Officer, on how to create more meaningful online engagement between the federal government and American citizens. They discussed her ideas and experiences serving as a
digital communications volunteer for the White House. Several weeks after their meeting, the White House announced
it would be holding the Conference on Aging to listen, learn,
and share with older adults, their families, caregivers, advo-

cates, community leaders, and experts in the aging field on how to best address the changing landscape of aging in the coming decade. When I learned about the conference, I demanded she ask Jason if he could help me get an invitation to attend the event. Thanks to him, we both received invitations. The day I received mine via email, I was on a natural high because it represented a major milestone in my work to support President Obama during his campaigns and administration.

On the day of the conference, I rode the Metro to the White House. My journey started on the Blue Line from the Largo Town Center station and ended at the McPherson Square station. As I got closer to the station, my excitement grew because this visit marked my first time being inside the White House. I had visited the White House once before when my wife and her students were invited to attend an event hosted on the grounds during the Reagan Administration. This visit was much different and historic for me as a Black man going to see the first Black U.S. President.

My daughter could tell how excited I was when she met me at the station's entrance and crossed Pennsylvania Avenue and walked towards the White House gates. I was dressed in my blue seersucker suit, blue pinstriped shirt with a white collar, and red tie. My outfit was a walking billboard for America. Once we arrived inside the People's House, we took several photos together to commemorate what I think was one of our best father-daughter moments. I have a hunch we were the only father-daughter team at the conference. When we entered the State Dining Room, one of the White House staffers pulled me to the side and asked me if I wanted to be seated in the front of the room. I responded, "Certainly." That's how my daughter and I ended up seated right behind the former U.S. Senator Claire McCaskill (D-MO) who is now a political analyst for MSNBC and NBC News.

Throughout the conference, I gathered lots of new information about the state of aging, heard firsthand accounts from older Americans, and received updates about the Obama administration's efforts to support the aging community. When President Obama addressed the audience, I quickly moved into my role as a senior digital citizen. My phone camera was moving quite fast as I listened to his remarks. Once he was done, he stepped down from the stage and started walking towards former Senator McCaskill. He was shaking people's hands. So, I reached out mine and he grabbed it. I could not believe I was shaking hands with President Barack H. Obama and had a chance to thank him for his great work. My son Matthew was working at WETA that day and was able to view the moment in the control room at the station. He created a photo from the video recording. That photo is a prized possession that also serves as my Facebook page background. Before the day ended, my daughter and I joined a small group lunch discussion where I was able to share my own experiences about aging. What a day we had! One I will never forget.

Immediately following my White House experience, I was asked to discuss my online activism on the award-winning *Ed Brown Show* that aired on Bowie TV. The invitation was made possible by my daughter's Sigma Gamma Rho Sorority

Soror Kamaria Richmond who worked as a producer for the show. After my first interview, I returned as a regular guest to discuss political issues, the importance of voting, how to discuss race relations, and how my family celebrates Kwanzaa and its history. Kamaria also invited me to share my online activism experiences and discuss political issues and voting on her podcast, *The Stroke Diva Fabulous Show.*

During the 2020 election, I recorded a series of podcast discussions on SoundCloud about the importance of voting. I shared the episodes on my social media platforms and engaged in conversations with my Facebook community. I used the same model to launch my *Dr. John Live!* on Facebook during the 2022 midterm elections. I invited my NEA colleague Deloris Rozier to join me for a conversation about her election work in South Carolina and insights about voting in her state.

In the 1980s, I had been involved in the Lake Arbor community where we were living, serving on the homeowner's association board. This was a new community in Prince George's County. It had many growing pains and underwent a major transition from the original developers, who had to turn things over to the bank. The bank delayed further development until a company that specialized in restarting unfinished developments took over. During this period, I again served on the re-activated association. Much later, I once again served on the homeowner's association as president. Along with the other members, I helped to make some changes. We changed the management company, reduced the number of delinquent association fees, and established a regular schedule of meetings. Shortly before I moved out and to an active-over-55 community in 2016, I resigned. During the first two years in the new community, I served on the social committee. While I don't hold a formal role in my current neighborhood, I participate in social events and stay engaged through conversation with my neighbors when I am out walking or working out at the community center.

CONSULTING WORK

Even though I had closed my firm and stepped into retirement, I was open to taking on short-term client projects like the two Dr. Tamara Hamilton, a 1991 NEA intern, invited me to work on in 2017. The first project gave me the opportunity to be part of a team focused on implementing diversity in a national physician's organization that transforms health delivery experience for providers and consumers.

In the second project, I served as a member of a coaching team, working with employees of a major air and space organization. The focus was understanding executive presence and how to make it work. The program extended what is known about leadership by augmenting them with the interpersonal skills needed to consistently garner the respect and influence that produce disproportionately positive results. It is the evolution of the complete leader. The exciting aspect of the two efforts was introducing me to several new approaches to the delivery of training. I learned it is never too late to learn new things.

NATIONAL BLACK STAFF NETWORK AWARD

Throughout my career, I received many awards, certificates, and other forms of recognition. The most significant award was the JEGNA Award I received during the National Black Staff Network's (NBSN) 35th Annual Conference in 2019. I have been a member since its beginning and attended most of the annual conferences. I've also been a presenter and speaker.

The JEGNA Award is given to individuals who are active NBSN members and have made outstanding contributions to the organization and advocacy on behalf of African American employees of the NEA and its affiliates. In the ancient Ethiopian kingdom of Abyssinian, the word JEGNA is a title of distinction that refers to a master teacher who embodies courage, strength, and protection of the culture, land, and people. A JEGNA recipient has:

- Been tested in struggle or battle.
- Demonstrated extraordinary and unusual fearlessness.
- Shown determination and courage in protecting his/her people, land, and culture.
- Shown diligence and dedication to our people.
- Produced exceptionally high-quality work.
- Dedicated themselves to the protection, defense, nurturance, and development of our young by advancing our people, place, and culture.

I was surprised and humbled to receive the award and had no idea it was going to happen. For me, it represented a lifetime achievement award. As I accepted the award, my emotions got the best of me because it was a beautiful thing to receive my flowers while I am still alive. Having many of my former NEA interns present to share in my joyous celebration was the icing on the cake.

ALUMNI SERVICE

I have always been active in my Archbishop Carroll High School alumni activities because the school gave me so much in terms of a stellar academic education and career preparation. Having received such a rich experience, I felt compelled to give back to the current students. The school continues to do an excellent job in preparing young men and women for their college and professional careers.

Over the years, I have served as my class representative in the Carroll Alumni Association. The role of a class representative involves organizing reunions, encouraging classmates to share their personal and professional news with the school, helping the school communicate with my class, and being an ambassador for the school. I have enjoyed working with my classmates in planning reunions. I am proud to say I have attended all of them. Serving as a class representative has provided an opportunity to keep in touch with my classmates and strengthen our relationships. It has also allowed me to develop connections with younger alumni and students. One of the most memorable moments I had as a representative was when I welcomed the graduates into the Association during the 1982 graduation ceremony.

In 2015, Archbishop Carroll High School President Beth Blaufuss invited me to serve on the President's Council which is made up of alumni. In her written invitation, President Blaufuss told me she valued my advice and consulting experience. She thought my consulting experience would enhance the school's recruitment efforts and sustain and invigorate the school's commitment to social justice activism. Naturally, I accepted her invitation and was honored to be included with a diverse group of alumni.

Supporting Carroll's sports program during my children's high school years gave us an opportunity to root for the Lions at home games during the 1980s. My daughter borrowed my high school letter sweater and wore it to several basketball and football games. It was a big hit among her Elizabeth Seton High School classmates. The basketball and football games also created a healthy competition with my sons who attended DeMatha High School.

I also supported Carroll's Hall of Fame Induction Ceremony which started in 2007. In 2008, I attended the induction of my classmate James Howell, a basketball player. My longtime friend Lloyd Hall was inducted in 2011 for his service as the manager of the baseball, basketball, and football teams from 1951 to 1955. In 2022, the school held the Legends of Carroll Basketball Luncheon that included a naming ceremony for the George H. Leftwich Gymnasium and the Carroll Holmes Court. I met George during my senior year. I learned about Carroll when he became the basketball coach. Following their remarkable careers and now seeing them being recognized for their contributions to the school was powerful. Hearing the tributes given by many of the former players, coaches, and others impacted me emotionally. They reminded me that you should give people their flowers while they are still alive.

DOWNSIZING

At some point, Theresa and I undertook the process of downsizing which was a huge undertaking. A lot of people may resist it until something drastic happens like a health issue or death. Our decision to downsize was intentional, which eliminated resistance to this great change. We had always lived in a house that was suited for a family of six. We began to experience a change when the last of our four children moved out of the house during his third year of college. We did feel our home would always be a place our children could come back to, if necessary, but none of them ever returned. We were truly "empty nesters."

In addition to our family home, we also owned a beach house in Oyster Harbor, a private community on the Annapolis Neck peninsula, just outside of Annapolis, Maryland in Anne Arundel County. It was 30 minutes away from our home in the Lake Arbor community in Bowie. Oyster Harbor was incorporated in the 1950s. At that time, most of the homeowners were African Americans. Oyster Harbor shares Oyster Creek with three historic African American communities, Bay Highlands, Venice Beach, and the Village of Highland Beach.

We purchased the beach house in 1992 after Theresa read a *Washington Post* article about abolitionist Frederick Douglass's summer cottage, Twin Oaks, that was built in Highland Beach in 1895. She and my daughter went to visit the cottage and discovered Oyster Harbor which was located across from Highland Beach. After Highland Beach was incorporated in 1922, it became the first African American municipality in Maryland. It is also known as the first African American summer resort in the United States. Well-known homeowners and guests included Paul Robeson, Judge Robert Terrell, Dr. Mary Church Terrell, Booker T. Washington, Robert Weaver, Dr. W.E.B. DuBois, Paul Laurence Dunbar, Langston Hughes, E. Franklin Frazier, and Alex Haley.

We always felt the house was on sacred ancestral land. That's why we filled it with African American memorabilia and African artwork. We used it for weekend getaways, family vacations, birthday parties, annual crab feasts, and Kwanzaa celebrations during our 25 years of ownership. My daughter used it for her artist and writing retreats, and recovery from her fibroid surgery.

In 2015, navigating the steps in both houses became an issue for Theresa that caused us to move forward on our downsizing. We began searching for a one-level home with no steps. After several years, we found what we were dreaming about in a predominately white, active-over-55 adult community. Selling two houses was not an easy task. It took us two years to sell both. Our greatest challenge was not in the readying of our homes or in the sale itself but in deciding what to keep. Getting rid of over 50 years of stuff wasn't easy. With the support of our children, we were able to release a lot of stuff. There are still some things in boxes in the garage which should let you know that downsizing remains a work-in-progress.

LIFE IN A NEW COMMUNITY

Moving into the new community was a blessing because I didn't have to worry about any landscaping issues such as cutting our grass and planting flowers. I now have access to a community center that has an indoor heated pool, fitness center and weekly classes like the tai chi class I am currently taking, ballroom for hosting events, and outdoor pool and recreation areas for family barbeques. In the section of my neighborhood, my neighbors and I are VERY social. Most of us chat with each other whenever we meet up at the mailbox or while walking throughout the week. We also gather for block parties and monthly potluck dinners and host a few Saturday morning coffee chats during the year.

The community association organizes a wide variety of social activities and clubs. It also maintains an active email listserv and Facebook group for sharing information and diverse points of view. When we first moved in, I joined the social committee and was active in organizing many events. Last year, I joined the Unity and Presence Club that sponsors an African American book club, cultural events that celebrate Black History and Juneteenth, and a weekly game night. Being a part of the book club has expanded my reading interests. My daughter was excited to learn that I read Octavia Butler's book *Parable of the Sower* and Stacey Abrams's book *Rogue Justice*. She even attended one of the book club discussions and was able to witness my enthusiastic participation. I thoroughly enjoy both the book club and game night. However, game night is my favorite because it brings me back to my passion for playing bid whist that started during my college years at Indiana State University in Terre Haute.

Theresa and John Leeke with their goddaughter Sharon Malachi

*Theresa and John Leeke
with their godson
John Adeleye, Jr.*

*Theresa and John Leeke
with their goddaughter
Olusayo ("Sayo") Adeleye*

*Theresa and John Leeke
with their godson
John Adeleye, Jr.*

*John and Theresa Leeke
with their godchildren
Olusayo ("Sayo") and
David Adeleye*

John Leeke and John Adeleye, Sr. at the wedding of Sayo Adeleye and Alexander Baldridge in 2022

John and Bosede ("Bose") Adeleye

Theresa and John Leeke's goddaughter Olusayo ("Sayo") Adeleye and Alexander Baldridge at their wedding in 2022

John Leeke with his fellow Obama campaign volunteers from
Prince George's County, Maryland in 2012

John Leeke encouraging his
fellow Obama campaign
volunteers from Prince
George's County, Maryland on
a bus ride to Virginia in 2012

John Leeke volunteering
as a phone canvasser for
the Obama campaign in
Prince George's County,
Maryland in 2012

John Leeke volunteering for Anthony Brown,
a Democratic candidate for Maryland Governor in 2014

John Leeke with fellow volunteers for Anthony Brown,
a Democratic candidate for Maryland Governor in 2014

*John Leeke shaking President Barack H. Obama's hand at
the White House Conference on Aging in 2015*

John Leeke, Ed Brown (seated), Kamaria Richmond, and William Murry on The Ed Brown Show *in 2015*

John Leeke and Ed Brown discussing Kwanzaa on The Ed Brown Show *in 2015*

*John Leeke receiving the National Black Staff Network's
JEGNA award from Dr. Tamara Hamilton and
another NEA staff person in 2019*

*John Leeke with his Archbishop Carroll High School
classmates at a barbeque. Seated (L–R): Richard Gaither,
James Howell, and Royce Wells. Standing (L–R):
Sameul Malachi, William Jameson, John Leeke, Lloyd Hall,
Arnold Hart, Herman Richards, and John Robinson.*

*John Leeke with his Archbishop Carroll
High School classmates Jim Beers, John Flood, and
Herman Richards at an awards ceremony*

CHAPTER 19 REFLECTION QUESTIONS

---

1. Individual: Have you thought about what your life would look like in retirement?

2. Individual: Have you helped a family member or friend prepare for retirement? What were some of their retirement concerns?

3. Group Discussion: Give each person 3–5 minutes to share their individual response with the group. As a group, list some of the similarities and differences highlighted in the sharing session. Also, discuss one or two lessons each person has learned.

CHAPTER 20

My Family

*"Family represents a collection of individuals who are
committed and bound together, always and forever,
to provide love and support to one another."*

—DR. JOHN F. LEEKE, a change agent

In the movie *Mahogany*, starring Diana Ross and Billy Dee
Williams, there was a powerful scene where he says to her,
"Success is nothing without someone you love to share it
with!" His words echo the love and support one gets when
they share their lives with others, especially in a family. His
words always remind me how important my relationships
with my wife and children are. My family relationships have
been and continue to be my lifeline of love, growth, friendship, and support. I am grateful to have them in my life.

For 62 years, my wife, Theresa Bernadette (Gartin) Leeke,
was my life partner, my best friend, my lover, and a mother to
our four children. I had a front-row seat in watching Theresa
move through life as a loving and supportive wife, mother,
daughter, sister, and aunt while wearing the hats of a mu-

sician, an educator, a social activist, and a church, sorority, and community leader. One of the greatest lessons she taught me was patience, especially when I wanted things to move faster in life or in a different direction. For example, I wrote earlier in the book about my year-long struggles as a teacher at Brown Junior High School during the second year of our marriage. There were many times I wanted to give up and resign. However, Theresa helped me have patience and faith by talking to and reminding me that God was watching out for us. Together we leaned into our Catholic faith through prayer and weekly worship services.

When she was born in Indianapolis, her parents, Dorothy Mae (Johnson) Gartin and Robert Warren Gartin, Sr., had her baptized at St. Rita Catholic Church. Her baptism was a Gartin family tradition that started with the children of her great-grandmother Millie Ann Gartin. She was educated at St. Rita Catholic School and St. Mary Academy. At an early age, she discovered her passion for music and began playing the piano and organ at St. Rita's. As she matured, she also began leading the church choir and playing music for the choir and glee clubs at St. Mary's during her high school years. When she graduated, she decided to study education at Indiana University, Butler University, and Indiana State Teachers College. She paused her college education after we married and began having children.

After we moved to Maryland and our youngest child entered school, she returned to college at Prince George's Community College and earned an Associate of Arts degree in Elementary Education. Immediately after completing this degree, she pursued a Bachelor of Science in Early Childhood Education with honors from the University of Maryland at College Park. Throughout these educational experiences, she took our four children to class with her as I was often on the road. After she began working as a teacher in a Catholic elementary school, she continued to pursue advanced work in early childhood education at the University of Maryland and completed a Master of Science degree in Curriculum and Supervision from Trinity University in Washington, DC. Throughout her academic endeavors, I witnessed a woman who was committed to continuous learning. I admired her drive, work ethic, persistence, determination, attention to detail, and energy that she invested in her education and passion for music.

Her professional career included being an elementary school teacher, assistant principal, and principal—all at Catholic elementary schools in the Archdiocese of Washington, DC. This allowed her to model and teach the importance of academic excellence and continuous learning to her students and staff. As a consummate networker, community builder, and collaborative leader, she: launched afterschool programs; developed teaching and training models; secured funding and in-kind donations; created a computer lab; increased parental support and participation; and incorporated the arts and music as core subject matters. Her efforts enhanced the overall academic experience of students and added to the professional growth of her staff. Theresa was asked to serve on the Middle States Association of Colleges and Schools to do peer evaluations and regional accreditation of public and private schools in the Middle Atlantic, USA. She served as chair for numerous school accreditations throughout the region from New York to Maryland.

Drawing on more than seven decades of musical passion and experience, Theresa served the St. Joseph Catholic Church Community for 53 years as the founder and Musical Director of the St. Joseph Gospel Choir. Under her leadership, she developed several music ministries that included cantors, a praise and worship band, small vocal ensembles, children and youth choirs, and Grow Our Own Musicians. Grow Our Own Musicians Program was her most cherished effort. The program allowed her to teach, train, and mentor children and youth on how to read liturgical music, play musical instruments, and participate as members of St. Joseph's liturgical music ministry. Many of the young people graduated from high school and college and were married. A few currently provide music where they reside.

In addition to serving her church community, Theresa served Sigma Gamma Rho Sorority, Inc. for 64 years. She was a life member and a Cultured Pearl, a highly respected distinction. She was inducted into Alpha Chapter at Butler University, under the direction of the founding members of the sorority. When we moved to Flint, Michigan, she became a charter member of Gamma Psi Sigma Chapter. Then when we moved to Landover, Maryland, she transferred into Phi Sigma Chapter and began working as an undergraduate advisor to Epsilon Lambda Chapter at Bowie State University.

She became charter advisor to Eta Beta Chapter at the University of Maryland at College Park, her alma mater. Later, she served as an advisor to Alpha Phi Chapter at Howard University. In addition, she has served three terms as Basileus (President), two terms as Anti-Basileus, historian, and secretary, and chaired and served on various committees on the regional and national levels.

Her commitment to being actively involved in organizations like the parent-teacher association and the neighborhood community homeowner association was something I always admired because it demonstrated her dedication to our family and the local community. Over the years, she was able to expand her activism by serving on the board of the Phyllis Wheatley YWCA and holding membership in the National Council of Negro Women, the American Association of University Women, Kappa Delta Pi, the NAACP, and the Gospel Music Workshop of America. In her retirement years, I watched her live out her commitment to make life better for others. She was a quintessential woman. A smart, confident, humble, beautiful, and stylish person who knew who she was and what she wanted out of life. I am grateful she was my wife, partner, lover, and friend.

FATHERHOOD

Having been an only child, I knew I wanted to have children. I had no idea what raising them required, but like other things in my life, I learned and have enjoyed the experience. One of the joys of being a father has been nurturing and seeing my children become loving, independent, contributing, and productive human beings. From their early years to now, I have witnessed the growth of four unique individuals who have carved out for themselves a direction for how they want to live their lives.

MICHAEL DAVID

My eldest son, Michael David (Mike), was our Montessori child. We believe that contributed to him being very organized and creative. As the first born, Mike became the leader of the pack and during his early years and into high school, he quietly set the pace for his siblings. Like many kids growing up in the suburbs, when he wasn't in school or hanging out with friends in the neighborhood, he was watching TV, mostly cartoons, science fiction, action, and adventure shows. The cartoon that most affected him was the *Justice League of America*. Mike would sit in front of the TV and try to draw the characters after watching them. Realizing his interest, we bought him a drafting table and enrolled him in an after-school art course where he began to learn the fundamentals of drawing.

In his senior year at Largo Senior High School, he received the Outstanding Graphic Artist award from the *Scholastic Magazine* on Senior Day. We were so surprised as he hadn't said a word, but this was Mike. His award gave me bragging rights at work. As a result, my colleague Jessie Muse hired him to create illustrations for the NEA's color filmstrip, *Inte-*

grating Handicapped Students into Regular Classrooms. His work was so good that another colleague hired him to work on a project.

His acceptance into the Philadelphia College of Art (now the University of the Arts) was a blessing because it gave him what I think was the perfect environment and community to major in art illustration. Mike's career started in his senior year of college when Comico Comics, a Japanese-based company, hired him as a freelance illustrator for the *Robotech: The Macross Saga* series. For the next seven years, he continued to be one of the principal artists for Comico.

After leaving Comico, he began working for Valiant Comics on *X-O Manowar*, *H.A.R.D. Corps*, *Deathmate*, and *Psi-Lords*. He later illustrated his first co-owned project, *Pantheon*, that was published by Lone Star Press. He also partnered with several artists to launch the *Gritz 'n' Gravy Magazine* featuring his own project, *The Cadre*. Throughout his career, I have gone to comic stores where he was the guest artist. Seeing him in his world surrounded by his fans was always a proud moment. I was proud to be called Mike Leeke's father.

In the past several years, he has worked on special commissioned projects, including a profile illustration of architect Julian Francis Abele for Temple University's *Black Lives Always Mattered* graphic novel. The graphic novel presents the history and impact of 14 Black Philadelphians. Abele was the primary designer of Duke University's West Campus. He also designed more than 400 buildings, including the Widener Memorial Library at Harvard University, Philadelphia's Central Library, and the Philadelphia Museum of Art.

Like me and my parents, Mike met his wife, Lu, when they were college students in Philadelphia. He introduced me to her during one of my visits. She was born in Hong Kong, China. She and her family moved to Norfolk, Virginia in the late 1960s. Shortly after settling in Norfolk, her parents opened a Chinese restaurant. Like Mike, Lu is an artist and a culinary genius. Throughout their long courtship, she shared her tasty dishes with our family.

When they married in 1993, I gained an amazing daughter and chef. Their wedding was very special. It was held the day before my parents' wedding anniversary at St. Joseph Catholic Church. It also reflected their commitment to honor African American, Chinese, and West African cultures in the wedding attire, decorations, music, and rituals. Lu sewed her own wedding dress and the Kente cloth vests worn by Mike and the groomsmen. Mike drew their portrait for the cover of the wedding program. Ghanaian Adinkra symbols and photos of Mike and Lu as children and their parents were included on the wedding program. They jumped the broom, an African American tradition that was established during slavery, at their wedding reception. African, Chinese, and African American soul food were served to their guests. At the end of the day, my wife and I hosted both families at our house and witnessed a Chinese tea ceremony that paid homage to Lu's parents and family.

Lu told me the purpose of the Chinese Wedding Tea Ceremony is to show respect, honor, and express gratitude for the couple's families. The newlyweds honor and conduct the tea service on their knees in front of the parents who are seated. When they receive and sip tea, their actions symbolize the acceptance of the marriage. Afterwards, they offer words of wisdom, give red envelopes containing money, and wishes of good luck, success, and fertility to the couple. The red envelopes are called "hong bao" in Mandarin or "lai see" in Cantonese. They are given by elders and married couples who enjoy passing good fortune to others, especially the young. New crisp bills and shiny coins are used in the amounts of the number eight which is the luckiest number in Chinese culture. The images or symbols on the envelopes are just as important as the money inside. One should use the money and save the envelope for luck.

Over the years, I have enjoyed visiting Mike and Lu in their home in Philadelphia and watching their marriage grow. I have also enjoyed celebrating many holidays with Lu's family. I got to know her brother Joe and his sons and her sister Sylvia. Sylvia lived with Mike and Lu and was a part of our family gatherings. Some of my favorite memories were spending time with Sylvia and Lu while they prepared Chinese New Year dinner each year. That's where I became aware of Chinese New Year and different Chinese dishes and traditions they learned from their mother. They taught me Chinese New Year is also referred to as Lunar New Year. It is a celebration that has a wide variety of traditions. Some of these practiced customs and traditions may be from myths, superstitions, symbolism, and even wordplay. Individuals can choose to celebrate a little differently depending on their preferences, beliefs, and locations.

During our family gatherings, Sylvia and I would spend hours talking about politics and social issues. She often asked me for advice about work, social issues, and life in general. I appreciate the time she and Lu spent with my mother during her final years. They both loved sports too. They were fans of the Buffalo Bills and Philadelphia Phillies who never passed up a great buffet. I'll never forget the time she and Lu volunteered during President Obama's first campaign and them coming to DC to attend his inauguration in 2009. Afterwards, we followed President Obama's administration closely and talked about civil rights frequently. I admired Sylvia's thirst for knowledge, quick wit, commitment to family, and work ethic. We kept in touch even during the pandemic through family Zoom calls. My heart was broken when she died of cancer in 2022.

MADELYN CHERYL

Before she was born, I had prayed for a daughter. When she arrived on a cold winter day, I became what folks now call a girl dad. We named her Madelyn Cheryl in honor of Madelyn Grace, Theresa's best friend and maid of honor in Indianapolis, and Cheryl Saunders, the daughter of my parents' friends Martha and Hallet Saunders in DC. Cheryl and her dad, Hallet, became her godparents. Cheryl's parents were Mike's godparents. Before we took her home, we gave her the nickname

"Puffy" because she had puffy jaws. "Puff the Magic Dragon" became a longer nickname that followed her into her college years when she pledged Sigma Gamma Rho Sorority at Morgan State University.

By the time Madelyn was two years old, Theresa and I noticed her independent and competitive nature. She also had the gift of gab and asking questions. She seemed to want to do everything better than her brother Mike. When we moved to Landover, Maryland, nothing seemed to get in the way of her playing with her brothers and their friends. She developed a strong interest in sports and watched football, basketball, and track. Whatever they were into, she would do it too. Playing kickball, soccer, and football, riding bikes, climbing trees, and going to gymnastics and karate classes at the recreation center. Digging in the dirt, running through the sprinkler, planting vegetables, and collecting insects in the backyard. Drawing, reading, playing with Hot Wheels, and pretending to be the Jackson Five in the basement. She also had her own friends and interests that included playing with Barbie dolls, listening to music on the radio and records on her record player, watching *Soul Train* and learning new dances, coloring, reading and writing poetry, making homemade cards, and making cakes and brownies with her Easy Bake Oven.

Like her brothers Mike and Mark, Madelyn attended Kenmoor Elementary School and Kenmoor Junior High School. When she was in the eighth grade, she decided she wasn't being challenged academically. During this time, she became friends with several students at St. John Baptist de la Salle, the school Theresa taught at. Her new friends talked to her about their plans to attend Catholic high school and their academic and extracurricular interests. She talked to Theresa about attending high school with them. They selected Elizabeth Seton High School. The first time I learned about her interest in attending Catholic school was the day she received her acceptance letter. I was surprised because we wanted our children to attend public school. Working at the NEA made me a strong supporter of public education. Although I was hurt and we did not have a conversation about their decision and the reasons for it, I supported her choice to attend Seton. Looking back, it was clearly the right thing for her to do.

Her choice opened the door to having the types of experiences and significant development Theresa and I had in Catholic school. A year after she started at Seton, we decided Mark and Matt would attend Catholic school. Mark was accepted into DeMatha High School. Matthew enrolled in St. Ambrose Catholic Elementary School. The location of their new schools created an easier commute. In the morning, Theresa dropped off Matthew at St. Ambrose, Madelyn at Seton, and Mark at DeMatha before heading to her teaching job at St. John's.

In her junior year at Seton, she took a practical law class and decided she would pursue a career as a lawyer. Following what she learned in school, she created a strategy for achieving her career goal which included extracurricular activities that would help her develop leadership and business skills. She held several offices in the Awareness of Black Culture Club at Seton and joined Junior Achievement and Toastmasters' International. Both experiences helped her develop her confidence and speaking skills. Along with the teaching methods at Seton, she became very organized and was always an avid reader.

During her junior and senior years, she applied to several historically Black colleges and universities (HBCUs) including Spelman College, Fisk University, Bennet College, Xavier University, and Morgan State University. Each week she seemed to be excited about a different one. Her mother told her she had to attend an HBCU. All of them were some distance away. Her final choices were Xavier in New Orleans and Morgan in Baltimore. We paid a room deposit on both schools because we knew she might not want to go so far away. On the day of her graduation, she walked up the aisle of the Basilica thinking she was going to Xavier. When she walked down the aisle with her diploma, she changed her mind and decided to go to Morgan because she realized she would not be able to come home regularly and get her hair done. Her hair was a major thing because she had it done every two weeks ever since she was four years old.

Attending an HBCU was exactly what she needed at the time. She decided to major in French because she was good at it and thought it would help her get good grades for law school. She learned early on from her French advisor and mentor, Dr. Sandye J. McIntyre, II, that majoring in French would not be easy. Dr. McIntyre was chair of the Foreign Languages Department and treated her like a daughter. He was always in her business and carefully monitored her academic and social activities. In 1986, she graduated with a Bachelor of Arts in French and a minor in Spanish. After graduation, she attended Howard University School of Law and graduated in 1989. Immediately after graduation, she worked as a law clerk for Administrative Law Judge Robert E. Duncan at the U.S. Commodities Futures and Trading Commission. During this time, she started her course work and later earned a Master of Laws in Securities and Financial Regulation from Georgetown University Law Center in 1991. She had accomplished many of her goals, but then experienced a major stumbling block as she took and failed the bar exam eight times.

While she was studying for the bar exam, she began to learn about and participate in African American history and political groups. She also became a vegetarian, studied world religions, and returned to writing poetry. To honor her African ancestors, she adopted the Swahili name "Kiamsha" which means "that which awakens me" in 1992. The name celebrated her creative spirit. That same year, she launched her first business, Sunsum Communications, and self-published her first chapbook of poetry, *My Soul Speaks*. When she turned 40, she adopted the name "Ananda" which means "God's eternal bliss" in Sanskrit to mark her commitment to yoga, meditation, and Buddhism.

After taking the bar exam for the eighth time in 1993, she decided she no longer needed a bar card to move forward in her career. With the support of our family and her friends and mentors, she pursued a career in finance. Shortly thereafter, she landed a job in municipal finance. Over the course of her diverse career, she has worn the hat of an entrepreneur and worked in investment banking, refugee resettlement, and digital communications in the DC Government, a woman-led investment banking firm, and various nonprofit organizations. As an entrepreneur, she has shared her gifts as a speaker, trainer, artist, yoga teacher, reiki practitioner, meditation teacher, coach, mindfulness consultant, and digital wellness educator. Currently, she leads Ananda Leeke Consulting, a wellness company. She also manages the Thriving Mindfully Academy, an online education platform and membership site, and hosts the *Thriving Mindfully Podcast*. Her three books are available on Amazon: *Love's Troubadours*, a self-love and yoga-inspired novel; *That Which Awakens Me: A Creative Woman's Poetic Memoir of Self-Discovery*; and *Digital Sisterhood: A Memoir of Fierce Living Online*.

Throughout her life, she has enjoyed traveling. Her first solo trip was to Indianapolis to see Theresa's family in 1972. Since then, she has traveled to numerous cities in the U.S. and countries including Brazil, Canada, China, Cuba, Egypt, Ghana, Haiti, Jamaica, Senegal, and Turkey.

Like her mother Theresa, great-grandmother Florida, and a great-grandaunt Lillian, she is a member of Sigma Gamma Rho Sorority. She acknowledges she is a Black American Princess (BAP) like her mother and grandmother Frederica. As a father, I had looked forward to escorting and dancing the waltz at her debutante ball during her freshman year at Morgan. Even though she put us through a lot more work and drama when her escort showed up late, it was one of my proudest moments.

Throughout high school, college, law school, and most of her work experiences, I have often played a role in and/or attended her activities. While she was in high school, I was working at the NEA. Many mornings I would drive her to school. We would listen to WHUR's morning show and sing Bob Marley & The Wailers song, "Three Little Birds." Her favorite part was, "Don't worry about a thing 'cause every little thing is gonna be alright." When she was at Morgan, I would stop by the campus on my way home from consulting jobs. I got to know most of her friends who would often go and tell her, "Your father is on campus." While she was at Howard, I even flew home to observe her first moot court assignment. During her blogging years, I attended local and national conferences with her. Her blogging friends also became my blogging friends. Most family members and friends consider her a daddy's girl. That makes me a girl dad.

As a girl dad of an adult woman, I have learned to appreciate her independence, assertiveness, intelligence, creativity, and empathy. She often sends me cards and emails expressing her feelings and thoughts. I have kept many of them over the years. When I turned 70 in 2009, she sent me a handwritten card with a message that read:

Happy 70ᵗʰ Birthday J, a father, a friend, a fan, a family man, a fabulous human being! May you continue to enjoy a fantastic life with family, friends, career opportunities, and fun times.

John @ 70, a poem

Seventy opens the door to Sensational Living
Special moments to reflect and grow
Sharing opportunities to bless others with your
    hard-earned wisdom
Service experiences to work towards fulfilling
    President Obama's plan.
So go for it all, Change Agent!

Love Puf

Her words echo the result of many of my life's choices. I am glad she can see and appreciate me in ways that affirm what I have tried to do as a father to all my children.

MARK ANDREW

Mark is our third child and second son. He was given the nickname "Tank" because when he was very young, he looked like a tank. During the pregnancy, we had a scare that he didn't seem to be in the correct position, but fortunately everything worked out perfectly. Mark, like our others, attended Kenmoor Elementary School. He completed two years at Kenmoor Junior High School before heading off to DeMatha Catholic High School. While there, he developed a serious interest in photography. By the time he reached his final year, he wanted to follow Mike and attend Philadelphia College of

Art. However, he ended up getting accepted to Atlanta College of Art which turned out to be a wonderful decision. In Atlanta, he studied photography, experimental sound, and video production. Mark, like his brother and sister, was taken and dropped off at college and returned home only for vacations and family celebrations. He became very independent and quickly adjusted to life in Atlanta. He also secured a part-time job as a bartender at the college.

His 1988 graduation was a major family celebration. My parents, Theresa, Mike, and myself flew down to Atlanta. Matthew and Madelyn drove from DC. We hosted a big dinner to celebrate his Bachelor of Fine Arts with his classmate's family at Paschal's Restaurant, a famous Black-owned soul food establishment that had been a meeting place for Dr. Martin Luther King, Jr., Aretha Franklin, Andrew Young, and others.

Shortly after he graduated, he began his career as a video journalist at Turner Broadcasting's *CNN Headline News*. His duties at CNN included studio camera, video editing, master control video playback, audio, technical directing, and directing a half-hour newscast.

In 1996, he took a position as a technical director at QVC, Inc. in the Philadelphia suburbs. At QVC, he worked in both the studio and control rooms, manning the switcher, robotic cameras, audio, graphics, and the studio camera. In less than a year, he was contacted by a former CNN colleague who was working at Reuters Japan in Tokyo, and invited Mark to join him as Director and Editor. He directed live newscasts and ran audio, robotic camera, and video editing. He was promoted to Senior Director in 2000 and took on additional duties that included videography, booking satellites, and training production staff. During his stay in Asia, he took advantage of traveling to other parts of Asia and Europe. He took up scuba diving and visited some of the best scuba sites in the world.

Theresa and I were excited about his opportunity to work in Japan but knew we would not see him for long stretches at a time. We did get the opportunity to visit him in Tokyo after one of my NEA assignments in Hawaii. Prior to traveling to Japan, we had taken a few international trips to Germany and various Caribbean Islands. When we arrived at Tokyo International Airport, Mark met us. We were amazed by its massive size. We witnessed a high-level of organization we hadn't seen before. The airport personnel were extremely courteous. They were quick to provide support and answer our questions. One thing we weren't prepared for was the two-hour long train ride from the airport to the center of Tokyo. It was exhausting.

Mark arranged for us to stay at a fabulous five-star hotel that had big rooms, glass showers, and a pot of green tea delivered twice a day. We enjoyed a delicious breakfast bar with an assortment of food. We really liked the fact that the hotel was located right next to a subway station. It made our local travel experience great because once we entered the subway, we saw firsthand what living in Tokyo was truly like. The first thing we noticed was how people travel to work in crowded trains during the rush hour. We were shoulder-to-shoulder with them. Even though we were too close for comfort, people managed to be polite and even offered Theresa a seat on one occasion. We also saw restaurants and all types of shops in the underground area. A person could actually stay underground and do everything like eating and shopping.

During the day, we visited temples, museums, and other historical sites. While we were at the museums, we noticed how Japanese children attended school on a half-day schedule four days a week. They had time to visit museums and explore the city on their own during their off time which was very different from our experience as educators and parents.

Each night during our visit, Mark and his friends took us to different restaurants. Our dining experience exposed us to many neighborhood restaurants with a variety of great-tasting Japanese food. At one of the restaurants, we sat on the floor around a table and watched a chef cook the food in front of us. He explained the ingredients and the reasons he was using them in our meal.

Two of the highlights of our trip were visiting Mark's apartment and Akihabara. Seeing his tiny apartment was eye-opening and exposed us to Japanese minimalism and efficiency. He had a washer with no inside dryer. That meant he had to dry things on a clothing line. Akihabara is known as "Electric Town," a famous shopping hub named after electronics retailers. There were all types of shops from tiny stalls to vast department stores that sold electronic products that take about five to 10 years to come to the U.S. Street vendors sold the same products at a cheaper price in the back alleys.

In 2002, Reuters (like other news agencies), engaged in downsizing and reorganizing that resulted in Mark being laid off. Initially, he stayed in Japan and began a contract position in the master control unit for the broadcast center at the World Cup Soccer Finals in Yokohama. Later that year, he returned home and began working at C-SPAN in DC. Shortly thereafter, he was hired by Comcast as a Director and Studio Manager for its Brookline Studios in Boston, Massachusetts. When Mark became homesick and fed up with Boston's cold weather and snow, he applied for a Technical Manager position at DCTV in 2006. DCTV gave him an opportunity to work directly with members of the DC community. It also allowed him to utilize his management and production skills as well as mentor and train students and professionals.

During the COVID-19 pandemic, he was laid off and began freelancing full-time in the fall of 2020. His clients included entrepreneurs and small nonprofit organizations that needed help using technology, creating audio and video content, and streaming online. Several of his former DCTV interns hired him to do contract work for their companies. A year later, he applied for and accepted a position as a Master Controller and Technical Director at the WBAL Channel 11 (NBC) in Baltimore. He wears many hats in this position. He manages audio, robotic cameras, and the master control. He also serves as the technical and floor director.

Mark, like other Leeke family members, has had a variety of experiences. He has also demonstrated other family traits and interests including a willingness to explore new opportunities, hard work, support of others, teamwork, commitment, and entrepreneurship. Our father and son bond has spilled over into our passion for sports. We are both self-proclaimed sports junkies who used to have season tickets to Georgetown University's basketball games. He has also become one of my tech gurus who provides in-person and phone training and technical assistance.

MATTHEW JAY

Matthew (Matt) is the last of the four M's. He was a surprise as we had skipped a year of Theresa being pregnant. Afterwards, she made it very clear we were done. Matt being the last experienced many indignities from his siblings. They teased and made him feel different. He didn't have to wear glasses and had different hair which was curly and difficult to be styled in a bush. The others even attempted to tell him he wasn't really a Leeke and was adopted. One of his goals was to get even one day.

When we moved to Landover, Maryland, Matt became close friends with our neighbor, Stanford Coleman. They were inseparable from the time they met. They even went to nursery school and Kenmoor Elementary School together. Their elementary school teachers thought Stanford was another Leeke. At dinnertime when Theresa would call the children in from playing outside to eat dinner, Stanford would always come with them and sit right down at the table like his was our fifth child. We always fed him. Surprisingly, his mother didn't figure out until much later the reason he was not so hungry was because he had already eaten at our house.

They remained close throughout high school.

After he completed the sixth grade, we enrolled Matt in St. Ambrose Catholic Elementary School. He followed Mark to DeMatha Catholic High School. Matt ran track, participated in fashion shows, and was very social at DeMatha. He loved to go to dances and talk to girls. He was also active in a Catholic Youth Organization's Substance Abuse Program, a local high school group that encouraged teens not to use drugs. While he was in the group, he met his lifelong friend, Andrew "Drew" Peace. They forged a strong bond that lasted until Drew's early death from cancer, which Matt took very hard.

While he was at home, he spent what we thought was way too much time watching television and listening to music. Little did we know his passion for television and music would lead him to his current career. By the time he was in his senior year, we didn't need to have a discussion as to whether he was going to college because we made it clear he was going. He only had to decide which school. Howard University was his only choice. He did apply to Towson State University, mainly to satisfy me. He thought a second option might help sway my concern for any potential girl-crazy distractions he might face from the beautiful Howard women.

Attending Howard University, one of the top HBCUs, turned out to be one of his best life decisions and biggest blessings. At Howard, he developed a serious attitude and focus about his major and career in radio and television. The School of Communications became a second home for him filled with mentors and peers who shared his interests. That one choice gave him access to some of the greatest Black television and radio professionals in the DC area like the late great Melvin Lindsey, host of WHUR's *Quiet Storm*. Matt grew up listening to him on the radio and had many opportunities to talk and work with him.

When I hear him talk about his career, he often shares how he has always been in the right place at the right time. During the first semester of his freshmen year, he started working at the student-run radio station, WHBC. Within a short time, he had his own show. During this period, he developed a friendship with Melvin who mentored and took him under his wing. Being a Howard alum, Melvin upheld the tradition, "Each One Teach One." Melvin also helped him develop a sense of community.

In his second semester, Matt enrolled in the WHMM-TV student training program. Upon completion, he began interning at the station. His internship paved the way for paid freelancing opportunities. He seized his first paid opportunity in the broadcasting industry when WHMM was looking for students to work at commencement. That one paid gig led to more than a decade of him working at the annual commencement.

Throughout his college career, he constantly searched for ways to enhance his skills and knowledge. He took the opportunity to learn about sound engineering and found his way to securing a job at Howard's Cramton Auditorium. While working there, he developed lifelong friendships and gained a mentor in Ralph T. Dines, the manager at Cramton. Mr. Dines was a second father to him at Howard. He not only trained Matt but made sure he was fed. Students affectionately referred to him as "Daddy Dines." He was given this nickname because he mentored and hired numerous students, and the fact that he was the first Black man in the International Alliance of Theatrical and Stage Employees (IATSE).

All his friendships were with students or recent college graduates who were a few years older than him. He formed very close relationships with Anthony "Bucky" Adams and David Green. They helped Matt form a brotherhood that became known as "Mr. Dines's boys." As a result of his relationship with Mr. Dines and Bucky, he started working at the Carter Barron Amphitheatre during the summers. After graduation, he continued to work there as the Technical Director of Stage Production. His job at the Carter Barron included family benefits, aka free tickets to concerts, that we took advantage of. Thanks to Matt, we enjoyed many blues, jazz, and R&B concerts.

His other mentors included Jim Brown, Director of Student Training at WHMM-TV, and Judi Moore-Latta, his faculty advisor. Jim worked with him on the student produced program, *Spotlight*. *Spotlight* gave Matt the complete foundation for television production. With Jim's guidance, he was able to direct 18 30-minute and two hour-long television shows. Having Judi as a mentor and faculty advisor helped him stay focused on managing personnel. She pushed him forward and instilled his confidence in trusting his own judgment that led him to be more confident. She mentored him when he was running WHBC, the student radio station, as the general manager.

During Matt's junior year, he broke one of the Leeke traditions by moving back home and commuting to school. Matt had also been the first to get his driver's license in high school and took advantage of having access to one of the family cars. In some ways, I think his mother enjoyed having him home. Matt was a momma's boy. His stay at home only lasted a year until his mother made arrangements for him to move into a studio apartment on the same floor as his sister in The Woodner on 16th Street in DC. I am told by my children that The Woodner was a popular apartment complex for Howard students. Since he was already driving our family Volvo station wagon, it moved with him too.

Matthew's commitment to hard work and entrepreneurial spirit began early as he and one of his lifelong friends, Erik Carey, started their own neighborhood business, E&M Enterprise. When it snowed, they shoveled driveways and sidewalks. During the summer, they cut grass and washed cars. After he graduated from Howard with a Bachelor of Arts in Radio and Television in 1989, he formed his own production company, MAJIK Productions, which was later incorporated in 2001.

In addition to starting his own business, he worked temporarily at AVS, an audiovisual company at the Capital Hilton Hotel in DC. He had been offered a job at CNN in Atlanta, but chose not to take it because he didn't want to be in the shadow of his brother, Mark. That proved to be a smart move on his part because WHMM-TV hired him a few months later. Within three years, he became the main Post-Production Editor and Sound Engineer. During his tenure, he received several awards for his work, including employee of the year and a PBS Gold Award. He also edited several Emmy Award-winning programs.

In 1994, Matt left the public television world and became a Post-Production Editor at WJZ-TV (CBS) in Baltimore, Maryland. This position gave him an opportunity to edit the news, do stage directing in the studio, work in engineering audio for all newscasts, and serve as a technical director. After 13 years, he returned to public television and began working at WETA-TV. WETA produces multiple network shows, such as *The PBS Newshour*, *Washington Week*, and *In Performance at the White House*. Matt has been able to work on many of these shows. Currently, he is the Production Tape Supervisor and Editor for both local and national programming. His work at PBS was celebrated when he received the George Foster Peabody Award for Editing for the News Coverage of COVID-19 in 2021.

As he matured and began his professional work career, he became very focused which led him to become a workaholic. During the 1990s, he was introduced to Pamela (Pam) Charity by their mutual friend. They initially became friends. Many years later, they began dating and maintained a long-distance relationship until they were married in 2011 in a beautiful ceremony in Cleveland, Ohio. Throughout the years, Pam and I have developed a close relationship. I have tried to show up in her life like I would my own daughter. One special highlight was when I traveled with Matt to Cleveland to join her family and friends in celebrating her on the day she received her Ph.D. in Urban Education from Cleveland State University. She is an educator with a longstanding career in higher education and programs specialized in serving under-represented students. We have a lot of conversations about life in the same way I spoke to Sylvia, Lu's sister. We also enjoyed attending Georgetown Hoya basketball games together or with Matt and Mark. We both love decorating our trees and homes together during the Christmas holiday season. Like Lu and Syl, Pam is one of the greatest blessings I could receive.

High school photo of
Michael D. Leeke

High school photo of
Madelyn C. (Ananda) Leeke

High school photo of
Mark A. Leeke

High school photo of
Matthew J. Leeke

Theresa and John Leeke celebrating their 25ᵗʰ wedding anniversary
with their children and parents, Dorothy Gartin and Frederica
and John L. Leeke, at St. Joseph Catholic Church in 1986

*Wedding program of Michael
and Lu Leeke in 1993
(artwork by Michael Leeke)*

*Wedding of Michael and
Lu Leeke at St. Joseph
Catholic Church in 1993*

*Wedding photo of Michael and Lu Leeke at
St. Joseph Catholic Church in 1993*

(L–R) Ricardo Marbury (best man), Michael and Lu Leeke, and Sylvia Eng (maid of honor) at Michael and Lu's wedding at St. Joseph Catholic Church in 1993

(L–R) Mark, Matt, John, Mike, Lu, Theresa, and Madelyn (Ananda) Leeke at Michael and Lu's wedding at St. Joseph Catholic Church in 1993

*Matthew and Pamela Leeke celebrating their wedding
with the Leeke Family in Cleveland, Ohio in 2011*

Family dinner celebrating Theresa's birthday in 2019

Theresa and John's photo from St. Joseph Catholic Church's member directory in 2019

John and Theresa at goddaughter Sayo Adeleye's wedding in 2022

Family page in St. Joseph Catholic Church's
Centennial Celebration Program Booklet *in 2022*

Family barbeque celebrating John's birthday in 2023

CHAPTER 20 REFLECTION QUESTIONS

—————————

1. Individual: How have you experienced family in your life?

2. Group Discussion: Give each person 3–5 minutes to share their individual response with the group. As a group, list some of the similarities and differences highlighted in the sharing session. Also, discuss one or two lessons each person has learned.

CHAPTER 21

Our Father's Journey: How My Children See Me

"It's the courage to raise a child that makes you a father."

—BARACK OBAMA, a change agent and
the 44th President of the United States

Being a father of four children who are now adults with different personalities, ideas, needs, and wants has not been easy. Some might call it an adventure into the unknown that never ends. Having the courage to embrace the adventure of being our father daily and raising us with our mother is one of the greatest gifts we have received in our lifetime.

In writing this book, our father has given us two more gifts that will live well beyond his lifetime. His first gift is blessing us with an inside look into his psyche and the people and experiences that have impacted him over the past eight decades. His second gift is the invitation to share our reflections about the man, father, and friend he has become during our lifetime. Through each decade we have known him, he has done his best to be emotionally, mentally, and physically present in our lives. The unconditional love, affirmation, energy, and time he and our mother, Theresa, gave us became our permission slip to live freely and fully as our authentic selves. With four children, they were able to create space for each of us to have our own relationship and experiences with them, individually and as a couple. Read on to see a glimpse of who our father has been in our lives.

REFLECTIONS FROM MICHAEL DAVID

As a child, I was not able to envision my life by having clear goals. Therefore, I had a limited view of my future. I would come to discover I had some talent as an artist; yet did not know where or how that would take shape in life. As a teenager, I became lazy and unfocused. But in a household with both parents who are educators, that would not remain the case. To this day I can remember the time I presented Dad with a failing report card and seeing the look of disappointment on his face. He told me in a firm voice that getting an education was the key to a good future and that I would do better because he knew I had it in me to do better.

What I learned from my father in my youth was how to be firm but patient, honest, loving, and respectful of others. He taught me that life as a Black man would not be easy or fair and that I would, at times, have to work harder than most to achieve the same level of success as others, but that should not deter me from pursuing my dreams.

While in high school, I was given my first freelance job as

an illustrator through his association with the National Education Association. It would be my first opportunity to conduct myself as a professional. Just as I began my college education, Dad began his freelance career. By observing how Dad interacted in the business world, I would use these lessons as blueprints to become the disciplined artistic creator I am today.

The husband and mentor I am today is directly influenced by Dad's relationship with Mom and with my brothers and sister. I will forever be thankful for having him as a role model as well as a trusted counsel.

REFLECTIONS FROM MADELYN CHERYL

Before former Los Angeles Laker Kobe Bryant coined the phrase "girl dad," and it went viral as a hashtag on social media after ESPN anchor Elle Duncan shared a memory of her conversation with him during a tribute to his life in 2020, my father lived and breathed it. For those who don't know, a girl dad is a father who wants his daughter to be treated equally. That means he wants her to have the same rights, opportunities, and privileges as any boy. For as long as I can remember, my father has shown me a fierce love wrapped in an endless bow of support and freedom of expression. His personal investment in my well-being as a child, teenager, young adult, and now as of this writing, a 59-year-old woman, is beyond words. He and my mother taught me I could be and do anything in the world because it was mine.

There are moments I can remember when he showed up

in my defense as only a girl dad could. Like the time he met with the two nuns at my all-girls Catholic high school and told them in his loud Black man voice that they were racist due to their mistreatment of me and the other members of the Awareness Black Culture Club. He has believed in me when I couldn't, especially during the eight times I took and failed the bar exam and each time I have written and published a book. He has even helped me write parts of my books over the telephone when I was running out of creative energy and patience. He has listened to me in my craziest moments and advised me before and after I have taken several risks in my career.

Ours is a rich, layered, and intense relationship that has allowed me to explore and express myself; experiment with my life, career, and creativity; and passionately pursue my healing and wholeness with confidence, freedom, and a safety net that he will always be in my corner no matter what. Being Dr. John F. Leeke's daughter has given me the honor of sitting in the front row of his life as a digital senior citizen activist, blogger, podcaster, storyteller, and author. As time moves us forward, our relationship is blessing me and my brothers with perhaps the greatest honor: supporting my father as he walks the path of a wise person in his aging process. What a gift to behold!

REFLECTIONS FROM MARK ANDREW

Growing up in the Leeke household, the importance of getting a good education was said often and, with that, "to be successful you have got to put in the work." My father used our love for basketball during my high school years to show me how hard work equals success, by pointing out different high school, college, and professional teams. This really resonated in college. There were countless all-nighters and weekends spent in school labs working for perfection on many projects. My father witnessed my success on the professional level early in my career on a visit to Atlanta. During the visit, I gave him a tour and I was able to demonstrate some of the many skills I had mastered at CNN.

As an adult, my relationship with my father has grown into both mentor and friend. Dad has been there for me countless times with professional advice on how to successfully supervise in the workplace as a person of color. One piece of advice that has stayed with me is to never define a person based on their race, gender, age, or orientation. You look at what skills they bring and their capacity to grow professionally. If my father did not have my back, I would not have grown into an individual that has lived and worked in so many different places.

REFLECTIONS FROM MATTHEW JAY

My parents shaped my work ethic and appreciation for hard work. I have a sense of self and compassion for others because of my parents. As a man, I model myself after my dad. He taught me what it means to be a man. As an adult, our relationship has grown far beyond father and son to best friends. It's the bond very few achieve and most desire to have. I remember a moment at church when one of the parishioners commented on how much my dad and I are alike. I immediately responded, "I am like him because I changed. He has always been like this."

During my high school years, we didn't see eye-to-eye, but little did I know Dad's influence was merging into my personality and mindset. I hear his voice when making life decisions. He taught me to stand up for myself and for others; a strength that comes from within. I have a love for education and a desire to never stop learning. To this day, I see my father continuing his learning.

He has shown me a love for family and a sense of responsibility. Responsibility is responding to the challenge of the day. I may not like it, but I must take on the challenge with a clear goal and purpose. It's okay to complain tomorrow, but it doesn't change the fact that it must be done today. I've seen my father express a full range of emotions. I've learned to be fearless with expressing mine.

As a husband, Dad has given me a great blueprint for marriage. Commitment, honesty, communication, and compromise are some of the keys demonstrated by my parents. Theirs is a partnership that is equal and unique. They are not perfect people, but their love is. I know it is possible because I have been lucky to see it with my own eyes. I am very proud to be his son.

CHAPTER 21 REFLECTION QUESTIONS

---

1. Individual: How have your parents and their life journey impacted you?

2. Group Discussion: Give each person 3–5 minutes to share their individual response with the group. As a group, list some of the similarities and differences highlighted in the sharing session. Also, discuss one or two lessons each person has learned.

CHAPTER 22

A Legacy Gift for You: Lessons Learned

"We write to leave legacies for the future."

—BELL HOOKS, a change agent,
a professor, a cultural critic, and an author

When I began my writing journey, my intention was to tell stories about parts of my life that would help my children understand me and what I have tried to do in the world. I am also leaving my stories as a legacy for future generations. As I am nearing the end of my life story, the one thing I can say is that it's been a rich life. One I am truly thankful for. I firmly believe I was placed on earth to make it a better place. Through the many roles I have played as a son, a grandson, a nephew, a cousin, a husband, a father, an uncle, a godparent, a friend, a Black Catholic man, a leader, a colleague, an entrepreneur, and a member of many communities and organizations, I think I've done my best to make this world better. Along the way, I have also learned lessons that you, my dear reader, may find helpful as you move forward in your life. The 10 key lessons I am sharing are part of the legacy I am leaving for you. They are not listed according to their importance. Enjoy reading them!

1. *Be clear about who you are.*

Disappointment and struggle will teach you who you are and what you value and believe. My first major disappointment as an adult happened when I truly believed I would be able to get a teaching job in St. Louis, Missouri. After I applied, I learned I needed a state teaching certificate I didn't have. That experience taught me I needed to do more research and preparation for my career. I faced a real struggle when I accepted a teaching position a year later at a junior high school. I needed that job. It was the only one I was offered. I quickly learned the teaching position was not in alignment with my values and beliefs when the principal told me I was hired not to educate the young Black men. He informed me in no uncertain terms that I was responsible for keeping them quiet and away from the other students and teachers. I had a hard time accepting his expectations because it would cause me to disrespect the students and block their opportunity to learn. I wish I could say that I didn't have moments where I lived out his expectations. Throughout that year, I learned to lean into my faith through prayer and support from my wife and family. They were my lifeline and reminded me of who I truly was. I also learned not to give up on myself and my dreams. As a result, I was able to find the courage and strength to seek better employment. A year later, I accepted a position that gave me exactly what I needed to show up as the teacher I wanted to be. My experience taught me the true meaning of African American civil rights leader, orator, writer, and statesman, Frederick Douglass's wisdom: "If there is no struggle, there is no progress."

2. *Relationships are essential to your development and the impact you make on the world.*

In 2020, I celebrated my 81st birthday. It was very different from previous celebrations because of the COVID-19 pandemic. My family chose to organize a Zoom birthday party which became a big moment for me. The big moment happened when I realized how humbling it was to celebrate with family and friends from many parts of my life. Hearing their words, stories, and laughter let me know how loved and respected I am. It also underscored why I constantly tell anyone who will listen that relationships are essential to one's own development and the impact you make on the world.

Relationships require time, commitment, authenticity, patience, and just plain ole' hard work. My relationships with family, friends, colleagues, clients, and others are a melting pot of diversity. I learned so much from being open to sharing my life experiences with them and listening to theirs. Taking the time to engage in dialogue has enriched my life and given me a greater understanding of the world I have lived in.

Many of the relationships you make are at a very conscious level. Some you are blessed with, and others come into your life by chance, accident, or a consequence of work. The ones I have experienced have all made significant contributions to my life. My most important relationships begin and end with my immediate family. They are the ones who support me no matter what's happening. They also keep me honest even when I am stubborn. You can learn more about the impact they have made on my life in Chapter 20.

My relationships with my Terre Haute buddies Warren Ross, Wally Webb, and Huerta Tribble are three of the closest friendships I have had since we met as infants and attended Indiana State College and joined Pi Lambda Phi Fraternity together. We've seen each other through many of life's changes. I shared a similar bond with my St. Augustine Catholic Elementary School and Carroll High School classmate, Samuel "Sam" Malachi. By the time we became parents of small children, and I moved back to the DC area, our friendship deepened in ways that created cousin bonds our children share with each other. They call each of us Uncle. I am also the godfather to his youngest daughter.

Another Carroll classmate, Lloyd Hall, and I established a close friendship when my family moved to the DC area in 1968. Our love of watching basketball, football, golf, swimming, tennis, and track created what some might say sports junkies. We talked on the phone, attended games, and had season tickets to see the Washington Commanders football team and the Georgetown Hoyas. Our sports adventures even took us on the road to the Big East Tournaments in Madison Square Garden in New York City.

3. *Having sponsors, mentors, and colleagues helps pave the way in your life and career.*

Throughout my life and career, I have been given freedom to grow and opportunities to expand my skills and experiences because of my relationships with people who have acted as sponsors, career mentors, and peer mentors. A sponsor is a person who serves in a senior role in your workplace or academic environment that knows and values your unique abilities and skills, work ethic, and performance track record. A sponsor also leverages their influence to support your upward mobility that translates into increased leadership, opportunities, promotions, and bonuses. My mentoring experiences have included career and peer mentors. A career mentor is a person who uses their knowledge and experience to advise, coach, and offer feedback to a less experienced mentee. A peer mentor is a professional colleague who works in a similar role as the mentee. The peer mentor shares their unique skills, knowledge, and experiences with their colleague in ways that may help both grow.

My very first sponsor was Mother Consolata, the principal of St. Augustine's Catholic Elementary School. If you recall, in Chapter 3, I talk about our relationship and how she selected me to represent the school and assigned me to take responsibility for school activities during my sixth, seventh, and eighth grade years. As a result, she witnessed my academic performance and work ethic, and knew what I could achieve. That's why she advised my parents to send me to

Archbishop Carroll High School. Her advice set me on a path for sustained success both in high school, college, and life after graduation.

George Jones was the most significant career sponsor and mentor. When George hired me to work at the NEA, he helped launch my career as a national change agent with an increase in salary. The salary increase allowed me to say goodbye to part-time jobs I held while teaching and counseling students. With his support and advice on how to engage high-level managers, leaders, and members, I was prepared and protected, especially when my suggestions were challenged by senior employees. Our relationship was also a mentoring experience. We would often spend time at the office and in his home where George coached and helped me develop a framework for working with change. I was the beneficiary of his wisdom and 20+ years of experience as a teacher association executive and dean at an HBCU. He was my secret weapon at the NEA.

Elsie Y. Cross and the EYCA colleagues were some of the most intentional and fulfilling peer mentor experiences I have had. EYCA began with a commitment to changing our clients and ourselves. We were intentional in how we interacted with each other as a team. Our growth as individuals was tied to the growth of the collective through structured training, coaching, constructive feedback, and regular evaluation. We developed a collaborative approach in our client engagement that was constantly updated as we learned what worked and did not work.

In my work with the NEA Intern Program, I served as a peer mentor to my colleague Deloris Rozier and as a career mentor to the interns. Deloris also served as my peer mentor. In all these experiences, I have learned and supported people at various stages in their lives and careers. While reading this book, if you have received some insights or guidance from me then I am probably serving as your mentor. Being a mentor allows you to give back what you received from your mentors and more.

Remember to share what you learned with others. Sharing with others is an investment in them and yourself.

4. Strive for competence by doing the very best you can.

My first years at the NEA and Ph.D. journey helped me to be tough-minded, analytical, and intellectually disciplined to succeed. That meant I needed to always strive for competence. My definition of competence is a personal dedication to scholarly pursuits which include reading, interactive discussions with others, and a commitment to being open and willing to change when new and different information, approaches, and individuals present themselves.

As you grow in your life and career, your experiences will influence the person you become and the quality of work you do. Make a commitment to yourself to strive for competence by being self-motivated, tough-minded, analytical, and intellectually disciplined.

5. *Take risks to expand your life and career.*

Most of the risks I have taken have been in my career. For example, I took a risk when I accepted the NEA's offer to work as a staff person on a one-year contract. At that time, I had a stable job as a guidance counselor. My principal had given me a lot of freedom to create a guidance counseling program. He was also serving as a career sponsor and grooming me for a school administrator position. Leaving this position for a one-year contract meant I had to move my wife and children with me. We sold our home and had to make a new life in a new place. All these factors increased the risk level of my choice. Taking this risk laid the foundation for the change agent I am today.

There will be lots of times in your life and career when opportunities present themselves. You must use your judgment to determine whether you are able to take the risks. Sometimes your choice to take a risk may not work out in the way you expected. No matter what happens, you must deal with the consequences. One way to move forward is to begin to accept what has happened and move on to the next opportunity.

6. *Learn to deal with professional disappointment.*

In my career at the NEA, I was once responsible for managing the team and production process for a guidebook on how to deal with institutional racism in schools. At the time, I was in my late thirties and had been working for the NEA for 10 years. Up until then, every project I managed had been successful. My team members were 15 to 20 years older and did not work at the NEA. They included a university professor and seasoned school administrators with diverse experience. My team and I gave our best effort only to be told it was too thorough. I took it personally and had a very hard time accepting the feedback. It took me a while to get over my anger and disappointment. When I spoke to my team and learned they did not have the same degree of disappointment, they helped me realize we could incorporate the feedback and produce a credible guidebook that could be used.

When you are hired to produce a work product, keep in mind it may not always be accepted by your employer or client. You may be asked to edit or change the content significantly. These changes may disappoint you or make you angry. If that happens, know you are human. You have a choice in how you respond. Before you do, talk to someone you respect and trust about what has happened. Seek to get clarity when you are calm and able to think clearly.

7. *Access the value of your career skills and expertise regularly.*

When I look at the arc of my career, I can see how I was able to develop and utilize my skills and expertise as a teacher, coach, and counselor in most of the positions I held. I also brought my entrepreneurial legacy to these positions. Nowadays, what I was doing is called intrapreneurship, the act of operating like an entrepreneur while working within an organization. In addition, my use of the Myers-Briggs® Type Indicator (MBTI) system confirmed many of the attributes, skills, and ways of being I possessed and consistently demonstrated in my career.

The MBTI is a personality type instrument that provides four preference pairs and 16 personality types. Each reflects different personality aspects and are labeled in the following manner: (E) Extraversion, (I) Introversion, (S) Sensing, (N) Intuition, (T) Thinking, (F) Feeling, (J) Judging, and (P) Perceiving.

As you navigate your career, I encourage you to do regular self-assessments of your skills and expertise. Consider using MBTI or a similar instrument. They can help you see the value you bring to the workplace. They can help you pursue salary increases, new employment, consulting work, and so much more.

8. *Get involved and serve a community.*

When you serve a community, you have an opportunity to pursue and discover new passions, share your skills and expertise in ways that benefit others, and cultivate and enjoy interracial, intercultural, and intergenerational relationships that offer friendship and lifelong learning. As I mentioned in Chapter 19 that discusses life in retirement, I have been able to pursue my passion for service in the St. Joseph Catholic Church community, Archbishop Carroll High School Alumni

Association, and national and local political campaigns. My active involvement helps me feel valued and stay healthy, informed, and connected to others.

9. *You can be a change agent.*

A change agent is a person who is committed to making things better in an organization and community. I've been a change agent since my early days as a teacher and guidance counselor in Flint, Michigan. When I worked as an NEA staffer and a consultant with my own firm and EYCA, I was able to make organizational change within institutions. In addition, I have leveraged my change agent skills to improve my civic and church communities. If you're interested in being a change agent, identify how you can use your skills and expertise to improve the organization you work in and the communities you live and serve in. Remember change is a process that takes time and energy. Remember what Vice President Kamala Harris had to say: "Change is never easy, but is always necessary." I encourage you to embrace the wisdom of science fiction author Octavia Butler: "All that you touch you change. All that you change changes you. The only lasting truth is change." So be patient and keep working on it as long as it takes. Make "play the long game" your mantra!

10. *Life will call you to be a change agent when you are faced with difficult changes such as the loss of a loved one.*

A few days after my family and I celebrated my wife Theresa's 84th birthday in 2023, my daughter Ananda and I were sitting in my office working on this book you are now reading. We were talking about the impact of Theresa's death which occurred on July 9, 2023. She asked me how I was doing living on my own for the past several months. I told her I was doing okay because my faith helped me accept that Theresa is in heaven with God. Although I miss her every day, I know she lived a full life, and we had a loving marriage for 62 years. I also know and trust God called her home on time in the same way he will call me home. My faith has been the essential ingredient I have leaned on when faced with difficult changes. When you encounter difficult changes such as the loss of a loved one, take the time to find strength and comfort in your own unique way.

CHAPTER 22 REFLECTION QUESTIONS

---

1. Individual: What lessons have you learned in your life and career?

2. Group Discussion: Give each person 3–5 minutes to share their individual response with the group. As a group, list some of the similarities and differences highlighted in the sharing session. Also, discuss one or two lessons each person has learned.

RESOURCES

Here is a list of books, magazines, journals, and resources that have contributed to my development and career as a change agent. They are organized in the following categories: Biographies, Diversity, Education, Gender and Sexism, History, Journals and Magazines, LGBTQ, Organization Development, and Race and Racism.

Biographies

- *Born to Rebel* by Benjamin E. Mays
- *The Souls of Black Folk* by W.E.B. Du Bois
- *Reconsidering the Souls of Black Folk* by Stanley Crouch and Playthell Benjamin
- *W.E.B. Du Bois: Biography of a Race* by David Levering Lewis
- *Long Walk to Freedom* by Nelson Mandela
- *Thurgood Marshall: American Revolutionary* by Juan Williams
- *Big Man on Campus: John Thompson and the Georgetown Hoyas* by Leonard Shapiro

- *Second Wind: The Memoirs of an Opinionated Man* by Bill Russell and Taylor Branch
- *Native Son* by Richard Wright

Diversity

- *The Diversity Factor: Capturing the Competitive Advantage of a Changing Workforce* by Elsie Y. Cross and Margaret Blackburn White
- *Managing Diversity: The Courage to Lead* by Elsie Y. Cross
- *Developing Competency to Manage Diversity* by Taylor Cox, Jr. and Ruby L. Beale
- *Teaching Diversity: Listening to the Soul, Speaking from the Heart* by Joan V. Gallos and V. Jean Ramsey
- *Cultural Diversity in Organizations* by Taylor Cox, Jr.
- *Privilege, Power and Difference* by Allan G. Johnson

Education

- *Pedagogy of the Oppressed* by Paulo Freire
- *Education and Racism* by National Education Association
- *The Mis-Education of the Negro* by Carter G. Woodson
- *What Black Educators Are Saying* by Nathan Wright, Jr.
- *Lies My Teacher Told Me: Everything Your American History Textbook Got Wrong* by James W. Loewen

- *Everyday Antiracism: Getting Real About Race in School* by Mica Pollock

- *"It's Being Done": Academic Success in Unexpected Schools* by Karin Chenoweth

- *Teaching Strategies for Ethnic Studies* by James A. Banks

- *Models of Teaching* by Bruce Joyce and Marsha Weil

- *Cultural Proficiency: A Manual for School Leaders* by Randall B. Lindsey, Kikanza Nuri Robins, and Raymond D. Terrell

Gender and Sexism

- *Our Separate Ways: Black and White Women and the Struggle for Professional Identity* by Ella L.J. Edmondson Bell and Stella M. Nkomo

- *Sister Citizen: Shame, Stereotypes, and Black Women in America* by Melissa V. Harris-Perry

- *The Androgynous Manager: Blending Male and Female Management Styles for Today's Organization* by Alice G. Sargent

- *Rebirth of Feminism* by Judith Hole and Ellen Levine

- *Black Women in White America: A Documentary History* by Gerda Lern

- *Breakthrough: Women into Management* by Rosalind Loring and Theodora Wells

- *The Rights of Women: An American Civil Liberties*

Union Handbook by Susan C. Ross

- *Affirmative Action: Equal Employment Rights for Women in Academia* by Jinny M. Goldstein

- *Sisterhood is Powerful: An Anthology of Writings from the Women's Liberation Movement* by Robin Morgan

- *The Black Woman: An Anthology* by Toni Cade Bambara

- *Women, Race & Class* by Angela Y. Davis

- *Men and Women of the Corporation* by Rosabeth Moss Kanter

- *The Potential of Women* by Seymour M. Farber and Roger H.L. Wilson

- *We'll Do It Ourselves: Combatting Sexism in Education* by Barbara Yates, Steve Werner, and David Rosen

- *Woman's Place: Options and Limits in Professional Careers* by Cynthia Fuchs Epstein

- *Toward a New Psychology of Women* by Jean Baker Miller

- *The Trials of Phillis Wheatley: America's First Black Poet and Her Encounters with the Founding Fathers* by Henry Louis Gates, Jr.

- *Feminism Is for Everybody: Passionate Politics* by bell hooks

<u>History</u>

- *Before the Mayflower: A History of Black America* by Lerone Bennett, Jr.

- *Bury My Heart at Wounded Knee: An Indian History of the American West* by Dee Brown
- *The Only Good Indian: The Hollywood Gospel* by Ralph and Natasha Friar
- *The Black Muslims in America* by C. Eric Lincoln
- *The Colonizer and the Colonized* by Albert Memmi
- *The Destruction of Black Civilization: Great Issues of a Race from 4500 B.C. to 2000 A.D.* by Chancellor Williams
- *LaRaza: The Mexican Americans* by Stan Steiner
- *Our Brother's Keeper: The Indian in White America* by Edgar S. Cahn and David W. Hearne
- *History of the American Teachers Association* by Thelma D. Perry
- *The National Education Association: The Power Base for Education* by Allan M. West
- *All the People: NEA's Legacy of Inclusion and Its Minority Presidents* by Al-Tony Gilmore
- *Hooded Americanism: The History of the Ku Klux Klan* by David M. Chalmers
- *The Black American Experience: From Reconstruction to the Present* by Arvarth E. Strickland and Jerome R. Reich
- *The Trail of Tears* by Gloria Jahoda
- *From Slavery to Freedom: A History of African Americans* by John Hope Franklin

Journals and Magazines

- *Black Enterprise*
- *Ebony*
- *Essence*
- *Harvard Education Review*
- *Jet*
- *Latina*
- *The Diversity Factor*
- *The Journal of Blacks in Higher Education*
- *The Journal of Race, Ethnicity, and Politics*
- *Urban Education*

LGBTQ

- *Is It a Choice?: Answers to the Most Frequently Asked Questions about Gay & Lesbian People* by Eric Marcus
- *On the Down Low: A Journey into the Lives of 'Straight' Black Men Who Sleep with Men* by J.L. King
- *One More River to Cross: Black and Gay in America* by Keith Boykin
- *Cracking the Corporate Closet* by Daniel B. Baker, Sean O'Brien Strub, and Bill Henning
- *The Dance of Difference: The New Frontier of Sexual Orientation* by Shirley Anderson Fletcher

Organization Development

- *Personal and Organizational Change Through Group Methods: The Laboratory Approach* by Edgar H. Schein

- *Group Dynamics and Social Action* by Kenneth D. Benne

- *Agent of Change: My Life, My Practice* by Richard Beckhard

- *Organization Development: Theory, Practice and Research* by Wendell L. French, Cecil H. Bell, Jr., and Robert A. Zawacki

- *SYMLOG: A System for the Multiple Level Observation of Groups* by Robert F. Bales and Stephen P. Cohen

- *Social Interaction* by Thomas M. Kando

- *Managing in the Age of Change* by Roger A. Ritvo, Anne H. Litwin, and Lee Butler

- *Temporary Systems* by Jack Gant, Oron South, and John Hansen

- *Managing Transitions: Making the Most of Change* by William Bridges

- *The Fifth Discipline: The Art & Practice of the Learning Organization* by Peter M. Senge

- *The Fifth Discipline Fieldbook: Strategies and Tools for Building a Learning Organization* by Peter Senge, Richard Ross, Bryan Smith, Charlotte Roberts, and Art Kleiner

- *Schools That Learn: A Fifth Discipline Fieldbook for*

Educators, Parents, and Everyone Who Cares About Education by Peter M. Senge, Nelda Cambron-McCabe, Timothy Lucas, Bryan Smith, Janis Dutton, and Art Kleiner

- *The Handbook of Organization Development in Schools* by Richard A. Schmuck and Philip J. Runkel
- *The Theory and Practice of Managing* by James Owens
- *Leading in Black and White: Working Across the Racial Divide in Corporate America* by Ancella B. Livers and Keith A. Caver
- *Breaking Through: The Making of Minority Executives in Corporate America* by David A. Thomas and John J. Gabarro
- *Cracking the Corporate Code: The Revealing Success Stories of 32 African-American Executives* by Price M. Cobbs and Judith L. Turnock
- *The Black Manager: Making It in the Corporate World* by Floyd Dickens, Jr. and Jacqueline B. Dickens
- *The Skilled Facilitator: Practical Wisdom for Developing Effective Groups* by Roger M. Schwarz
- *A Union of Professionals: Labor Relations and Educational Reform* by Charles Taylor Kerchner and Julia E. Koppich
- *Rules for Radicals* by Saul Alinsky
- *Eugene Debs: Rebel, Labor Leader, Prophet* by David F. Selvin

Race and Racism

- *Critical Race Theory: The Key Writings That Formed the Movement* by Kimberle Crenshaw, Neil Gotanda, Gary Peller, and Kendall Thomas

- *The Nature of Prejudice* by Gordon W. Allport

- *Dark Ghetto* by Kenneth B. Clark

- *Pathos of Power* by Kenneth B. Clark

- *Race, Racism and American Law* by Derrick A. Bell, Jr.

- *Racial Oppression in America* by Robert Blauner

- *Racism and the Class Struggle: Further Pages from a Black Worker's Notebook* by James Boggs

- *The Fire Next Time* by James Baldwin

- *Black Power: The Politics of Liberation in America* by Stokley Carmichael and Charles V. Hamilton

- *Racism in America and How to Combat It* by Anthony Downs

- *The Political Economy of Racism* by Raymond S. Franklin and Solomon Resnik

- *Black Rage* by William H. Grier and Price M. Cobbs

- *White Over Black: American Attitudes toward the Negro, 1550-1812* by Winthrop D. Jordan

- *Toward the Elimination of Racism* by Phyllis A. Katz

- *Institutional Racism in America* by Louis L. Knowles and Kenneth Prewitt

- *White Racism: A Psychohistory* by Joel Kovel
- *Racism in American Education: A Model for Change* by William E. Sedlacek and Glenwood C. Brooks, Jr.
- *Blaming the Victim* by William Ryan
- *For Whites Only* by Robert W. Terry
- *Mindful of Race: Transforming Racism from the Inside Out* by Ruth King
- *Racial Sobriety: Becoming the Change You Want to See* by Clarence E. Williams, Jr.
- *Member of the Club: Reflections on Life in a Racially Polarized World* by Lawrence Otis Graham
- *The New Jim Crow: Mass Incarceration in the Age of Colorblindness* by Michelle Alexander
- *White Like Me: Reflections on Race from a Privileged Son* by Tim Wise
- *Dear White America: Letter to a New Minority* by Tim Wise
- *Black and White Styles in Conflict* by Thomas Kochman
- *White Awareness: Handbook for Anti-Racism Training* by Judith H. Katz
- *Fire in the Heart: How White Activists Embrace Racial Justice* by Mark R. Warren
- *The Isis Papers: The Keys to the Colors* by Frances Cress Welsing
- *Between the World and Me* by Ta-Nehisi Coates

- *Can You Hear Me Now?* by Michael Eric Dyson
- *What's the Matter with White People?* by Joan Walsh
- *Killers of the Dream* by Lillian Smith
- *The Failures of Integration: How Race and Class are Undermining the American Dream* by Sheryll Cashin
- *Race, Religion and Racism, Volume 1 and 2* by Frederick K.C. Price
- *Race Matters* by Cornel West
- *Black Wealth/White Wealth: A New Perspective on Racial Inequality* by Melvin L. Oliver and Thomas M. Shapiro
- *Racism 101* by Nikki Giovanni
- *Loving: Interracial Intimacy in America and the Threat to White Supremacy* by Sheryll Cashin
- *Black, White, Other: Biracial Awareness Talk About Race and Identity* by Lise Funderburg
- *Beyond the Burning: Life and Death of the Ghetto* by Sterling Tucker
- *The Choice: The Issue of Black Survival in America* by Samuel F. Yette
- *The Spook Who Sat by the Door* by Sam Greenlee
- *Black Professionals' Perceptions of Institutional Racism in Health and Welfare Organizations* by Charles L. Sanders
- *Black Protest* by Joanne Grant
- *Racial Crisis in American Education* by Robert L. Green

- *Black Man's Burden* by John Oliver Killens
- *The White Use of Blacks in America* by Dan Lacy
- *Black Skins, White Masks* by Frantz Fanon
- *White Attitudes Toward Black People* by Angus Campbell
- *The Rightness of Whiteness* by Abraham F. Citron
- *Black Families in White America* by Andrew Billingsley
- *One Drop of Blood: The American Misadventure of Race* by Scott L. Malcomson
- *Mississippi: Conflict and Change* by James W. Loewen and Charles Sallis
- *Convicted in the Womb* by Carl Upchurch
- *The Autobiography of Malcolm X* by Malcolm X
- *Martin & Malcolm & America: A Dream or a Nightmare* by James H. Cone
- *Invisible Man* by Ralph Ellison
- *Breaking Barriers: A Memoir* by Carl T. Rowan
- *Vernon Can Read!: A Memoir* by Vernon E. Jordan, Jr.
- *Becoming* by Michelle Obama
- *Dreams from My Father: A Story of Race and Inheritance* by Barack Obama
- *The Audacity of Hope: Thoughts on Reclaiming the American Dream* by Barack Obama
- *Obama: From Promise to Power* by David Mendell

ACKNOWLEDGMENTS

First and foremost, I am grateful to God and my ancestors. Thank you for loving and guiding me through my life and this book-writing journey.

I am deeply grateful to my wife, Theresa, and children, Mike and Lu, Madelyn (Ananda), Mark, and Matthew and Pam, for their love and support.

I would like to extend a special thanks to Madelyn (Ananda), my co-author, daughter, and friend, for helping me to write and publish this book.

Special thanks to my four children for writing about me as their father.

Many thanks to my son Matthew for identifying and scanning numerous photos for the book.

I thank my cousin Barbara Toles Bluiett for sharing photos and stories about the Jones side of my family.

I appreciate and give thanks to everyone who educated and mentored me in my life.

Thanks to everyone I worked with and learned from in my career.

Many thanks to my NEA and EYCA colleagues and the clients I served.

Special thanks to the former NEA interns who graciously shared their reflections in this book: Nas Afi, Eric Beck, Demetrice Davis, Candace Lilyquist, and Bryant Warren.

A deep bow of gratitude to everyone who read the early drafts of my book and book description: Michael Burkart, Deleyte Frost, Ed Hill, Wayne Henry, Tracy Mickens-Hundley, Garnet Jackson, Deborah Kirby, Reginald Lawson, Pamela Charity Leeke, Jessie Muse, Barbara Riley, Deloris Rozier, and Meico Whitlock.

I appreciate the amazing support I received from my photographer, Leigh Mosley, my copy editor, Yael Flusberg, and my book and graphic designer, Gigi Mascareñas.

AUTHOR BIOS:
DR. JOHN F. LEEKE, PH.D.

John F. Leeke, Ph.D., is a change agent and trailblazer in the field of diversity, equity, and inclusion with over 60 years of lived experience. "Dr. John" is also an organizer, an advocate, a digital senior citizen activist, a podcaster, and a blogger. Prior to retirement, he was President of John F. Leeke Associates, Inc., and served as a senior associate in Elsie Y. Cross Associates, Inc., a pioneering diversity firm providing organizational development strategies to fortune 100 companies.

His organizational development career began as a staff member of the National Education Association (NEA) in 1968. For 17 years, he provided services to NEA members and local and state affiliates in problems and issues of urban education, human and civil rights, and teacher training and certification. He developed and trained teachers and NEA professional staff members in racism and sexism awareness.

As President of John F. Leeke Associates, Inc., he worked with clients in the private sector, state and federal agencies, universities, school systems, and NEA and its affiliates. One of his most significant efforts was designing and delivering an affirmative action program for the NEA that identified and prepared over 200 people of color and white women to become professional staff employees who served teachers and others in the United States. The program lasted 27 years.

Dr. John is a proud graduate and active alumnus of Archbishop Carroll High School. He holds a Bachelor of Science degree in Education from Indiana State University, a Master of Science degree in Guidance and Counseling from the University of Michigan, and a Doctorate degree in Organizational Behavior from the Union Institute and University. He also has extensive training from the National Training Laboratory of Applied Behavioral Science and has been a member for many years. The NEA National Black Staff Network honored his legacy with the JEGNA Award, its highest recognition of service in 2019.

Currently, he lives in Maryland and is actively involved in his local church and high school alumni association.

Visit anandaleeke.com/drjohn to learn more. Connect with him on social media:

- Blog: drjohnleeke.tumblr.com
- Facebook: facebook.com/john.leeke1
- Instagram: @drjleeke
- LinkedIn: linkedin.com/in/john-leeke-51580b165
- Soundcloud: soundcloud.com/john-leeke
- YouTube: youtube.com/@drjohnleeke

Contact Ananda Leeke, ananda@anandaleeke.com, for media, speaking, and training inquiries.

AUTHOR BIOS:
ANANDA KIAMSHA MADELYN LEEKE

Ananda Kiamsha Madelyn Leeke discovered mindfulness, self-care, and wellness when her career as a lawyer, an investment banker, and a digital communications professional stressed her out, caused burnout, and did not produce the level of success she expected. During Ananda's healing journey, she studied and practiced meditation, yoga, reiki, journaling, art-making, and creative writing. They helped her develop self-care practices, navigate change, and become resilient. As a result, she became a certified yoga + mindfulness meditation teacher, a digital wellness educator, a reiki master practitioner, a sound healer, and an artist-in-residence for the Smith Center for Healing and the Arts at Howard University Hospital and Walter Reed National Military Medical Center.

Today, she shares her gifts and expertise and makes an impact in the world as an artist, an author, a coach, a digital wellness educator, a human design doula, and a mentor. She leads Ananda Leeke Consulting, a wellness company that specializes in helping people, organizations, and communities navigate change. She also oversees the Thriving Mindfully Academy, an online education platform and membership community that supports people in being present, well, and their real selves in their lives, relationships, and careers. In addition, she hosts and produces the *Thriving Mindfully Podcast.*

In 2019, Ananda was selected by lululemon to serve as a lululemon luminary, received Acquisition International's Influential Businesswoman in Professional Development—USA Award, and was named a Well-Being Warrior by the Well-Being and Equity Bridging Network. Her books, *Love's Troubadours*, a yoga-inspired novel; *That Which Awakens Me*, a mindful creativity memoir; and *Digital Sisterhood*, a mindful technology memoir, are available on Amazon. Currently, she is writing her third memoir, *Thriving Mindfully as Theresa's Daughter.*

She speaks at conferences and events, conducts trainings, and leads coaching sessions for Amazon, Automattic/WordPress, #BlackTechFutures Research Institute, Georgetown University Law Center, InsightLA, Insight Meditation Community of Washington, Institute for Medicaid Innovation, Keela, Marisla Foundation, National Association of Corporate Directors, National Collective for Health Equity, Nonprofit Technology Network, Pennsylvania Association of Nonprofit Organizations, Sierra Club, Sigma Gamma Rho Sorority, Inc., Sistas 4 Digital Equity, Smith Center for Healing and the Arts, The Conference Board, World Wildlife Fund, and Wonder Women Tech Summit.

Ananda is a proud alumna of Georgetown University Law Center, Howard University School of Law, Morgan State University, and Elizabeth Seton High School. She is a member of Sigma Gamma Rho Sorority, Inc. She lives in Washington, DC. Visit anandaleeke.com to learn more. Follow @anandaleeke on LinkedIn, YouTube, and Spill; and @anandaleeke.bsky.social on Bluesky.

www.ingramcontent.com/pod-product-compliance
Lightning Source LLC
Chambersburg PA
CBHW071659120626
46550CB00001B/32